# Marketing

## EVERYBODY'S BUSINESS

## Second Edition

*covering European and International Marketing*

**DAVE NEEDHAM**

**ROB DRANSFIELD**

Heinemann

Heinemann Educational Publishers
Halley Court, Jordan Hill, Oxford OX2 8EJ
A division of Reed Educational & Professional Publishing Ltd

OXFORD   MELBOURNE   AUCKLAND
JOHANNESBURG   BLANTYRE   GABORONE
IBADAN   PORTSMOUTH (NH) USA   CHICAGO

First edition published 1991
Second edition published 1995


99  00  01  02
10  9  8  7  6  5  4


British Library Cataloguing in Publication Data
Needham, David
Dransfield, Robert
658.8.
ISBN 0 435 450255


Designed by Mike Brain
Typeset and illustrated by TecSet Ltd, Wallington, Surrey
Printed by The Bath Press, Bath

# Acknowledgements

The authors and publishers would like to thank the following people and organisations for their help in the preparation of this book.

Margaret Berriman
Sheri Hill
Roger Parker
Chris Sefton
Laura Schuster
Bryan Oakes
Shell UK
National Westminster Bank PLC
Sainsbury's
*Marketing*
British Airways
Lyons Tetley

# Contents

# Preface

In the first edition of this book we tried to show that, in a rapidly changing world, power has shifted from the producer towards the consumer. The marketing process has helped this to happen and, as a result, many organisations have found that strategies developed to satisfy consumer needs more effectively gain them many competitive advantages. In the modern business environment, where choice and competition exist, consumers have the ultimate power – they do not have to buy! Marketing is, therefore, not the business only of the producer, but also of the consumer – it is everybody's business. Today's consumers are more articulate and informed about what they want to buy than ever before. Producers have not only to satisfy their requirements, they also have to be sensitive to them.

Another theme of the first edition which has been carried through to this book is that marketing is a strategic planning discipline that caters for the health of the whole of an organisation. Effective marketing involves providing a coherent and well-planned strategy as well as tactical flexibility and clarity.

This edition has been fundamentally changed to take into account the fact that we are moving towards the era of the global village. In a world of constant change, new ideas, stiffer competition and improved communications, more organisations now trade beyond national boundaries in a much wider marketplace. This book therefore makes the assumption that marketing is an international activity, and reflects throughout the different approaches necessary to cater for this.

As in the first edition, each chapter contains a number of Case Studies. We have added Assignments at the ends of chapters.

We believe that marketing is exciting. It helps organisations to succeed but, if carried out badly, it will contribute towards failure. If we have communicated well some of the more dynamic elements of the subject within this book, and this helps students to pursue their interests, then we can claim that we have developed a product that is market-led!

Dave Needham                                                    Rob Dransfield

# From Little Acorns . . .

by **Chris Sefton**
Group Marketing Manager, J.N. Nichols (VIMTO) plc

At the beginning of the twentieth century not many people knew the word 'marketing'. Yet one person was about to embark on the road to making history by creating a product (dare we say a 'brand'?) which would be developed on to the world marketplace.

To state simply that this person was the creator of an imaginative soft drink understates his real ability. Looking back it is relatively easy to see the path he used to develop and then exploit the huge potential for his unique drink, but we should recognise that he was a pioneer on his own.

Perhaps this is a way of looking at 'marketing' as we know it today in a different light. Many modern marketers have the benefit of joining an existing business and, by using a variety of skills gained in their careers, manage to provide some new direction, some new thinking to identify and then take advantage of a previously undiscovered consumer requirement. They do all these things with the added demand of 'making profit'. But almost a hundred years ago would we have recognised these basic attributes as 'marketing skills'? I doubt it.

This scenario happened with a product which is known today as Vimto. It is a unique blend of fruits, herbs and spices made to a closely guarded recipe.

It started life with the name Vimtonic, which was quickly shortened to its present name. Initially it was sold through herbal shops and temperance bars in the north-west of England. Now it is sold throughout the world.

How did a locally manufactured product develop into an international brand?

- Was it planned?
- Was it a necessity?
- Had the UK market dried up?

In the first instance (in the mid-1920s) the product was taken abroad by British civil servants travelling by land overseas to parts of India.

Their journeys took them through the Middle East where in 'alcohol-free' countries the drink Vimto soon became a desirable commodity.

Back in England the inventor, John Noel Nichols, recognised the opportunity (the first step in marketing!) and took action (the second step) to make enquiries with local agents on how best he could supply their demands (a word that is essential in every marketing person's vocabulary!).

Even at this early stage of international marketing he decided to retain a number of his fundamental principles; i.e. to market the concept and retain control of the unique selling point or USP (the secret recipe), but allow local knowledge to dictate sales methods and distribution. He did not try to be 'all things to all people' but adhered to the maxim: 'Do what you do best and let someone else take the risk.'

He recognised that local people understand local markets; they understand their own culture (especially important on the international scene); they relate better to their own social and economic climates. This policy was carried down to the next generations in the family business and enabled Vimto to be sold in over 40 countries at the start of 1994.

Certain aspects of marketing the Vimto brand have been carried into all territories, in particular the use of the Vimto logo, with red lettering against a white background. Even when the style of lettering was changed in the UK in 1988/89, this was carried across packaging throughout the world – again, local knowledge decided the best timescale in which to achieve the changeover. It does not always pay for the brand owner of international products to dictate the pace of changes. What has presently happened in this country probably is not appropriate throughout the world, but as the brand progresses and develops, changes must be implemented at the earliest possible opportunity.

Another aspect of Vimto's international marketing policy is to encourage 'self-sufficiency'. This doesn't usually appear in the textbooks as such, but closer understanding of what is meant should help.

When dealing on the world stage it is extremely difficult to nurture enthusiasm in every trading area. If you can encourage 'self-sufficiency' the local contact sees the benefits of investing time, capital and (most importantly) people in the development of the product. In our example, Vimto is readily available in a concentrate form which allows local manufacturing to be set up. Thus savings are made in packaging and transportation costs, but equally vital is that local people are provided with employment. This in turn brings about a commitment – another essential ingredient in the marketing mix.

People often talk about 'global marketing' as being the answer to controlling a brand's performance. The use of international advertising and the linking of world-wide sponsorships might work – probably do work – for some exceptional brands, but there is no universal method of marketing products throughout the world.

In international marketing you definitely need to recognise the needs of individual countries, and you may need to be flexible in your approach to packaging. But I would suggest that there is one thing on which there is *no compromise*, and that is QUALITY. The quality of your product or your service should be the rock upon which your international marketing policy is founded.

# Introduction to Marketing

## WHAT IS MARKETING?

Marketing is everyone's business! Every person working for an organisation should understand the importance of marketing. So, what is it and why is it important?

The **Chartered Institute of Marketing** uses the following definition:

> Marketing is the management process responsible for identifying, anticipating and satisfying consumer requirements profitably.

This definition places **consumers** at the centre of an organisation's activities – whether they be a doctor's patients, the pupils or parents of children at the local school, or people queueing to buy fish and chips. Some organisations are physically very close to their consumers – for example, a post office in a small town. For other organisations consumers may be thousands of miles away – for example, Mars selling sweets and chocolates around the world. The principle that the 'Consumer is King and Queen' is just as relevant to the organisation engaged in international marketing.

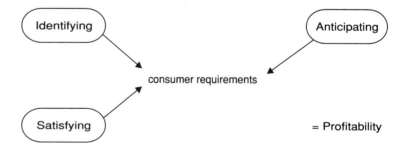

FIGURE 1.1
*The ingredients of marketing*

There are a number of key words in the definition given above:

- **Identifying** – This will involve answering questions such as 'How do we find out what the consumer's requirements are?' and 'How do we keep in touch with their thoughts and feelings and perceptions about our good or service?' As we shall see in Chapter 3, this is a key purpose of market research.

- **Anticipating** – Consumer requirements change all the time. For example, as people become richer they may seek a greater variety of goods and services. Anticipation involves looking at the future as well as at the present. What will be the Next Best Thing that people will require tomorrow?

- **Satisfying** – Consumers want their requirements to be met. They seek particular benefits. They want the right goods, at the right price, at the right time and in the right place.
- **Profitability** – Marketing also involves making a margin of *profit*. An organisation that fails to make a profit will have nothing to plough back into the future. Without the resources to put into ongoing marketing activities, it will not be able to identify, anticipate or satisfy consumer requirements.

For an organisation to continue to make profits it must find out *in good time* what its consumers want to buy and then satisfy these requirements.

## THE BUSINESS ENVIRONMENT

Organisations operate in an environment of **change**. Today we live in a **global marketplace** for many goods and services in which technology, purchasing power and many other factors change on a regular basis. One of the key functions of marketing is to find out how these changes affect consumer wants and needs and to develop organisational **strategies** and **plans** that will ensure that the organisation meets these challenges.

> Marketing finds out how the changing environment affects consumers' wants and needs in order to produce organisational marketing **policies**.

The **marketing function** of an organisation therefore has to find out what goods or services are required by consumers now and in the future. The organisation needs to be **consumer-orientated**. Assessing customer needs is a process of discovery, so that the organisation can direct its activities towards supplying consumers with the good-quality products and services they want.

Today, more and more organisations emphasise the marketing function. General Electric is often regarded as one of the first organisations to have recognised the importance of marketing. The General Electric view was and is that marketing is not just something that you 'bolt-on' to an organisation's activities; rather it is a *key part* of all activities – from product innovation and development, through to manufacture and delivery, and even to after-sales service. All decisions that an organisation makes should be based on consumer requirements.

## CASE STUDY *Marketing failure*

Few organisations operate in a static world. Today we live in a global market-place for many goods and services, in which technology, purchasing power, tastes as well as many other factors are all changing at the same time. In adapting to many of these changes good marketing is a key factor.

*Good marketing involves looking OUTWARDS in order to respond to changes in markets, business conditions and competition as well as INWARDS in order to meet all of those consumer needs which have been identified by the marketing process (see Figure 1.2).*

The classic example from the UK of failure to monitor customer requirements comes from the motor cycle industry.

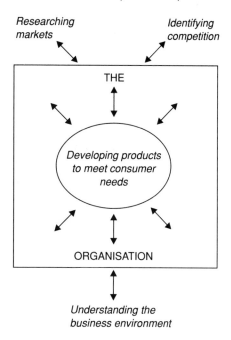

FIGURE 1.2
*Linking opportunities outside the organisation with the development of products*

Thirty years ago foreign motorbikes were hardly ever seen on British roads. Great names such as BSA, Triumph, Ariel and Norton graced the highways with 'heavy, slow-revving, large-capacity machines'. The few imports available at the time were from Italy in the form of lightweight, high-revving machines and these were hardly given a second glance by British manufacturers. As British manufacturers did not make them customers could not have them. At the

3

time there was virtually no link between both the market and the marketing environment and the products which the manufacturers were producing.

For British bike manufacturers this did not matter. They were profitable and did not have to reinvest in costly research activities. However somebody else had identified that British manufacturers were failing to match the wishes of consumers in the marketing environment with the products they were making. Thousands of miles away research and development programmes were under way. Japan was about to enter the marketplace.

Today the transformation is complete. We only have to look on our roads to notice that motorbikes are nearly all Japanese and there are very few British manufacturers left. If the British had looked outwards and identified customer requirements the position today might be very different.

**Questions**
1  Explain why the marketing process involves looking outwards and inwards.
2  What marketing activities should British motorcycle manufacturers have been carrying out in the 1960s?
3  Why did Japanese companies have a competitive edge?
4  Why do you think that it might be difficult to regain a competitive edge once it has been lost to a rival manufacturer?

# MARKETING STRATEGY

Every organisation needs to have clear **goals**, and the major route to achieving organisational goals will depend on **strategy**. It is important, therefore, to be clear about the difference between strategy and **tactics**.

These terms originate from military use (military strategy before and during a battle is the general policy overview of how to defeat the enemy). Developing a strategy involves establishing *clear aims and objectives around which the framework for a policy is created*. Having established its strategy, an organisation can then work out its day-to-day tools and tactics to meet the objectives.

Marketing can thus be seen as the process of developing and implementing a strategy to plan and coordinate ways of identifying, anticipating and satisfying consumer demands, in such a way as to make profits. It is this strategic planning process that lies at the heart of marketing.

# MARKETING SERVICES

**Marketing services** are the tools used by the marketing department. The marketing department will set out to identify the most appropriate marketing services to employ in order to make profits. These services may include public relations, trade and consumer promotions, point-of-sale materials, editorial, publicity and sales literature.

Any communication with consumers should ideally come under the responsibility of the marketing function. The traditional areas of advertising, public relations and sales promotion are clearly marketing services. In addition, marketing services should also include the production of statements, invoices and even final demands, because the perception of the organisation by customers is too important to be neglected in any way.

Today many markets for goods and services have evolved to the point where the consumer has become of primary importance and has substantial control. In response to this changing balance of power, the successful business must produce the goods or services required to an appropriate standard at an acceptable price and distributed in a convenient manner. In terms of immediate service to the present clientele of a business, the marketing function is essential for:

- market research
- product development
- pricing
- distribution.

This constitutes the tactical side of marketing. Each of these topics is covered in later chapters in this book, so they will be described only briefly here.

## Market research

The subject of **market research** could fill many volumes in its own right. It is far more complicated than asking 100 people if they like a product and saying 'good' if 60 of them do. That, however, is really where it all starts.

Consider what is involved in bringing to market a new product and the research required to achieve success. In the following list the second column gives some of the research requirements:

| | | |
|---|---|---|
| ● | *Product concept* | Size and nature of total market? |
| | | Projected profitability? |
| | | Competition? |
| | | Demographic trends? |
| | | Production capability? |
| ● | *Product development* | Product variations? |
| | | Pricing |
| | | Packaging etc.? |
| ● | *Promotion* | Do advertisements work in the target market? |
| | | Media selection? |
| | | Other promotional techniques – direct mail, sales promotion? |
| ● | *Distribution* | Methods – direct, via third party, via distributors? |
| ● | *After-sales* | How best to maintain contact with consumer sector to detect changes in consumer profile? |

## Product development

Marketing ensures that products are developed to meet demand profitably – the aim of every business.

## Pricing

Pricing is by no means straightforward. The price 'weapon' has many uses in business. For example, by deliberately keeping its prices low to achieve high sales (a large 'market share') a business can attempt to starve competitors into vulnerability. Alternatively, by setting its prices high for a 'quality' product, a business can establish 'premium' status for the product – then, the desired profit can be achieved with a lower number of sales.

## Distribution

The means of effective distribution are, of course, vital to any business, but all too often they are an afterthought. For example, is a direct sales force more cost-effective than using a network of agents or wholesalers? Are salespeople or distributors necessary at all, or can the product or service be distributed direct to the consumer?

These questions and more need to be answered, but the final solution must be cost-effective to the company and acceptable to the consumer.

## CASE STUDY *Shell and the identification of a top-up society*

This case study is intended to exemplify the nature of the marketing function. It shows how the company Shell, faced with 'saturated' markets for petrol sales, identified a new opening in the marketplace. It shows how every aspect of meeting the requirement of this newly identified market has been consumer-orientated, from the detailed research of consumer requirements to ensuring the quality offered in the Select shop outlets.

A **market-conscious** organisation should always be on the lookout for fresh changes and opportunities in the marketplace. In the early 1990s, Shell UK commissioned a specialist market research company to research motorists' shopping habits, and the results indicated that regular 'topping up' is a way of life for 90 per cent of people.

### What is topping-up?

In addition to their major supermarket 'spend', many people regularly buy 'little extras' such as groceries, toiletries, snacks and drinks. Some of these are traditional so-called 'emergency' or 'distress' purchases, but there may also be other 'top-up' requirements such as sweets and snacks to satisfy a late-night craving, flowers or chocolates for a gift, or simply a break from a long car journey.

### Moving on from saturated markets

Shell's move into the top-up market was partly a response to the saturation of the existing market for petrol and other fuel sales. Fuel is no longer a growth market – and an increasing number of competitors are chasing a share of the cake. Practically every family now has a car, so it is unlikely that there will be significant increases in fuel demand as a result of car purchases. Shell

7

therefore saw the need to branch out and give motorists other reasons to spend their money on further Shell products.

Shell's first thought was to move into selling traditional motoring-related goods – tyres, batteries and accessories. However, it was not possible to compete head-on with suppliers who specialise in these things. Shell's marketing arm then turned to the 'top-up' society.

'Top-up' defines *how* we shop rather than *where*, and involves a number of different types of retailers including the old-style corner shop, convenience chains, and petrol stations. As yet no one dominates this market.

### Meeting the needs of the top-up shopper

To meet the needs of the top-up shopper it is necessary to have a suitable range of products in a shop. The shop should be easy to get to, have long opening hours and a quick, efficient service.

Market research reveals the following:

- Top-up shoppers are mainly 16–44 year-olds.
- 71 per cent of people top-up at least three times a week as part of their normal routine, and 90 per cent do so about once a week.
- Extra items bought in this way account for a quarter of the average weekly grocery bill.
- Most top-up purchases are made outside conventional shopping hours.

A number of factors have contributed to make this a real niche in the market. These factors include:

- the growth of single households
- an increase in the number of working women
- extended travelling times to and from work
- a growing tendency for family members to eat at different times
- a lengthening of the desired shopping day resulting from the other factors.

### The development of Select shops

Shell already had an excellent base from which to move into this market:

- It had a network of service station shops.
- It had a large customer base.
- It had a first-class brand image (and one of the best known logos in the world).

The company therefore developed a strategy for the 1990s to build on this foundation. Between 1988 and 1993 it launched and developed 360 Select shops and invested a further £250 million on converting all Shell-owned sites to cater for the top-up society.

Shell already had a chain of service stations. It had the staff already working extended opening hours, and had a well organised distribution network. Site layouts provide easy access with high standards of safety and good lighting. Therefore the cost of adding extra business to existing lines is relatively small. Shell has the ability to create at least 1000 Select sites to cater for a market which in 1992 was worth over £30 billion a year. The pictograph shows some of the items sold in Select shops in 1993.

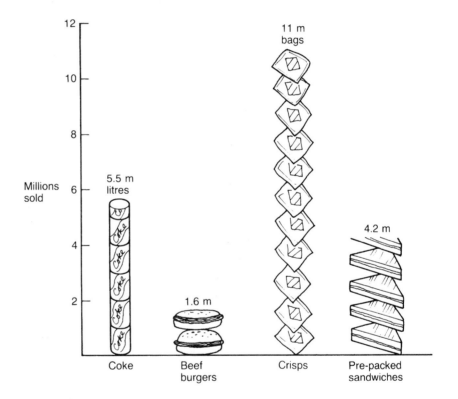

## A franchise operation

Many Select shops are currently run as franchise operations (for more information on franchising, see Chapter 7). By franchising, Shell is able to specify the core range of goods that must be stocked, but cannot dictate where the franchisees buy stock.

However, it is possible to insist on tight standards of excellence and professionalism across the network. This is combined with a pledge from the franchisee guaranteeing the level of service. Shell insists on the highest standards of goods and services from suppliers (e.g. by visiting the egg-mayonnaise factory to monitor what goes into sandwiches).

A key ingredient of the product that Shell provides is its emphasis on *quality*. This starts with the recruitment of franchisees, who undergo an intensive selection procedure. It is not enough to have the necessary capital; they also need a broadly based business awareness and the right attitude towards the customer. This is reinforced with staff training, and monitored by a 'mystery motorist', a professional researcher who visits outlets frequently to assess their performance.

The public face that the company wants to present is one of friendly, efficient, courteous service, and this is enhanced by investment in technology. Select shops are the smallest retailers to have bar-code scanning, and sales are logged electronically to monitor performance of particular lines. Each shop's stock can then be tailored to suit the customer but the franchisee can contribute greatly to this by using local knowledge. For instance, in some areas of Scotland a particular brand of drink is very popular, and Shell's flexibility makes room for that in the shop. There is thus a common core of products combined with a degree of local demand – this is called 'micromarketing'.

**Questions**

1  In what ways has Shell's decision to cater for the top-up market been a response to changes in its marketing environment?

2  How does Shell's move into the top-up market exemplify the process of strategic marketing?

3  What evidence is given in the case study that marketing activity is a key ingredient of everything that an organisation does?

4  What do you understand by the following terms used in the case study?

| | |
|---|---|
| **a** top-up shopper | **e** franchise |
| **b** range of products | **f** broadly based business awareness |
| **c** niche in the market | **g** micromarketing. |
| **d** brand image | |

# STRATEGIC DECISION-MAKING

In recent years a lot of emphasis in Business Studies has been given to **strategic decision-making** in organisations. G. Johnson and K. Scholes, in their key text *Exploring Corporate Strategy* (Prentice Hall), identify the characteristics of strategy as follows.

Firstly, strategic decisions are likely to be concerned with the **scope** of an organisation's activities. For example, should the organisation concentrate on just one part of the chocolate market (e.g. filled bars) or should it produce a wide variety of sweets, confectionery, ice-creams etc.?

Secondly, strategy is to do with the matching of the activities of an organisation to its **environment**. For example, does an organisation operate in a local, national or Europe-wide market? Clearly this decision is of key importance in deciding many other things, such as how the product is marketed, the finance required etc. An organisation needs to weigh up the opportunities and threats presented by the environment in which it operates – for example, the opportunities from increased sales, and the threats of increased competition in a larger market.

Thirdly, strategy is concerned with the matching of the organisation's activities to its **resource capability**. Clearly the organisation needs to understand its resource limitations if it is to make best use of opportunities. An organisation that fails to advertise may find that nobody knows about it. An organisation that spends too much on advertising may find that it has not enough resources available for research and development, production, and a thousand and one other things. Any organisation that chooses to spread its sphere of influence into international markets needs to have the resources to be able to do so.

Fourthly, strategic decisions have major **resource implications**. Decisions need to be made to ensure that the organisation has the most appropriate resources to move forward. For example, in the late 1980s Mars produced an ice-cream version of the successful chocolate bar in order to compensate for the fall in sales in the summer months. This required a considerable research programme and tooling the company up with new capital equipment, as well as expenditures on sales and promotion.

Fifthly, strategic decisions are likely to affect **operational decisions**. For example, when Mars moved into ice-cream it needed to set in motion a whole new training programme for employees, as well as changes to sales and distribution methods.

Sixthly, the strategy of an organisation will be affected by the **values and expectations** of those who have power in the organisation. Those groupings of stakeholders that have most influence in the organisation will be able to shape the strategy according to their values and expectations. For example, an influential group of senior managers and directors may have a vision of their company expanding to dominate a market.

Seventhly, strategic decisions are likely to affect the **long-term direction** of a company. Strategic decisions tend to involve thinking about where the organisation is going in the longer period. Today more and more organisations place marketing at the heart of this strategy.

Finally, strategic decisions are usually **complex**. This complexity arises because strategic decisions involve a high degree of **uncertainty**. They are likely to require an integrated approach involving all elements of the organisation. We can see, therefore, the importance of the marketing function being at the heart of this integrated approach. Strategic decisions are also likely to require and involve major changes in an organisation.

Johnson and Scholes have identified three major ingredients of the strategic management process (see Figure 1.3). We can see clearly how these three elements underpinned Shell's decision to move into the top-up market and Mars' decision to produce ice-creams.

- **Strategic analysis** is concerned with understanding the strategic position of a company (e.g. What is our scope of operation? How can we match our activities to our environment? How can we match our activities to our resource capability?).
- **Strategic choice** involves setting out a menu of options to choose from, weighing up these options, and then choosing the 'best' strategy for the organisation.
- **Strategic implementation** involves putting the 'best' strategy into practice.

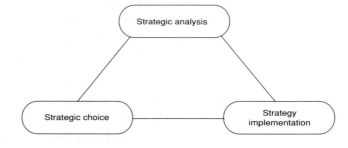

FIGURE 1.3
*The three parts of the strategy management process*

---

## CASE STUDY *Competition in confectionery ice-cream*

The market for confectionery ice-cream grew dramatically in the early 1990s. In 1989 it did not exist, but by 1993 it was worth £150 million a year (in a total ice-cream sector that was worth only £770 million).

The first confectionery ice-cream to come to the market was the Mars ice-cream bar in 1989. It was introduced to balance the traditional slump in sales of Mars bars in the winter months.

Very quickly new competitors came to the market. For example, Walls teamed up with Cadbury to produce ice-cream versions of some of its popular chocolate lines. Nestlé also entered the market.

Walls, which has more than 60 per cent of the impulse market (mainly lollies bought from shops), and Nestlé's Lyons Maid (12 per cent) supply freezers free of charge to small retailers and corner shops on condition that they stock only their ice-creams in the cabinet. Manufacturers do not just supply freezers to shops, they also maintain and service them – all the shops have to pay is the electricity bill.

A major problem for Mars, despite its early start, was in getting its ice-creams into retail outlets. Some experts feel that if Mars had had access to freezers at an earlier date it could have made its market position unbeatable. Instead it has become just one competitor in the field. Walls has spent over £20 million on supplying freezers to retail outlets.

Mars now offers a range of other well-known brands such as Bounty, Twix and Snickers in ice-cream forms. Walls has Cadbury's Dairy Milk and Nestlé sells its Milky Bar, Kit Kat and Aero.

The Mars company is frustrated that it cannot compete on equal terms in small shops.

**Questions**

1  Explain how Mars' move into confectionery ice-cream involved strategic decision-making.

2  How does the case study indicate that there have been some major weaknesses in Mars' strategic thinking that have prevented it from dominating the market?

3  What relative weaknesses does the case indicate in Mars' position relative to its competitors?

4  Explain how Walls and Nestlé's move into this market has involved strategic decision-making.

5  What key lessons would you draw out of this case about strategic decision-making?

## A CYCLE OF MARKETING ACTIVITIES

In Chapter 12 we shall look at marketing planning in greater depth. For the time being it will be helpful to make a few general points about the marketing process. The implementation of marketing policy can be viewed as an **ongoing cyclical process**.

**Reconnaissance** involves carrying out market and product research to find out what customers want, how well the products are performing, and the strengths and weaknesses of competitors. This research should enable an organisation to make forecasts and predictions of likely future trends.

**Strategy** involves deciding on objectives and priorities for an organisation as well as laying down clear plans for marketing activities (e.g. what range of products will be made, their prices, and how they will be delivered to customers).

**Operations** involves putting the plans into practice – organising advertising and selling campaigns, getting the goods to the right place at the right time, etc.

**Control** involves checking on the effectiveness of the marketing operation (e.g. checking on the volume of sales made, measuring the effectiveness of advertising, analysing the profitability of operations). Once again, *this feeds back into reconnaissance.* If sales are falling, why is this so? Why has an advert been so effective? The information that stems from control activities should feed back into fresh research (see Figure 1.4).

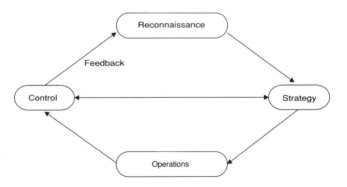

FIGURE 1.4
*A cycle of marketing
activities*

**Marketing planning** is essential for an organisation. It enables the organisation to plan for the present and for the future and to learn from the past. The three main objectives of planning are:

- to assess how well the organisation is doing in the various markets in which it operates
- to identify the strengths and weaknesses of the organisation in each of these markets
- to establish goals and objectives, so that resources can be used in an appropriate way.

## PLANNING FOR INTERNATIONAL MARKETING

Marketing on an international scale usually involves increasing the scope of operations. It may also involve new considerations such as language translation, coping with different currencies and other factors that do not exist in the home market. In today's global economy, goods and services can be moved very quickly from one area to another. Businesses also need to be constantly aware of the threat of competition from international competitors in what they traditionally regard to be their home markets. Remember how we saw in the earlier part of this chapter how quickly Japanese competition decimated the UK motorcycle industry.

The key questions that any business should consider before moving into international markets include the following:

- How is the market, including the UK market, changing for our business?
- Should we become an international business, looking upon wider geographical areas as our primary market rather than just the UK?
- Would becoming an international business alter the scale of the targets in our plans?
- In what ways will we be vulnerable to more competition in our present markets, whether solely in the UK or on an international scale?
- Should we form links, merge or acquire businesses to strengthen our market presence, broaden our range of products and services and spread our financial risk?
- Is our management and structure appropriate to exploit new opportunities or defend our position?
- What training, in languages and other skills, do we need to be able to trade on an international scale?
- Who in the firm is going to be responsible for deciding how to make the most of international opportunities?

# BEYOND STRATEGIC PLANNING

The sheer uncertainty of the business environment today has meant that business thinking has had to move beyond strategic planning. The unpredictability of the future, the rapid rate of change of events, the time taken to feed back from the results given by control mechanisms to new reconnaissance, often means that we have got to think faster than existing planning mechanisms allow. This does not mean that strategic planning has no place in the modern environment; rather it means that *some decisions have to be made so quickly that they require fast on-the-ground decision-making*.

The emphasis in today's modern corporation is on being lean and fit, and being able to 'think on your feet'. If an opportunity arises such as the reunification of Germany or the opening of Eastern Europe, then you need to be able to grasp the opportunities presented, as the advertising agency Saatchi & Saatchi did with their campaign 'First into Eastern Europe'.

The implication for marketing is that all members of an organisation need to be aware of the importance of a marketing philosophy which sees the consumer as being at the centre of all organisational activities. Individual members of organisations need to take on board this philosophy for themselves so that they can react in appropriate ways in novel circumstances. Marketing is thus everyone's business – it is not just something that you leave to the strategic planners to sort out.

**ASSIGNMENT** A case study in this chapter has described how Shell UK was the first oil company to identify the top-up market. Because of the nature of its existing operations it was in a good position to win a handsome share of this market. However, there are competitors in the market – for example, other oil companies with networks of service stations, corner shops, hypermarkets etc. Many of these competitors can quickly copy some of the ideas that Shell has adopted.

For this assignment you should imagine that you are a researcher working for the retailing department at Shell. You have been asked to produce a short report for the company outlining the strengths and weaknesses of the current strategy of moving into the top-up market. You also need to identify the opportunities and threats that exist in the top-up market. Produce a 1500-word report supported by three overhead projector transparencies to be presented to the retail manager at Shell head office. Your report should include the following:

**Task** **a** A brief explanation of what the 'top-up society' is.

**Task** **b** An explanation of why it is important for Shell to continue to expand its presence in this market.

**Task** **c** An outline of Shell's existing strengths which will make it a major player in this market (e.g. existing network of service stations).

**Task** **d** An outline of any weaknesses that Shell may have in this market (e.g. that in some regions service stations are few and far between).

**Task** **e** An explanation of the existing and possible future opportunities which will enable Shell to expand its presence in this market (e.g. the recent development of a new Shell logo giving it a more up-to-date image).

**Task** **f** An explanation of the existing and possible future threats which are dangers to Shell's performance in this market (e.g. the development of competitors, including hypermarkets selling cut-price fuel).

**Task** **g** An analysis of what Shell's major objectives should be in the top-up market.

**Task** **h** An explanation of how these objectives can be built in to every aspect of Shell's operation in the top-up market.

**Task** **i** Three OHPs for a 15-minute presentation to an invited audience.

# Understanding the Marketing Environment and the Customer

It has been said that the only constant thing in life is change. Organisations today exist in a far more complex business environment than ever before and this has increased the importance of the marketing function. Influences in the environment might be friendly or hostile and pose many varied threats and opportunities. Marketing involves understanding this changing environment so that organisations can develop their activities to deliver appropriate goods or services more effectively than their competitors. Such an understanding should therefore be the driving force behind the decisions they make.

In the modern world, no individual or group can make decisions which are not affected by a wide range of external factors. The internal structure and functioning of an organisation and the wider market and business environment in which it exists are constantly changing. Such **interdependence** is a basic fact of business life. Some changes are cosmetic and almost imperceptible, while others – such as the takeover of another company, higher interest rates or the creation of the European single market – may have a dramatic impact on an organisation's activities.

An appreciation of the importance of interdependence is vital for understanding how an organisation functions and which way forward it should move. A marketer should not only be aware of his or her own market and the actions of competitors, and have the ability to research and help with the development of new ideas and products, but should also be aware of changing business conditions within a wider environment and be able to suggest strategies and tactics which respond with appropriate measures.

## PEST ANALYSIS

One useful way of analysing an organisation's external environment is by grouping external forces neatly into four areas by using a **PEST** analysis. These forces are shown in Figure 2.1.

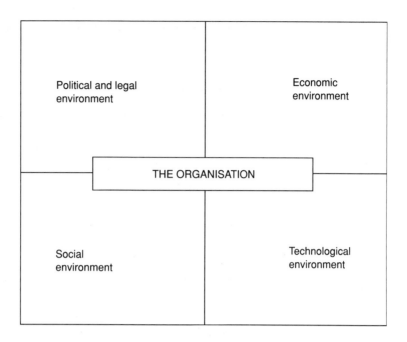

FIGURE 2.1
*The wider business
environment*

### Political and legal factors

Business conditions are influenced by both political decisions and legal controls. For example, the move towards supply-side economics during the 1980s encouraged many people to become self-employed. In contrast, unfavourable political conditions or political instability may create a lot of uncertainty in business.

### Economic factors

Though the economic environment is influenced by domestic economic policies, it is also dependent on world economic trends. For example, both domestic economic decisions and world recession dramatically affected the UK business environment during the recessions of the 1980s and 1990s. All types of organisations, no matter how successful, were in some way affected by such trends. Rates of economic growth, inflation, consumption patterns, income distribution and many other economic trends will determine the nature of products or services required by customers.

### Social factors

To understand the social environment involves close analysis of the behaviour of society. Demographic changes such as population growth, movements and age distribution will be important, as will changes in cultural values and social trends such as family size and social behaviour.

### Technological factors

In marketing goods and services, organisations must become aware of new materials as well as developments in manufacturing techniques and business processes. At the same time organisations have to look at the nature of their products and, in particular, their cost-effectiveness and their performance in relation to competitors.

---

# THE INTERNATIONAL MARKETING ENVIRONMENT

Marketing overseas poses many additional risks. It is, therefore, vital that the overseas environment be carefully scrutinised.

The *political* environment is made up of laws, regulations and various ways of doing business which an international marketer should have regard to before marketing to a particular country. Regular changes of government or political uncertainty may make it difficult to guarantee continuity of operations. The political beliefs of governments may also influence legislation. These laws may affect pricing policy, restrict advertising, create minimum standards and influence distribution systems. Other areas which might need to be investigated are monopoly and merger legislation, import controls, laws of ownership and acceptance of international trademarks, patents and copyrights.

In the *economic* environment many factors affect the consumers' ability to buy goods and services. For example, the purchasing power of the average consumer in Switzerland is roughly thirteen times that of the average consumer in Turkey. Ownership of consumer durables is, therefore, widely different, as are demands for different types of products. Infrastructure is an important economic consideration in overseas markets: road developments, transport, communications and even the availability of power may influence marketing decisions.

*Social* and *cultural* behaviour has a strong bearing on how people behave as consumers. In an overseas market consumers may have different attitudes towards ownership, designs, product usage, styles, colours, symbols and words. Such cultural differences are of great relevance to the marketer and may result in a need to modify or redevelop products for certain markets.

We frequently take different types of *technology* for granted. The nature of technology available is extremely important in international marketing. Technological awareness, support and service industries as well as the distribution system may influence the success of a project and determine its effectiveness in an overseas market.

---

## CASE STUDY *Euro Disney experiences problems*

As a result of massive losses Euro Disney has shelved plans to build a second theme park. The company set considerable store by the second park, which they argued would give the resort 'critical mass' and ensure that visitors had so many attractions to see that they would want to stay at least overnight in the resort's hotels. These hotels have experienced dismally low occupancy rates in the region of 45 per cent.

The chairman of Euro Disney feels that the current economic situation does not allow the company to proceed with the second park. The feeling is that it is necessary to be prudent in the short term and hope that things get better in the future. The company blames many of its problems on the downturn in the European economies and the devaluation of the pound, lira and peseta against the franc, which has made France a much more expensive holiday destination.

One analyst has stated that the Euro Disney project needs rethinking. Although it has been hit by the economic downturn, unrealistic assumptions were made about European consumers. It would have to look at other strategies to fill its hotels.

**Questions**   1   Using the PEST format as a guide, make a list of the positive and negative factors that may have affected Euro Disney.
2   To what extent do you feel that the marketing environment influenced the performance of Euro Disney?

---

## THE MARKET

An organisation can use the picture of its external environment created by the PEST analysis to help it to identify marketing opportunities. Such opportunities will exist in the **marketplace**.

> **A market exists when buyers and sellers come into contact.**

In some markets the buyer and the seller may meet face-to-face. In others they may rarely meet and simply contact each other using some form of external business communications, such as letter, phone or fax.

Organisations tend to be classified according to the goods or services they supply, and the markets for these goods or services are known as either consumer markets or organisational markets.

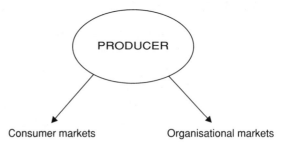

FIGURE 2.2
*Types of markets*

**Consumer markets** are made up of individuals who purchase items for personal or domestic consumption. Consumers typically buy from retailers and their transactions tend to be of low value. They include:

- rapid-turnover consumer goods with a short shelf life, manufactured for immediate consumption – for example, food and confectionery
- durable consumer goods with a much longer life which are bought less frequently – such as cars, televisions and videos.

**Industrial markets** or **organisational markets** consist of buyers who purchase goods and services to use towards the production of other goods or services. They include:

- industrial consumption goods which have a frequent purchase pattern but a limited life – such as chemicals and lubricants
- industrial durable goods which have a longer life – such as machinery and equipment.

Some organisations sell products in both consumer and industrial markets. A motor manufacturer may produce cars for individuals to buy as well as commercial vehicles for manufacturers to use.

Among the factors affecting an organisation within the marketplace is that of **competition**. Competition occurs where two or more organisations act independently to supply their products to the same group of consumers. Some markets are signified by an abundance of products and services so that customers have a massive choice. In other markets there may be little competition (if any) and consumers may only be able to make a limited choice from the range of goods or services on offer.

*Direct competition* exists where organisations produce similar products which appeal to the same group of consumers. For example, the Ford Mondeo is in direct competition with the Vauxhall Cavalier.

Even when an organisation provides a unique end-product with no direct competition, it will still have to consider *indirect competition*. This occurs where potential customers examine slightly different ways of meeting the same needs. For example, instead of going on holiday to St Ives they might go to Majorca; instead of buying a newspaper they might buy a magazine.

---

## CASE STUDY  *BT's war with cable firms*

British Telecom is squaring up for open warfare with Britain's cable TV industry. Both sides have been sniping at the other over speculation that BT wants to provide an entertainment service down its telephone lines.

Iain Vallance, BT's chief executive, is expected to announce plans to press ahead with the development of a video-on-demand (VOD) service, which would enable customers to dial up videos from their living-room sofa without paying cable subscriptions. Such a service would threaten the billions of pounds that cable companies are investing in the UK and could trigger one of the most bitter and expensive commercial scraps for years.

Cable companies are enraged that BT is encroaching on their patch and are threatening a legal battle that will have corporate lawyers salivating with delight. The cable companies have asked the government to stand by its current ban on BT entering this business. Restrictions have been put on BT (and Mercury) from sending entertainment services over their networks to allow the new cable franchises the opportunity at least to get off the ground. BT is barred until at least 1998 from going into conventional cable entertainment, but the sector is becoming so important that the company wants a slice of the action sooner.

Given the nature of this battle, if BT enters the fray the scrap is likely to be as interesting as any of the programmes it may broadcast.

**Questions**

1 Would you describe the competition between BT and the cable companies as direct or indirect?

2 Who would benefit and who would lose out if BT enters this market?

Markets involve customers, so an important characteristic of any market is its nature and size. For consumer goods markets, published figures on market size are normally readily available. As well as this, it is possible to obtain information on areas such as:

- population size, distribution and growth
- age distribution
- changing family patterns
- social trends and fashions
- trends in income and expenditure.

It is often the case that figures for organisational markets are more difficult to obtain. If a company knows the size of its market and knows that it can achieve a certain share, it can make much more accurate decisions about stock levels, production and sales forecasts. If only limited information was available it would have to invest more in primary research techniques (see Chapter 3).

## CASE STUDY *The changing nature of the housing market*

Examine the figures in the four accompanying tables which refer to the UK housing market in 1993.

**Questions**

1 Comment on the changing nature of the housing market in the UK.

2 Explain how such information might influence the actions of housebuilders.

**House-building starts (thousands)**

|      | Private sector | Housing assocs | Local authority | All houses |
|------|---------------|----------------|-----------------|------------|
| 1983 | 172 | 14 | 35 | 221 |
| 1984 | 158 | 13 | 27 | 198 |
| 1985 | 166 | 13 | 22 | 200 |
| 1986 | 180 | 13 | 20 | 213 |
| 1987 | 197 | 13 | 20 | 230 |
| 1988 | 221 | 14 | 16 | 252 |
| 1989 | 170 | 16 | 15 | 201 |
| 1990 | 135 | 19 | 8 | 162 |
| 1991 | 135 | 22 | 4 | 161 |
| 1992 | 120 | 33 | 2 | 156 |

**Average prices of modern semi-detached houses**

|  | £ | Annual change (%) |
|---|---|---|
| Northern | 51 373 | −2.4 |
| Yorks & Humb. | 51 858 | +1.8 |
| E. Midlands | 47 564 | −5.2 |
| E. Anglia | 48 247 | −6.9 |
| Greater London | 79 297 | −11.7 |
| Outer Metropolitan | 72 546 | −6.5 |
| Outer South East | 58 373 | −7.4 |
| South West | 59 621 | −2.9 |
| W. Midlands | 55 480 | −5.3 |
| North West | 52 544 | −9.9 |
| Wales | 52 525 | +9.6 |
| Scotland | 50 429 | −2.0 |
| N. Ireland | 35 930 | +2.8 |
| **UK overall** | **58 653** | **−5.0** |

**Age of dwelling**

|  | % |
|---|---|
| Pre-1918 | 20.1 |
| 1918–38 | 19.9 |
| 1939–59 | 18.9 |
| 1960–71 | 17.7 |
| 1972–82 | 14.8 |
| 1983–93 | 8.6 |

**Type of dwelling**

|  | % |
|---|---|
| Detached house | 14.8 |
| Semi-detached house | 29.6 |
| Terraced house | 28.0 |
| Bungalow | 9.0 |
| Flat/maisonette | 18.3 |
| Other | 0.3 |

A market's size must be large enough and have sufficient purchasing power to generate profits for the organisations operating within it. It is frequently argued that competition is good for both consumers and the business community. It forces businesses to offer new and improved products and wide selections at reasonable prices. As a result, consumers have a more varied selection of goods and services from which to choose. Without competition, consumers would have to accept a limited range of products and services at higher prices.

# CUSTOMER BEHAVIOUR

The process of buying a good or service is not as simple as it might seem. People or organisations do not just go to their supplier without thinking carefully about what they want. Wherever there is a choice, decisions are involved and these decisions may be influenced by complex motives.

Markets fall into two broad categories of *consumer* and *organisational*, and the buying patterns within each are quite different.

## 1  Consumer markets

We can sum up the information gathered so far in the following few sentences.

The ultimate consumers are persons or households that purchase products or services for personal or family use. The needs and wants of consumers affect their purchasing decisions. Businesses must determine what products or services consumers need and want and then make sure these items are available. This is why organisations require detailed knowledge about the age, sex, occupation, social grouping, etc. of their consumers. Such detail enables them to match the needs of each group of their consumers with an appropriate product.

Marketing therefore calls to attention such needs and enables organisations to provide goods and services in order to satisfy them. For example, Iceland, the frozen food retailer, identified the need of many households for a quick method of organising meals without the drudge of having to prepare them from scratch and identified the massive growth of the freezer market.

Much has been written about why consumers buy. There are many influences on their behaviour and these all affect each individual in a slightly different way.

---

## CASE STUDY  *Having seen the show, eat the cheese*

In December 1993 Dairy Crest launched Emmerdale, a new marbled cheddar, into shops. The cheese is first being distributed through Asda stores nationwide and will then be rolled out to other chains.

The product is the latest in a line of TV-associated brands which capitalise on the success of TV programmes which are household names. The great benefit is that the product has a pre-prepared **brand name** and a ready-made set of **brand values** with a loyal following of over 10 million TV viewers. Using TV programmes is a marketing technique which has become increasingly popular over recent years.

The Emmerdale name carries a gentle, rural image which suggests health, an outdoor life and fitness. The new brand has been developed to capture the tone and lifestyle of the series. Recognition of the brand name in the supermarket will surprise consumers and generate interest in the product which should help it to sell. The greatest benefit, however, is that the brand name is broadcast several times a week on national TV.

**Questions**   1   Explain why it is important to understand how consumers might react to this product.

2   Describe the characteristics of the type of consumer you might expect to buy Emmerdale cheese.

3   Link five other TV programmes with possible product developments. Give a brief description of the type of consumer the products might appeal to in each case.

A group of important factors which clearly affect consumer behaviour are the **economic determinants of consumer demand**. These include:

- The real disposable incomes available to consumers to spend on goods and services. An increase in real incomes will generally increase the demand for goods and services unless a commodity is an inferior one (e.g. synthetic fibre clothing).
- The relative prices of substitute products whose purchase might be preferred or seen as better value for money.
- Population size or composition. For example, if the birth rate increases, Mothercare products could be in greater demand.
- Government influences in areas such as credit regulations and safety requirements. These could influence demand for a host of commodities.
- Tastes, fashions and habits, which constantly influence the pattern of demand for goods and services (e.g. compact discs instead of records).

Another area that the marketer must understand are the needs or wants that inspire **individual motivation** and give rise to particular forms of purchasing behaviour. The best known theory of motivation is that of Abraham **Maslow** who suggested that, although it is difficult to analyse individual needs, it is possible to

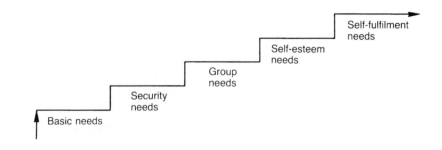

FIGURE 2.3
*Abraham Maslow's
hierarchy of needs*

develop a hierarchical picture which can be split into five broad categories (see Figure 2.3).

- *Basic needs* are concerned with acquiring food, shelter and clothing.
- *Security needs* are concerned with physical well-being and the need to provide protection, perhaps with a house in a safe trouble-free environment, with protected and reliable items within it.
- *Group needs* centre on the desire for acceptance, the need for affiliation, and purchases associated with belonging to a community.
- *Self-esteem needs* stem from one's desire for status, for a sense of achievement and for respect for one's accomplishments. This might lead to the possession of prestigious items, through living a lavish lifestyle, or self-esteem generated, for example, through making donations to charities.
- *Self-fulfilment* is concerned with full personal development and individual creativity. To achieve this level, individuals try to ensure that their individual skills and capacities are being fully utilised.

The implications of Maslow's theory are easy to perceive as different products and services are related to different needs. For example, life assurance is rooted in a desire for safety, a BMW is related to self-esteem needs, etc. It is noticeable that in Western societies there are far more products related to self-fulfilment needs than in third-world countries. Such a theory helps an organisation to bear the consumer more closely in mind when undertaking marketing and advertising activity.

Another theory of motivation is the **self-image theory**. The 'self' is an individual's image of himself or herself. Within this 'self' there are various ways to maintain and enhance this image. The individual will make choices of car, music, clothing, places to shop which fit into his or her perception of 'self'. By discovering how customers wish themselves to be perceived in terms of an image, organisations can design, promote and retail goods which are consistent with those sought by prospective purchasers.

## Building up a consumer profile

One important area of interest to the marketer is the need to understand the **personality** of their customers. If any of their customers have similar personalities, then it may be possible to divide the market up on the basis of such **stereotypes**. For example, various models of cars, records and fashion products all reflect the personality traits of customers. Think of products you use which reflect your personality. They may include clothes, the way you have your hair cut or styled or the car you drive.

**Culture** encompasses standard patterns of behaviour and also plays an important role in shaping our purchasing patterns. It stems from traditions, beliefs and values of the community in which we live. For example, the consumption of alcohol is an essential feature of western life. It is, however, forbidden to Muslim communities. Though a nation might be characterised by one culture, there may be a series of sub-cultures existing within it. Sub-cultures are important for organisations that wish to target their brands to those who share the values of that particular sub-culture – for example, youth markets, ethnic groups, senior citizens, etc.

Expenditure and consumption patterns can be broken up according to the 'social class' of the consumer through **socio-economic grouping**. Dividing groups up into different classes according to income is called **social stratification**. Each class will have its own pattern of behaviour which will serve to reinforce its purchasing and consumption patterns. Socio-economic groups classify people according to their similarity of income, occupation and education. One of the best known classifications used to divide people in the UK is shown in Figure 2.4.

This form of socio-economic grouping provides a reliable picture of the relationship between occupation and income. Members of each group will have similar priorities in behaviour which will influence their needs. For example, we would expect As and Bs to spend more of their income on private education, private health care and antiques than the other socio-economic groupings.

| Socio-economic group | Social class | Type of occupation | Examples |
|---|---|---|---|
| A | Upper/upper-middle class | Higher managerial, administrative, professional | Surgeon, director of a large company |
| B | Middle class | Intermediate managerial, professional, administrative | Bank manager, headteacher, surveyor |
| C1 | Lower middle class | Supervisory, junior managerial or administrative, clerical | Bank clerk, nurse, teacher, estate agent |
| C2 | Skilled working class | Skilled manual workers | Joiner, welder, foreman |
| D | Working class | Semi-skilled and unskilled | Driver, postman, porter |
| E | Those at lowest level of subsistence | Low-paid/unemployed | Casual workers, state pensioners, unemployed |

FIGURE 2.4
*Socio-economic groupings*

## CASE STUDY *Newspaper readership*

Examine the chart on page 31 and then answer the questions.

**Questions**
1 Describe the differences between the type of consumers who read *The Star* and those who read *The Independent*, as suggested by the chart.

2 Explain why this chart would be useful for a publishing group wishing to introduce a new national daily.

Another way of defining consumers which has proved popular with market researchers is by means of **sagacity life-cycle groupings**. The basic idea behind sagacity grouping is that people have changing behavioural patterns and aspirations as they go through life. Four main stages of life-cycle are defined which are then further sub-divided according to income and occupation groups (see Figure 2.5).

**Sales and readership profiles of national daily newspapers (1993)**

| | Tabloid/ broad-sheet | Circu-lation (000) | Adult readership (000) | Adult readership (%) | Adult readership profiles | | | | | | | |
| | | | | | Sex | | Age | | | Class | |
| | | | | | Men (%) | Women (%) | 15/34 (%) | 35/54 (%) | 55+ (%) | ABC1 (%) | C2DE (%) |
|---|---|---|---|---|---|---|---|---|---|---|---|
| *Population profile:* | | | | | 48 | 52 | 37 | 32 | 32 | 45 | 56 |
| Sun | T | 3 517 | 9 857 | 22 | 56 | 44 | 45 | 30 | 24 | 27 | 74 |
| Daily Mirror | T | 2 680 | 7 864 | 17 | 55 | 45 | 35 | 32 | 32 | 28 | 72 |
| Daily Mail | T | 1 775 | 4 723 | 10 | 50 | 50 | 30 | 35 | 35 | 61 | 39 |
| Daily Express | T | 1 497 | 3 903 | 9 | 53 | 47 | 29 | 31 | 39 | 56 | 44 |
| Daily Telegraph | B | 1 025 | 2 715 | 6 | 55 | 45 | 23 | 36 | 41 | 84 | 18 |
| Star | T | 773 | 2 478 | 5 | 65 | 35 | 49 | 35 | 16 | 22 | 77 |
| Daily Record (Scotland) | T | 755 | 1 941 | 4 | 52 | 48 | 39 | 34 | 27 | 31 | 69 |
| Today | T | 538 | 1 743 | 4 | 61 | 39 | 41 | 38 | 21 | 43 | 56 |
| Guardian | B | 416 | 1 457 | 3 | 56 | 44 | 42 | 37 | 21 | 77 | 23 |
| Times | B | 366 | 1 185 | 3 | 59 | 41 | 36 | 40 | 25 | 84 | 16 |
| Independent | B | 347 | 1 148 | 3 | 58 | 42 | 43 | 40 | 17 | 81 | 18 |
| Financial Times | B | 290 | 745 | 2 | 68 | 32 | 36 | 45 | 18 | 88 | 13 |

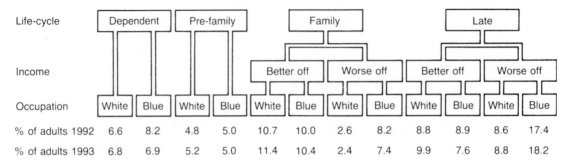

| Life-cycle | Dependent | | Pre-family | | Family | | | | Late | | | |
|---|---|---|---|---|---|---|---|---|---|---|---|---|
| Income | | | | | Better off | | Worse off | | Better off | | Worse off | |
| Occupation | White | Blue | White | Blue | White | Blue | White | Blue | White | Blue | White | Blue |
| % of adults 1992 | 6.6 | 8.2 | 4.8 | 5.0 | 10.7 | 10.0 | 2.6 | 8.2 | 8.8 | 8.9 | 8.6 | 17.4 |
| % of adults 1993 | 6.8 | 6.9 | 5.2 | 5.0 | 11.4 | 10.4 | 2.4 | 7.4 | 9.9 | 7.6 | 8.8 | 18.2 |

FIGURE 2.5
*Sagacity life-cycle groupings*

The *life-cycle stages* are defined as follows:

- *Dependent* – mainly under-24s, living at home or full-time students
- *Pre-family* – under-35s, who have established their own household but have no children
- *Family* – parents, under 65, with one or more children in the household
- *Late* – includes all adults whose children have left home or who are over 35 and childless.

The *occupation groups* are:

- *White* – head of household in the ABC1 occupation group.
- *Blue* – head of household in the C2DE occupation group.

Over recent years, organisations have paid increasing attention to the **life-style** of their consumers. A life-style is a behaviour pattern adopted by a particular community or a sub-section of it. By understanding such a life-style, they can develop products and

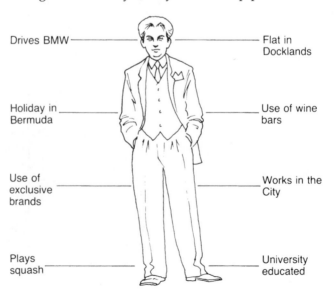

Drives BMW
Holiday in Bermuda
Use of exclusive brands
Plays squash

Flat in Docklands
Use of wine bars
Works in the City
University educated

FIGURE 2.6
*The 'Yuppy' image*

target them to this group. For example, someone upwardly mobile and ambitious would seek an affluent life-style and a higher material standard of living. The British 'Yuppy' is reputed to be a young (24–35), well-educated and upwardly mobile professional. Affluence comes from working hard in particular areas (e.g. in high finance) and is spent on expensive clothes, cars and homes in high-status districts. Agencies frequently advise their clients on how to design and position new products to appeal to groups with similar life-style patterns.

---

## CASE STUDY *The return of the Mighty White*

Allied Bakeries is relaunching its softgrain sliced-bread brand Mighty White with new packaging and a return to TV advertising after an absence of over two years. The £2 million advertising push is an attempt to revitalise the eight-year-old brand in the face of increasing external pressures.

The new adverts revert to a communication strategy last seen five years ago and aimed at children. The campaign now targets mothers – who often feel guilty about giving their children white bread – by explaining the nutritional benefits of Mighty White over its rivals. The adverts are set in Australia to reinforce the brand properties of health and fun and continues the theme of the small child who achieves feats of strength by eating Mighty White.

**Questions** 1 Explain how the Mighty White advertisement might appeal to potential consumers. In your answer refer to at least two of the following: self-image, personality, culture, socio-economic grouping, sagacity life-cycle grouping, life-style.

**2** Explain why consideration of some of the factors listed is important for providers of a product or service.

### Consumers in international markets

Consumer needs in international markets may be more complex. Individuals with incomes and backgrounds similar to those in the UK may display completely different patterns of consumption. This can be explained by their living in different cultures and social environments.

Thus, much of the research we have looked at on consumer behaviour in the UK market may not always be transferable to other societies. For example, though our understanding of motivation through theories such as that of Maslow may relate closely to cultures in western societies, the ideas are difficult to transfer to developing societies where many consumer needs may be at the lower end of the hierarchy. Similarly, socio-economic groupings such as A, B, C1, C2, D and E, though relevant in the UK, may sometimes not relate to societies overseas, particularly former Eastern Bloc countries such as Russia. In the USA a six-point classification is frequently used which bears no relation to the UK model; these six class groupings are upper upper, lower upper, upper middle, lower middle, upper lower and lower lower.

## 2 Organisational markets

Every day in towns and cities across the UK, car dealers hand the keys of new cars to their customers. A complex manufactured product such as this will be made up of numerous parts and materials from many suppliers. Whereas it may be easy to think about the sale of a car from a showroom, we tend not to think of the vast number of sales transactions which have taken place beforehand to bring together the components to manufacture the car.

An organisational market is one where organisations buy products and services which are used directly or indirectly in the production of other goods and services or are to be resold.

Many people are unaware of the significance of the organisational market. Consider again the number of transactions required to manufacture a car. Iron ore is mined and transported to a plant to be made into steel. The steel is bought and formed into the chassis and body. In order to construct a car with about 12 000 different parts, a manufacturer will probably produce about 6000 parts and then buy the other 6000 from other companies. Many of these companies will only supply one part, so the car manufacturer will

have to buy components from several thousand companies. The companies supplying these parts will also have suppliers from whom they buy raw materials and components. Ford is the biggest purchaser in the British motor industry with purchases close to one and a half billion pounds per annum as well as several hundred million pounds worth of purchases from Ford companies abroad. Ford is also the biggest single customer of the British machine tool manufacturing industry, its orders exceeding the rest of the motor industry put together.

When a company is selling to other organisations it still needs to understand the behaviour of its customers. But whereas a consumer product might have a potential market of 56 million users, there are fewer than 3 million organisations in the UK and the likelihood is that the product on offer will appeal to only a very small number of them.

The demand for organisational products and services is called **derived demand** because the amount purchased is determined by the demand for related goods and services. For example, the number of tyres purchased by a motor manufacturer will depend on the demand for vehicles. The industrial supplier is therefore aware that goods are being supplied to help produce someone else's product so that the demands of the final customer can be met.

Depending on derived demand can have serious limitations. Organisational markets are subject to **business cycles** and the demand for industrial products and services may fluctuate violently when the pace of business activity changes. Recessionary economic conditions can therefore lead to severe cutbacks in derived demand for inputs and cause a business to close down plants and lay off workers.

Companies supplying goods in organisational markets face constantly changing circumstances which are often called **contingency factors**. Marketers need to be constantly aware of information relating to such specific conditions. For example:

- The average value of an order follows a lengthy negotiation period and credit facilities will be very important.
- There is a risk of a takeover by the customer.
- Buyers often deliberately exercise buying power to influence the conditions of supply such as terms and prices.
- Large companies often seek out small companies so that they can exercise their buying power more easily.
- Large buyers may pursue a deliberate policy of delaying payment for goods and services received. This can have serious implications for the cashflow of suppliers.
- There is a risk of supplier dependency on the customer.

Organisational markets are described as either vertical or horizontal (see Figure 2.7). Where an organisational product or service is used by only a small number of buyers, it has a **vertical market**. For example, there are few buyers of passenger aircraft or electric locomotives. The main problem for British Coal over recent years has been that the electricity industry has looked for alternative sources of supply not just of coal but also of other sources of energy. An organisational product has a **horizontal market** if it is purchased by many different kinds of organisations in many different industries. For instance, the supply of stationery and lubricants has a broad usage.

FIGURE 2.7
*Vertical and horizontal markets*

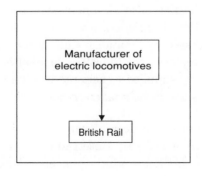
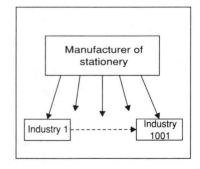

The process of selling in an organisational market differs greatly from selling in consumer markets. Selling can often require technical knowledge, particularly if products are complex or specifications need to be altered (or 'customised'). Decisions may also involve numerous people across a range of departments. For example, the purchase of a computerised management information system should involve discussions with representatives from a range of departments likely to be using the machine. Whereas consumers are influenced by a variety of behavioural factors, the main concern of most organisational customers is to obtain the necessary products at the lowest possible costs.

### Business in international markets

Prime behavioural characteristics affecting business in international markets include religion, differences in education, the use of language, and even bribery. The way in which people do business may be completely different and require some research. For example, in many Middle East countries business relationships may be as important as the business deal itself.

## CASE STUDY *Marks & Spencer*

M&S owns no factories nor does it make any of the goods that it sells. The firm works with manufacturers who supply to the company's high specifications. M&S set up this practice of direct dealing with producers in the 1920s. It is openly proud of the 'personal and friendly' relations it has with suppliers – not only does this help speed the response to customer needs, it also helps to anticipate them.

Sales of clothing account for almost half of the £5 billion plus turnover at M&S. To maintain such a position, numerous suppliers create new lines and ranges. Highly experienced buying teams determine the specifications for new lines, assess the suppliers' ability to produce the manufactured goods, and negotiate price, quantity and delivery. Many of the suppliers have worked with M&S for a considerable number of years and have seen their businesses grow in a similar fashion – although maybe not to similar proportions!

**Questions**

1  List the benefits available to a small garment manufacturer from supplying goods to M&S.

2  What factors must a small business take into consideration and be aware of when supplying to such a large organisation? Are there any dangers involved?

3  If you were working for a marketing department, would you prefer to be involved in marketing consumer products or services or industrial products and services? Support your answer with an explanation.

4  Comment generally on the sort of image generated by M&S. What type of customer are their clothing products directed at?

**ASSIGNMENT**

The market for ice-creams in the UK was worth £785 million in 1993. It comprised:

|  | £million |
|---|---|
| Choc-ices | 144 |
| Lollies | 89 |
| Cups/tubs/filled cones | 61 |
| Frozen yoghurt/fromage frais | 9 |
| Other multipacks | 3 |
| Complete desserts | 65 |
| Premium | 128 |
| Standard take-home packs | 286 |

**Task**  **a**  Working in groups, conduct an investigation into **one** of the above segments in this market. List the brands in this segment and then describe the differences between each brand. Explain how and why each brand is targeted. In your answer, refer to different groups of consumers you feel that each brand is directed towards.

**Task** **b** From your analysis of a part of this market, discuss and then develop some ideas for a new form of ice-cream product. In doing so, focus upon the group of consumers to whom your product is to be directed.

**Task** **c** If possible, present your findings back to the class.

# Researching the Market

The first stage in the marketing process is to understand **customers**, the **markets** in which they buy as well as the **business environment** in which all of this activity takes place (see Figure 3.1). To find out about each of these three areas an organisation requires **information** which directs activities, helps to satisfy customer needs and, at the same time, reduces the risks involved in decision-making. The overall success of the marketing process will, therefore, be dependent upon the *quality* of information gathered and then on how this information is used.

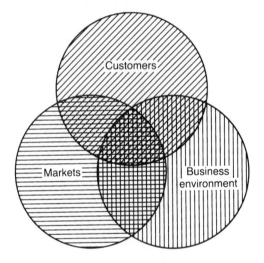

FIGURE 3.1
*The link between customers, markets and the business environment*

The purpose of **market research** is to provide answers to questions. By doing so it helps an organisation to use precise techniques which enable it to plan ahead with greater certainty rather than rely on unsubstantiated guesswork and hunches.

The American Marketing Association uses a simple working definition of market research:

> Market research is the systematic gathering, recording and analysing of data about problems relating to the marketing of goods and services.

We can break this definition down into its various ingredients:

- *Systematic* – in other words, using an organised and clear method or system
- *Gathering* – knowing what you are looking for, and collecting appropriate information

- *Recording* – keeping clear and organised records of what you find out
- *Analysing* – ordering and making sense of your information in order to draw out relevant trends and conclusions
- *Problems relating to marketing* – finding out the answers to questions which will help you to understand better your customers and other details about the marketplace.

Another frequently used interpretation of market research is: *to keep those who provide goods and services in touch with the needs and wants of those who buy the goods and services.* So market research is a vital link in the chain between buyers and suppliers.

The process of market research should not be a 'one-off' activity which takes place as part of a new product development. It should be ongoing, so marketers should constantly be collecting and analysing information and feeding it through for planning and decision-making purposes. There are five identifiable stages in the setting up of a market research programme. These are shown in Figure 3.2.

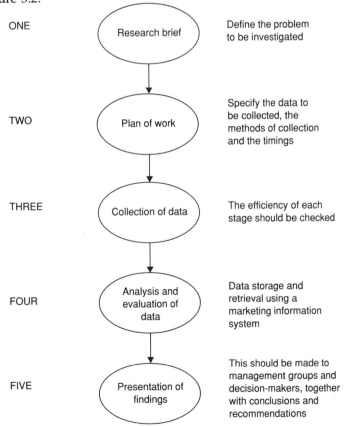

FIGURE 3.2
*The five stages of a market research programme*

ONE — Research brief — Define the problem to be investigated

TWO — Plan of work — Specify the data to be collected, the methods of collection and the timings

THREE — Collection of data — The efficiency of each stage should be checked

FOUR — Analysis and evaluation of data — Data storage and retrieval using a marketing information system

FIVE — Presentation of findings — This should be made to management groups and decision-makers, together with conclusions and recommendations

Before undertaking any market research an organisation must try to identify *what* information it requires. Research is neither easy nor cheap, so it is important to ensure that what is done is relevant to an organisation's information requirements. For example, specific objectives of market research might include the following:

- to identify new markets
- to monitor changes in customer needs and preferences
- to identify new product opportunities
- to improve the quality of information available for tactical and strategic decision-making
- to improve the organisation's understanding of changes in the marketplace, particularly of competitors' strategies
- to identify opportunities and threats
- to monitor the effects of political, economic, social and technological trends (PEST – see Chapter 2); this would be particularly important when marketing products overseas.

## CASE STUDY *Starting a games business*

Dave Robinson, Heather Roberts and Pete Hartley have attended pub quizzes for many years. As a development of this interest they built up a substantial database of questions which they sell in sets for quiz nights. For many months they talked about developing this business sideline futher and, early in 1994, they developed a board game.

The board game is for adults and is significantly different from other 'quiz' games on the market. It gets participants actively involved in developing alternative strategies, and the ability to do crosswords and solve puzzles and problems is useful. One possible use for the game is that of a management tool for training purposes.

The board game industry is worth about £150 million a year. Dave, Heather and Pete are conscious that they have little business experience and limited knowledge of marketing. They think they have developed 'a winner' but, before they take their ideas further, they know that a lot of research must be done.

**Questions**  **1**  What sort of information should Dave, Heather and Pete attempt to obtain before investing their money in this proposition?

**2**  How might such information influence the decisions they have to make?

## SOURCES OF INFORMATION

There are three broad areas in which market research can take place. Existing organisations may have **internal information** kept within their own systems. Secondly, a lot of information may already be published as **external** or **secondary information**. The third source of information will not already exist in any identifiable form and will have to be collected first-hand. This is **primary information**.

FIGURE 3.3
*Sources of information*

## INTERNAL SOURCES OF INFORMATION

Much of the information that an organisation requires is already held within its various departments (see Figure 3.4). A lot of this internal information might be in filing cabinets, and at least some of it will be out-of-date. The secret is to know what you need to discover, where to find it and then how to retrieve it.

Nowadays a lot of internal information is held on **computer files**. Databases have revolutionised the way information is stored, retrieved and analysed, and this has made the task of dealing with internal information much easier.

For example, in the past it was often difficult to get regular and reliable feedback from sales representatives, because their 'paperwork' was kept in their vehicles, was often disorganised and bulky and was rarely filed. This information was potentially enormously valuable as it represented **feedback** from first-hand experience with customers – it is often said that a sales force is an organisation's 'eyes and ears'.

| Purchasing | Stock levels, units costs, usage rates |
| Production | Output, materials, labour inventory, physical distribution, overheads, machine use |
| Personnel | Wage costs, efficiency levels, absenteeism, staff turnover |
| Marketing | Promotional and administration expenditures, brand and market data |
| Sales | Measured by product volumes, value, contribution, order size |
| Finance | Cost and accounting data |

FIGURE 3.4
*Some sources of internal data*

Computers have provided the means whereby information can be recorded in a simple manner, and contacts with each customer can be 'processed' so that information can be retrieved very quickly and then displayed in a way that is easy to understand. Techniques like this improve the quality of the market research process and enable organisations to direct goods and services to those customers who are most likely to make a purchase.

## CASE STUDY  *An electricity distribution company*

We can see how one type of database works by looking at the activities of an electricity distribution company. The relationship with a customer starts with a name, address and the nature of the property – whether it is a home or a business. Once the market research function has received these details, it gives to these groups a unique reference number at the relevant address called a *customer reference number* (CRN).

The CRN is crucial to all dealings with that customer, and it is with reference to the CRN that many of the financial transactions take place. To the CRN the company can attach all manner of information held *internally* that tells it more about that particular customer. For example:

*Tariff type* – The price a customer pays for electricity can vary according to whether they are a home or business, a large or small customer. Profitability to the electricity company will vary according to the type of customer.

*Consumption* – The company can track the amount of electricity a customer uses and when it is used.

*Method of payment* – Some people prefer prepayment rather than credit, others prefer to pay monthly rather than quarterly.

*Change of tenancy* – The company is informed when people move out of and into a property.

*New buildings* – The company knows when and where new buildings that use electricity are being erected because they apply for an electricity supply.

From such information it is possible to obtain answers to questions like:

- What is the size of the market?
- What type of user uses the most/least electricity?
- How do different types of customers prefer to pay?
- What is the average credit period?
- What type of customers are bad payers?
- How many new users are coming on-stream?
- How many users is the company losing?
- What is the average consumption per user?
- What is the average profitability from each type of user?
- How does electricity usage vary during the day?
- Where is the market expanding/contracting?

**Questions**  1  Explain how the answers to the questions asked above help to improve the ways in which an electricity company is managed.

2  Think of five other questions which could be answered from this type of database.

Internal information also has a valuable second purpose, and this is to know as much as possible about an organisation's capability of fulfilling the demands both within its main market as well as its potential to work outside this market. However, the scope of the projects which an organisation might be developing and the information needs may require other methods of research.

# EXTERNAL SOURCES OF INFORMATION

Internal information needs to be put into context, since on its own it simply provides a snapshot of an organisation and its customers. In particular it tells an organisation nothing about how effective its performance is relative to that of its competitors, nor how the business could be threatened by those competitors.

External information is more commonly called **secondary data** because it is often in the form of published materials, collected by somebody else (see Figure 3.5). It can provide a broader dimension to data previously collected and can be used in two main ways.

Firstly, external information can enhance an organisation's existing knowledge. For example, postcodes help to group customers geographically. By identifying and labelling characteristics of its customers, an organisation may be able to make assumptions about their needs. Two examples of useful external sources are:

- *Domestic socio-economic data* – Certain assumptions can be made about life-styles.

- *Industrial classification* – Organisational customers may be classified according to the nature of their activities. Certain organisations can then be expected to have predictable demands for certain services.

Secondly, external sources may complement an organisation's own information by providing useful comparisons with competitors. It may also help to identify markets offering potential and put performances into context by relating them to the economy/industry as a whole.

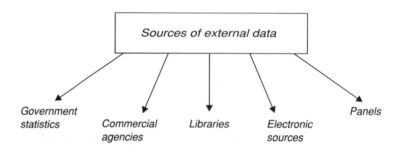

FIGURE 3.5
*Some sources of external data*

## Government statistics

The government's statistical service is coordinated by the Central Statistical Office (CSO). Government departments prepare statistics and the CSO publishes both a monthly and an annual analysis. In addition, *Business Monitors* are published quarterly to provide a range of information about various markets.

Government information on particular groups of industries is identified by a code which relates to a **Standard Industrial Classification** (SIC). As the SIC is the government's official way of classifying organisations and markets, it is frequently used in market research:

DIVISION 0 – AGRICULTURE, FORESTRY AND FISHING

Farming and horticulture

Forestry

Commercial sea and inland fishing

DIVISION 1 – ENERGY AND WATER SUPPLY INDUSTRIES

Coal-mining and manufacture of solid fuels

Extraction of mineral oil and natural gas

Production and distribution of electricity, gas and other forms of energy

DIVISION 2 – EXTRACTION OF MINERALS AND ORES, MANUFACTURE OF METALS, MINERAL PRODUCTS AND CHEMICALS

Metal manufacture

Extraction of stone, clay, sand and gravel

Manufacture of non-metallic mineral products

Chemical industry (includes paints, varnishes and inks, pharmaceutical products, some perfumes, etc.)

DIVISION 3 – METAL GOODS, ENGINEERING AND VEHICLE INDUSTRIES

Foundries

Mechanical engineering

Electrical and electronic engineering

Manufacture of motor vehicles and parts

Instrument engineering

DIVISION 4 – OTHER MANUFACTURING INDUSTRIES

Food, drink and tobacco manufacturing industries

Textile industry

Manufacture of leather and leather goods

Timber and wooden furniture industries

Manufacture of paper and paper products, printing and printing products

Processing of rubber and plastics

DIVISION 5 – CONSTRUCTION
Construction and repairs
Demolition work
Civil engineering

DIVISION 6 – DISTRIBUTION, HOTELS AND CATERING, REPAIRS
Wholesale distribution
Retail distribution
Hotel and catering (restaurants, cafes and other eating places, public houses and hotel trade)
Repair of consumer goods and vehicles

DIVISION 7 – TRANSPORT AND COMMUNICATION
Railways and other inland transport
Air and sea transport
Support services to transport
Postal services and telecommunications

DIVISION 8 – BANKING, FINANCE, INSURANCE, BUSINESS SERVICES AND LEASING
Banking and finance
Insurance
Business services
Renting of movables
Owning and dealing in real-estate

DIVISION 9 – OTHER SERVICES
Public administration, national defence and social security
Sanitary services
Education
Medical and other health services, veterinary services
Other services provided to the general public
Recreational services and other cultural services
Personal services (laundries, hairdressing and beauty parlours)
Domestic services
Diplomatic representation, international organisations, allied armed forces

Another useful source of information, particularly for industries working in consumer markets, is **census data** published by the Office of Population, Censuses and Surveys. A full census is carried out every ten years, the last one being in 1991. This office also carries out two continuous surveys on Family Expenditure and General Households which might also be useful for organisations to analyse for market research purposes.

# CASE STUDY  *Population statistics in the UK*

Examine the three charts shown here. Prepare a statement (up to 200 words) explaining how these figures may be of use to a manufacturer and distributor of *fashion shoes*.

## Resident population

|  | 1980 (000) | 1980 (%) | 1985 (000) | 1985 (%) | 1991 (000) | 1991 (%) |
|---|---|---|---|---|---|---|
| England | 46 787 | 83.1 | 47 112 | 83.2 | 48 208 | 83.4 |
| Wales | 2 816 | 5.0 | 2 812 | 5.0 | 2 892 | 5.0 |
| Scotland | 5 194 | 9.2 | 5 137 | 9.1 | 5 107 | 8.8 |
| N. Ireland | 1 533 | 2.7 | 1 558 | 2.8 | 1 594 | 2.8 |
| UK overall | 56 330 | 100.0 | 56 618 | 100.0 | 57 801 | 100.0 |

## Distribution of the population by social class

| Social class | Adult men (000) | Adult men (%) | Adult women (000) | Adult women (%) | Main shoppers (female) (000) | Main shoppers (female) (%) |
|---|---|---|---|---|---|---|
| A | 714 | 3.3 | 677 | 2.9 | 554 | 2.8 |
| B | 3 617 | 16.5 | 3 489 | 14.9 | 2 949 | 14.9 |
| C1 | 5 316 | 24.3 | 6 338 | 27.0 | 5 280 | 26.7 |
| C2 | 6 192 | 28.3 | 5 564 | 23.7 | 4 656 | 23.5 |
| D | 3 775 | 17.3 | 3 913 | 16.7 | 3 305 | 16.7 |
| E | 2 248 | 10.3 | 3 456 | 14.7 | 3 047 | 15.4 |
| Totals | 21 863 | 100.0 | 24 437 | 100.0 | 19 791 | 100.0 |

## Projected population of Great Britain at mid-year

|  | 1991 | 1995 | 2000 | 2010 | 2020 |
|---|---|---|---|---|---|
| Home population (millions) | 56.1 | 56.9 | 57.9 | 59.3 | 60.1 |
| Males (%) | 48.8 | 48.9 | 49.1 | 49.3 | 49.5 |
| Females (%) | 51.2 | 51.1 | 50.9 | 50.7 | 50.5 |
| Age distribution (%) |  |  |  |  |  |
| 0–4 | 6.7 | 6.7 | 6.5 | 5.8 | 5.8 |
| 5–14 | 12.3 | 12.8 | 13.1 | 12.4 | 11.5 |
| 15–29 | 22.4 | 20.5 | 18.8 | 19.2 | 18.7 |
| 30–44 | 21.1 | 21.5 | 22.4 | 19.9 | 18.2 |
| 45–64 | 21.6 | 22.7 | 23.4 | 26.1 | 26.6 |
| 65+ | 15.8 | 15.8 | 15.7 | 16.5 | 19.2 |

The governments of many other countries also provide statistical pictures of their populations and their economies. The table in Figure 3.6 is drawn up from statistics provided by various national statistical offices and Eurostat.

| | 1995 | 2000 | 2005 | 2010 | 2015 | 2020 |
|---|---|---|---|---|---|---|
| Austria | 7977 | 8091 | 8162 | 8201 | 8221 | 8172* |
| Belgium | 9914 | 9893 | 9820 | 9713 | 9580 | 9423 |
| Denmark | 5192 | 5233 | 5224 | 5172 | 5095 | 5019 |
| Finland | 5078 | 5096 | . . | 5076 | . . | 4984 |
| France | 57061 | 57883 | 58451 | 58766 | 58821 | 58664 |
| Germany | 81096 | 81126 | 80224 | 78858 | 77065 | 74964 |
| Greece | 10110 | 10335 | 10448 | 10554 | 10571 | 10594 |
| Ireland | 3503 | 3486 | 3456 | 3466 | 3461 | 3463 |
| Italy | 57585 | 57611 | 57257 | 56411 | 55089 | 53484 |
| Luxembourg | 387 | 394 | 399 | 403 | 406 | 410 |
| Netherlands | 15497 | 16020 | 16419 | 16688 | 16857 | 16979 |
| Norway | 4308 | 4373 | 4414 | 4437 | 4455 | 4470 |
| Portugal | 10491 | 10577 | 10639 | 10703 | 10612 | 10460 |
| Spain | 39217 | 39381 | 39333 | 38940 | 38200 | 37231 |
| Sweden | 8795 | 8950 | . . | 9167 | . . | 9507† |
| Switzerland | 7087 | 7380 | 7546 | 7591 | . . | 7533 |
| Turkey | 62732 | 70440 | 79420 | . . | . . | . . |
| United Kingdom | 58240 | 59039 | 59599 | 59966 | 60306 | 60674 |

FIGURE 3.6
*Population forecasts
(thousands)*

* 2025   † 2030

In addition, many international organisations provide useful statistics and publications. Examples are the United Nations, European Union, IMF and OECD. The United Nations publishes a Directory of International Statistics, a Demographic Yearbook, a Yearbook of National Accounts Statistics and a monthly Bulletin of Statistics. The European Union publishes various bulletins and publications, including a General Statistical Bulletin and an Economic Survey of Europe. The International Monetary Fund publishes a Balance of Payments Yearbook, and an annual Directory of Trade. The Organisation for Economic Co-operation and Development publishes various surveys and forecasts, including Main Economic Indicators.

## Commercial agencies

Information supply is a very important business in itself. There exist different types of agencies which buy or gather information, compile it into reports and then sell these reports to anyone who needs them.

Mintel is a **commercial research organisation** which, in return for a fee, provides a monthly journal containing reports on a variety of consumer markets – for example, bread, alcoholic drinks and insurance. The Mintel reports are up to about 20 pages long, with information such as market size, main competitors, projected growth, market share of main producers, advertising spend of main brands, trends, etc. Mintel also produces in-depth reports on certain markets.

Another research outfit which operates in a similar way to Mintel is **Euromonitor**. Key Note Reports cover a range of businesses and, at around 75 pages long, provide a good introduction to markets.

Some research establishments work exclusively in one particular sector. For the food industry, for example, there is the Leatherhead Food Research Association and the Food Policy Research Unit. Business-to-business reports are also available for many sectors.

A. C. Nielson and Retail Audits are research organisations which collect data from retail sales through supermarkets and large chains, and sell the figures to organisations wishing to buy them. These figures enable suppliers to work out their share of the market, the sales of different products, and the effects of any recent strategy such as a price change or a promotion campaign. These audits, therefore, offer a window directly on to the marketplace.

Specific data may often be obtained through **trade associations**. These relate to specific industries and can be contacted using the Directory of British Associations. Useful information may also be obtained from the Advertising Association, the Incorporated Society of British Advertisers, the Market Research Society and the Chartered Institute of Marketing.

Research for overseas markets is usually carried out by contacting either the same or similar types of agencies. The British Overseas Trade Board helps UK organisations by supplying an Export Intelligence Service.

## CASE STUDY *'Third-age' life-styles*

In 1993 Mintel published a report on 'third-age' life-styles for £795. The report, which was based on interviews with more than 5000 people, showed that better health, more money and leisure time, fewer worries about children, work and mortgage rates have produced some of the happiest pensioners ever.

According to this study, a person's middle years between 35 and 54 are those of 'peak satisfaction'. No matter what people say about youth or schooldays being the best days of one's life, this research shows otherwise. For example, 38 per cent of the over-50s now think that life is more satisfying than when they were younger, compared with 33 per cent in 1988. Among those aged 50–54 the figure rises to 47 per cent, much higher than for people aged 15–34. Even among the over-70s, satisfaction levels are rising – from 24 per cent in 1988 to 28 per cent in the early 1990s.

|  | 1988 | 1992 |
|---|---|---|
| All 50+ | 33 | 38 |
| Men | 34 | 43 |
| Women | 31 | 34 |
| 50–54 | 46 | 47 |
| 55–59 | 40 | 47 |
| 60–64 | 29 | 39 |
| 65–69 | 23 | 38 |
| 70+ | 24 | 28 |
| AB | 37 | 47 |
| C1 | 30 | 40 |
| C2 | 36 | 41 |
| D | 37 | 32 |
| E | 26 | 28 |
| Married | 38 | 43 |
| Not married | 22 | 28 |

Percentage more satisfied now than when they were younger, by various groupings

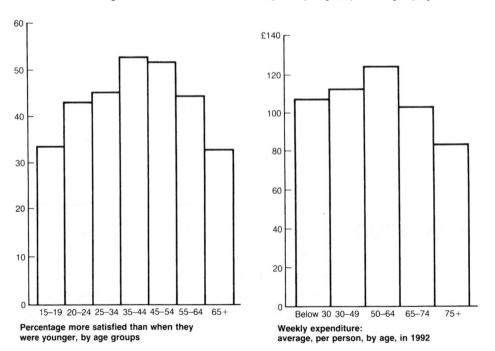

**Percentage more satisfied than when they were younger, by age groups**

**Weekly expenditure: average, per person, by age, in 1992**

During the 1990s the number of over-50s will grow by 9 per cent compared with only a 3 per cent growth in the population. By 2001 there will be a staggering 31 per cent increase in the number of adults in their early-50s and a 15 per cent rise in people in their late-50s.

As these 'baby-boomers' become more elderly, many are taking parts of their own youth culture into middle age. For example, in 1985, 27 per cent of men aged 45–54 bought jeans, but by 1993 this figure had risen to 45 per cent. Another aspect of getting older is appearance. Women aged 55–64 spend more at the hairdressers than any other age group. Perhaps they seem to think that more effort is required to keep looking young. With more surplus income and leisure time, many elderly people spend their money on holidays, visits, pets, gardening, reading books and newspapers, eating out and watching videos. The 55–64 age group is also the keenest on gambling.

Despite these images of the 'wealthy elderly' the picture is not uniform.
Dreams of retirement for some have led to poverty and there is a polarisation between those who retire on favourable terms and those dependent upon state pensions.

**Questions**

1   What sort of organisations would be interested in buying this type of report?

2   How might they intend to use this type of information?

## Libraries

There is a rich store of information in libraries. College, university and town libraries often have a wide range of useful reference materials such as those below which may be of use for research.

For example, there are many sources providing **information about the media**. These are useful for organisations wishing to look at how to get their promotional messages across to prospective customers. Benn's *Media Directory* provides details of TV and radio companies, newspapers and magazines. *British Rate and Data* (BRAD) provides comprehensive coverage of virtually all the media that sells advertising space, together with rates. The *Advertisers Annual* makes detailed comparisons of advertising agencies.

**Information about companies** is available from several sources. Kompass publishes two volumes of products and services listed by the SIC codes mentioned earlier. Extel provides details extracted from the published accounts of all the public companies and from many of the larger private companies. The annual publication *Who Owns Whom* gives details of the ownership of subsidiary companies.

## *Electronic sources*

The electronic transmission of information is in the process of transforming traditional reference sources and the ways in which information is handled. Teletext transmits information through the broadcast media and Viewdata sends information through the telephone network. Over the next few years the new era of **'on-demand information'** is likely to render traditional reference sources obsolete. Information may be called up either through the use of laserdisks/CD-ROMs or by access via the telephone network to a massive central database which may be called from anywhere in the country.

## *Panels*

Another way of finding out what is happening in the marketplace is to set up or buy information from **panels**. These are groups of consumers who record their purchases and/or media habits in a diary. The purpose of this diary is not just to record purchases but also to provide research information which relates purchasing habits with social status, occupation, income, demographic details and neighbourhood.

## PRIMARY SOURCES OF INFORMATION

Internal and external data may not answer all of the questions an organisation wants to ask. It may be out-of-date or it may not cover exactly the right market sector. Then, to meet an organisation's specific needs, **primary research** has to take place.

Primary data is first-hand knowledge, 'straight from the horse's mouth'. Information an organisation compiles from its own research efforts is called primary. This type of research involves the collection of new data which are to be used for a specific purpose. For example, before a supermarket chain opens a new supermarket it will commission a local shopping survey.

**Surveys** are the most common method used to collect primary data; they involve contacting **respondents** to find out how they react to a range of issues contained in a **questionnaire**. There are two types of survey, a census and a sample. A **census** involves questioning everybody in a particular market – but, unless the market is very small, this is unlikely to be practicable. Taking a **sample** involves questioning a *selection* of respondents from the target market. In order to ensure that the results of a sample survey are accurate, the market research process must identify a representative cross-section of customers. If the selection of the sample is fair and accurate, then information should be **statistically reliable**. If the sample is incomplete and does not accurately represent a group of consumers, misleading data are obtained – the sample is said to be **biased**.

### Choosing a sample

Samples may fall into either of two categories. **Probability samples** are so constructed that every customer or element has a known *probability* of selection and the limits of possible error are known in advance. Included in this category are simple random sampling, stratified random sampling and cluster sampling. **Non-probability samples** are based simply upon the choice of the selector and may be subject to error in sample selection. These include quota sampling, convenience sampling and judgement sampling.

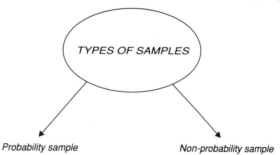

FIGURE 3.7
*Categories of samples*

### Simple random sampling

With this method the researcher chooses the size of the sample required and then picks the sample on a random basis. The sample must be selected in such a way that every item in the **sampling frame** has an equal chance of being selected. One way of doing this is to use a computer to draw names or numbers from the list at random.

### Systematic sampling

Another way is to use **systematic sampling**, which involves selecting items from the list at regular intervals after choosing a random starting point. For example, if it is decided to select a sample of 20 names from 1000, then every 50th name (1000 divided by 20) should be selected, after a random start in the first 50. If 18 is chosen as the starting point (possibly by using a table of random numbers), then the sample series would start:

18 . . . 68 . . . 118 . . . 168 . . . etc.

## Stratified random sampling

If some customers are more important than others, then simple random sampling can distort the results. **Stratified random sampling** therefore weights the sample on the basis of the importance of each group of customers in the market.

For example, if an organisation has 5000 small users of products accounting for sales of £1 million, 4000 medium users accounting for £1 million, and 1000 big users accounting for £2 million, a random sample of 200 would not be representative of the market. To make the sample more representative would involve allocating the big users half the sample because they make up half the total sales, with one-quarter of the sample to medium users and one-quarter to small users. The stratified random sample would then include 100 big users, 50 medium users and 50 small users, all randomly chosen from their respective categories.

## Cluster sampling

With **cluster sampling** the population/customers are divided up into small areas, but instead of sampling from a random selection of these areas, sampling is carried out in a few areas which are considered to be typical of the market in question. For example, you might divide the city of Newcastle into 200 segments and then, because of the nature of your survey, decide that you will only sample from a segment which contains at least one school, one church and one shopping centre, and any segments without these facilities are avoided.

## Quota sampling

Although random sampling, if properly conducted, produces the best results, it can be expensive and time-consuming, and in some situations it is not possible to identify a random sample. In these situations **quota sampling** is more commonly used.

Interviewers are given instructions as to the number of people to interview with certain characteristics – such as sex, age, socio-economic group or other demographic detail. For example, if the interviewers are asked to investigate housewives aged 36–50, they will quiz every housewife 'fitting the bill' (possibly in interviews in the high street) up to their maximum quota. The problem is that there is no assurance that the housewives interviewed are typical of housewives in that band, and the statistical accuracy of such sampling is questionable.

## Convenience and judgement sampling

**Convenience sampling** involves gathering information from anybody available for the interviewer to survey, no matter what their background. **Judgement sampling** involves selection of the respondents by the interviewer based on his or her judgement that they seemed to be and looked representative of the group of consumers in the market being researched.

### Preparing a questionnaire

When the sampling problems have been settled, the researcher must design a questionnaire. This is a systematic list of questions designed to obtain information from people about:

- specific events
- their attitudes
- their values
- their beliefs.

**Questionnaire design** is probably the most crucial part of a survey. Though it is easy to design questions, it is very difficult to produce a good questionnaire – and a badly designed questionnaire may lead to biased results. For instance, if the people completing the questionnaire are unaware of its purpose, they may place the wrong emphasis on the questions. Figure 3.8 shows an example of an unsatisfactory questionnaire – its weaknesses should become apparent when you have studied the remainder of this section!

Another problem may arise if very few completed forms are returned, or if those returned are only partially completed. In addition, if the questionnaire is being administered by an interviewer, there is always the danger that the interviewer may misinterpret the questions and introduce his or her own personal bias in a way which prompts certain answers from respondents.

A good questionnaire will:

- ask questions which relate directly to information needs
- not ask too many questions
- not ask intimate questions

- fit its questions into a logical sequence

- have unambiguous questions.

It will also have been extensively **tested**, possibly with trial interviews, before being administered.

---

**Kettle Ownership Questionnaire**

Name .................. Address ................

....................... Telephone Number ......

1  Do you use a kettle? Yes/No

2  What make is it? ..............................

3  Have you had other kettles before? ..............

4  Which of them was best? ......................

5  Have kettles that you bought had major faults?

   ...........................................

6  What type of kettle do you currently have? ......

7  Is it: Reliable ☐ Unreliable ☐ Average reliability ☐

8  Which of the following makes would you choose if price did not matter?

   Swan Cool Touch Cordless ☐
   Kenwood Cordless Automatic ☐
   Russell Hobbs Country Style ☐
   Tefal Freeline De Luxe ☐
   Haden Automatic ☐

9  How many company names do you remember from advertising?

10  Is price an important consideration? Yes/No

11  How often do you use your kettle. Often/Sometimes/Hardly Ever.

12  What do you use your kettle for? ................

13  How did you pay for your last kettle? ...........

14  Which in question 8 wouldn't you choose? ......

15  Who else has a kettle like yours? ...............

16  Do they use it: Very often ☐ Hardly Ever ☐ Frequently ☐ Rarely ☐ Mainly at weekends ☐ Never ☐ Sometimes ☐

17  Are you: Upper Class ☐ Upper Middle Class ☐ Lower Middle Class ☐ Upper Working Class ☐ Lower Working Class ☐

FIGURE 3.8

*A messy questionnaire with a number of flaws (see later)*

The questions in a questionnaire may be 'open' or 'closed'. **Open questions** allow the person answering to give an opinion and may encourage him or her to talk at length. **Closed questions** usually require an answer picked from a range of options (which may be simply yes/no). Most questionnaires use closed questions, so that they can be answered quickly and more efficiently, and the answers are easier to analyse (see Figure 3.9).

| Do you find that the speed with which your kettle boils water is: | | | | |
|---|---|---|---|---|
| Very fast | Fast | Satisfactory | Slow | Very slow |
| | | | | |

(tick where appropriate)

**b** Very fast ☐☐☐☐☐ Very slow

tendency to
(tick where appropriate)

Which of the following methods of payment do you use most regularly? (Tick the relevant box)

| | |
|---|---|
| Notes and coins | ☐ |
| Cheque payment | ☐ |
| Credit card | ☐ |
| Other means | ☐ |

FIGURE 3.9
*Examples of closed
questions*

The purpose of a closed question is to get people to commit themselves to a concrete opinion. If you ask an open question, the likelihood is that your survey will prompt a wide range of answers which are very difficult to analyse. Closed questions tie respondents down so that they have to make a decision within a range of choices.

To help interviewers operate a questionnaire, sometimes a **prompt card** is used. This means that several or all of the questions in the questionnaire have the same range of set answers; these can be numbered and the respondents' answers can be recorded as numbers (see Figure 3.10).

| National Westminster | 01 |
| Barclays | 02 |
| Lloyds | 03 |
| Midland | 04 |
| Abbey National | 05 |
| Yorkshire | 06 |
| Others | 07 |

FIGURE 3.10
*An interviewer's prompt card*

Some questionnaires are designed so that respondents can concentrate on the questions that are relevant, and then skip over questions which do not relate to them (see Figure 3.11).

Question 1  **Do you have a bank account?**

☐ **YES**

☐ **NO**

**If your answer is no** proceed straight to question 20

FIGURE 3.11
*An example of a 'skip' question*

## CASE STUDY  *Kettle ownership questionnaire*

Look back to the questionnaire presented in Figure 3.8. This is not very effective for a variety of reasons.

**Questions**  1  Identify the weaknesses.
2  Suggest how you could rewrite the questionnaire to make it more effective both in terms of questions and layout.

(An alternative task involving design of a questionnaire is set out as an assignment at the end of the chapter.)

## CASE STUDY  *Getting to know their customers better*

The long questionnaire reproduced on pages 61–66 was issued to a sample of National Westminster Bank customers by their Personal Financial Services Department. In its introductory letter the bank says (see page 67):

OFFICE USE ONLY:
SERIAL NO. _____ (1-6)
DATE _____ (7-12)
VER = N          1(13)
CARD             1(14)
COLOUR = 1       (15)
BLANK            (16-25)

# ♻ National Westminster Bank

## CUSTOMER SERVICE MONITOR

*All of your answers should relate to your personal dealings with NatWest, rather than any other dealings you may have with the bank for business purposes.*

*Please answer all questions by putting a ✓ in the appropriate circle, or by writing in the space provided.*
*Please use ink to fill in the questions, not pencil.*

**1** Please write in the address of the NatWest branch where your account is held.

Address:

Please write in the sort code for your branch. This is shown at the bottom of the letter accompanying this questionnaire as well as on your cheques and Servicecard or Cashcard. (e.g. 68-06-08).
(26-31)

**2** Is this the branch of NatWest you visit most often? (By visit we mean go into the branch, not just to use the cash machine outside).
(32)

| | | |
|---|---|---|
| Yes | O₁ | Go to **5** |
| No, I visit another branch most often | O₂ | Go to **3** |
| No, I have no regular branch for visiting | O₃ | Go to **8a** |
| No, I never visit a branch | O₄ | Go to **9** |

**3** If you visit another NatWest branch most often, what is the address of this branch? If you are unsure of the exact address then please indicate the street and town where it is.
BLANK (33-43)

Address:

(44-49)

**4** Does the branch you visit most often have a cash machine outside the branch?
(50)

Yes O₁     No O₂

**5** How often do you visit this branch? (That is actually go into the branch, not just to use the cash machine outside)
(51)

| | | | |
|---|---|---|---|
| More than once a day | O₁ | Once a fortnight | O₆ |
| Once a day | O₂ | Once a month | O₇ |
| 2-3 times a week | O₃ | Less than once a month | O₈ |
| Once a week | O₄ | Rarely | O₉ |

**6a** As far as you know, what are the weekday opening hours of this branch?
(52)

| | | |
|---|---|---|
| Opens at 8.30 am and closes at: | 4.30 pm | O₁ |
| | 5.00 pm | O₂ |
| | 5.30 pm | O₃ |
| Opens at 9.00 am and closes at: | 3.30 pm | O₄ |
| | 4.30 pm | O₅ |
| | 5.30 pm | O₆ |
| Opens at 9.30 am and closes at: | 3.00 pm | O₇ |
| | 3.30 pm | O₈ |
| Don't know | | O₉ |

**6b** How acceptable do you find these weekday opening hours?
(53)

| | |
|---|---|
| Very acceptable | O₁ |
| Fairly acceptable | O₂ |
| Not very acceptable | O₃ |
| Not at all acceptable | O₄ |

**7** At what time of day do you normally visit this branch on a weekday? (Again, we mean actually go into the branch for a service, not just to use the cash machine.)
(54)

Weekdays:

| | | | |
|---|---|---|---|
| Before 9.00 am | O₁ | On a weekday, but | |
| 9.00 - 9.30 am | O₂ | no normal time | O₉ |
| 9.31 - 11.00 am | O₃ | Not normally on | |
| 11.01 - 12 noon | O₄ | a weekday | O₁₀ |
| 12.01 - 2.00 pm | O₅ | | |
| 2.01 - 3.30 pm | O₆ | | |
| 3.31 - 4.30 pm | O₇ | | |
| 4.31 - 5.30 pm | O₈ | | |

BLANK (55-60)

61

## SATURDAY BANKING

**8a** What are the opening hours of the branch you use on a Saturday?

(61)

Never use a NatWest branch on Saturday ○₁ Go to **8d**
Open Saturday morning only (9.30 - 12.30) ○₂
Open all day Saturday (9.30 - 3.30) ○₃ Go to **8b**
Don't know ○₄

**8b** At what time of the day do you normally visit this branch on a Saturday (we mean actually go into the branch, not just use the cash machine outside).

(62)

Saturdays:

9.30 - 12.30 pm ○₁
12.31 - 3.30 pm ○₂
No normal time ○₃

**8c** How acceptable do you find these Saturday opening hours?

(63)

Very acceptable ○₁
Fairly acceptable ○₂ Go to **9**
Not very acceptable ○₃
Not at all acceptable ○₄

**8d** Why do you never use a branch on a Saturday?

(64)

I don't need to use a branch on a Saturday ○₁
There is no branch open on a Saturday near to me ○₂
The services I need are not provided on a Saturday ○₃
Other reason (please write in) ○₄

BLANK (65-70)

## TELEPHONING THE BANK WHERE YOUR ACCOUNT IS HELD

**9** How often do you telephone the NatWest branch where your account is held?

(71)

Weekly or more often ○₁
Every 2-4 weeks ○₂ Continue
Every 1-3 months ○₃ to **10**
Every 4-6 months ○₄
Every 7-12 months ○₅
Less often than once a year ○₆ Go to **13**
Never ○₇

**10** When you telephone this branch about how long does it usually take for them to answer your call?

(72)

The phone is usually answered within 3 rings ○₁
The phone is usually answered within 4-6 rings ○₂
The phone is usually answered within 7-10 rings ○₃
The phone usually takes more than 10 rings to be answered ○₄

**11** Overall, how acceptable do you find the length of time it takes staff at this branch to answer your call?

(73)

Very acceptable ○₁
Fairly acceptable ○₂
Not very acceptable ○₃
Not at all acceptable ○₄

**12** When you telephone your branch... (Please give one answer to each question)

| | Yes always | Yes often | Yes some times | No |
|---|---|---|---|---|
| (a) do you have to give all the details to more than one person before they find someone who can answer your question properly? | ○₁ | ○₂ | ○₃ | ○₄ (74) |
| (b) do you have to hold the line for long periods while someone is found who can handle your enquiry? | ○₁ | ○₂ | ○₃ | ○₄ (75) |
| (c) do staff seem to be giving you their full attention on the telephone? | ○₁ | ○₂ | ○₃ | ○₄ (76) |
| (d) do staff give you the impression that you are interrupting their work? | ○₁ | ○₂ | ○₃ | ○₄ (77) |
| (e) if staff leave you holding the line while they obtain information, do you have to wait for long periods without any explanation for the delay? | ○₁ | ○₂ | ○₃ | ○₄ (78) |

BLANK (79-80)

## HOW ACCURATELY YOUR BRANCH HANDLES YOUR ACCOUNT

DUPLICATE (1-13) CARD 2 (14)

Please indicate the quality of service provided to you by the NatWest branch *where your account is held*. If you have no experience of the service then please tick the 'NO EXPERIENCE' box.

**13** How well instructions are followed (eg. standing orders, direct debits)

(15)

They always carry out my instructions correctly ○₁
They get it right most of the time ○₂
They more often than not make a mistake ○₃
They always seem to get it wrong ○₄
NO EXPERIENCE ○₅

**14** Experience of mistakes

(16)

The bank never makes mistakes on my account $\bigcirc_1$

The bank occasionally makes mistakes on my account $\bigcirc_2$

The bank frequently makes mistakes on my account $\bigcirc_3$

The bank makes frequent and repeated mistakes
on my account $\bigcirc_4$

NO EXPERIENCE $\bigcirc_5$

**15** How any mistakes are handled (Please answer 'Yes' or
'No' to each statement)

|  | Yes | No |
|---|---|---|
|  | (17) | (18) |
| They are generally open and admit the mistake | $\bigcirc_1$ | $\bigcirc_1$ |
| They generally apologise for the mistake | $\bigcirc_2$ | $\bigcirc_2$ |
| They generally take action to sort the mistake out | $\bigcirc_3$ | $\bigcirc_3$ |
| NO EXPERIENCE | $\bigcirc_4$ | $\bigcirc_4$ |

BLANK (19-20)

## ABOUT THE NATWEST BRANCH YOU VISIT

If you never visit a branch please go to **33**

Please give your opinion of the service provided to
you by the NatWest branch you visit most often (this
may also be the branch where your account is held).
If you do not have one branch you visit most often,
but visit a number of different branches (as indicated
at Q2), please give your opinion of the service
provided overall by these branches. If you have no
experience of any of the elements of service below
please tick the 'NO EXPERIENCE' circle.

## THE STAFF

**16** Knowledgeable staff

(21)

Staff tend to know about all the Bank's
products and services $\bigcirc_1$

Staff tend to know about most of the Bank's
products and services $\bigcirc_2$

Staff tend to know about only some of the
Bank's products and services $\bigcirc_3$

Staff tend to know about very few of the
Bank's products and services $\bigcirc_4$

NO EXPERIENCE $\bigcirc_5$

**17** Confidence in staff

(22)

Staff appear very competent and I have
complete confidence in them $\bigcirc_1$

Staff seem to know what they are doing
and I feel reasonably confident in them $\bigcirc_2$

Staff don't always seem to know what they are
doing and I have little confidence in them $\bigcirc_3$

I have no confidence in the staff at all $\bigcirc_4$

NO EXPERIENCE $\bigcirc_5$

**18** Availability of appropriate person in branch to answer
my queries

(23)

There always seems to be someone who can
deal with my queries $\bigcirc_1$

There is sometimes someone who can
deal with my queries $\bigcirc_2$

There never seems to be anyone who can
deal with my queries $\bigcirc_3$

NO EXPERIENCE $\bigcirc_4$

**19** Politeness of counter staff

(24)

Generally speaking the counter staff
are polite to me $\bigcirc_1$

Counter staff are reasonably polite to me
but could do better $\bigcirc_2$

Counter staff are off-hand with me and
make little effort to be polite $\bigcirc_3$

Staff tend to be rude and abrupt $\bigcirc_4$

NO EXPERIENCE $\bigcirc_5$

**20** Attentiveness of staff

(25)

I know I have the staff's full attention
throughout the whole transaction $\bigcirc_1$

The staff serve me adequately, but I don't feel
they are really concentrating $\bigcirc_2$

Staff don't concentrate on serving me and chat
to other staff while they are doing it $\bigcirc_3$

NO EXPERIENCE $\bigcirc_4$

**21** Attitude of counter staff towards dealing with the
public

(26)

Counter staff seem to enjoy dealing with
the public and are generally good at it $\bigcirc_1$

Counter staff seem indifferent to dealing with
the public, it's just one job they have to do $\bigcirc_2$

They don't seem to enjoy dealing with the
public and are not particularly good at it $\bigcirc_3$

NO EXPERIENCE $\bigcirc_4$

BLANK (27-30)

## SPEED OF COUNTER SERVICE

**22** Frequency of having to queue to see a cashier

(31)

I never have to queue $\bigcirc_1$

I sometimes have to queue $\bigcirc_2$

I usually have to queue $\bigcirc_3$

I always have to queue $\bigcirc_4$

NO EXPERIENCE $\bigcirc_5$

**23** When I do have to queue to see a cashier, I:

(32)

Usually get to the counter within a minute $\bigcirc_1$

Usually wait 1-5 minutes $\bigcirc_2$

Usually wait 6-10 minutes $\bigcirc_3$

Usually wait more than 10 minutes $\bigcirc_4$

NO EXPERIENCE $\bigcirc_5$

**24** When I have to queue

(33)

Most tills are usually open ○₁

More tills are usually open than closed ○₂

About the same number of tills are open and closed ○₃

More tills are usually closed than open ○₄

NO EXPERIENCE ○₅

**25** Staffing levels at busy times

(34)

The branch appears to do everything it can
to provide enough staff to satisfy demand ○₁

The branch goes some way towards providing
enough staff to satisfy demand ○₂

The branch makes no effort to provide enough
staff to satisfy demand ○₃

NO EXPERIENCE ○₄

**26** Overall, how acceptable do you find the length of time you have to queue in the branch?

(35)

Very acceptable ○₁

Fairly acceptable ○₂

Not very acceptable ○₃

Not at all acceptable ○₄

BLANK (36-40)

### PRIVACY

**27** Privacy to discuss personal matters

(41)

Discussions always seem to be out of
earshot and out of sight ○₁

People can see and hear discussions
if they try ○₂

All discussions seem to be overheard
and overseen ○₃

NO EXPERIENCE ○₄

**28** Where do discussions about personal matters usually take place in this branch?

(42)

In a private room ○₁

In a screened off area in the banking hall ○₂

In the main area of the banking hall
at a desk or table ○₃

In the main area of the banking hall, but
not at a desk or table ○₄

Over the counter ○₅

Somewhere else ○₆

NO EXPERIENCE ○₇ Go to **30**

**29** How satisfied are you with this arrangement?

(43)

Very satisfied ○₁

Fairly satisfied ○₂

Not very satisfied ○₃

Not at all satisfied ○₄

NO EXPERIENCE ○₅

BLANK (44-45)

### BRANCH DESIGN

**30** How well do the signs and notices show you where to go when entering the branch?

(46)

It is clear where I should go for the
service I want ○₁

It is clear where to go for the main bank
services but not for anything else ○₂

I find where to go in the bank very confusing ○₃

NO EXPERIENCE ○₄

**31** Which of these words and phrases describe your overall impression of the design and atmosphere of this branch?

**PLEASE INDICATE AS MANY OR AS FEW AS APPLY.**

(47) (48)

| | | | |
|---|---|---|---|
| Friendly | ○₁ | Lacking privacy | ○₁ |
| Secure | ○₂ | Welcoming | ○₂ |
| Too formal | ○₃ | Too noisy | ○₃ |
| Too informal | ○₄ | Tidy | ○₄ |
| Spacious | ○₅ | Cluttered | ○₅ |
| Cramped | ○₆ | Efficient | ○₆ |
| Professional | ○₇ | Clean | ○₇ |
| Airy | ○₈ | Display racks well stocked | ○₈ |
| Too modern | ○₉ | Display racks accessible | ○₉ |

BLANK (49-50)

### CHANGES IN QUALITY OF SERVICE

**32** Compared to a year ago, how would you describe the quality of service offered by the branch you visit most often?

(51)

Much better ○₁

Slightly better ○₂

Slightly worse ○₃

Much worse ○₄

Unchanged, but already excellent ○₅

Unchanged, but acceptable ○₆

Unchanged, room for improvement ○₇

Account held for less than 1 year,
so unable to comment ○₈

BLANK (52)

*Now please turn over and complete the questionnaire.*

**33** If you were asked to recommend a bank to someone who was considering opening a bank account

(a) how likely would you be to recommend the branch where your account is held?

(53)

| | | | |
|---|---|---|---|
| Very likely | $\bigcirc_1$ | Not very likely | $\bigcirc_3$ |
| Quite likely | $\bigcirc_2$ | Not at all likely | $\bigcirc_4$ |

(b) and how likely would you be to recommend the branch you visit most often?

(54)

| | | | |
|---|---|---|---|
| Very likely | $\bigcirc_1$ | Not very likely | $\bigcirc_3$ |
| Quite likely | $\bigcirc_2$ | Not at all likely | $\bigcirc_4$ |
| | | Not applicable | $\bigcirc_5$ |

**34** Have you complained, or felt like complaining about the service you have received from NatWest within the last 6 months? If so, what was it about? (PLEASE USE BOTH COLUMNS, IF APPROPRIATE).

| | Have actually complained | Felt like complaining |
|---|---|---|
| | (55) | (57) |
| **Bank in General:** | | |
| Bank does not keep me informed eg. charges | $\bigcirc_1$ | $\bigcirc_1$ |
| Charges are too high | $\bigcirc_2$ | $\bigcirc_2$ |
| Poor understanding of customer needs | $\bigcirc_3$ | $\bigcirc_3$ |
| Too pushy about offering me things I don't need | $\bigcirc_4$ | $\bigcirc_4$ |
| Cash machines not working | $\bigcirc_5$ | $\bigcirc_5$ |
| Lack of cash machines available | $\bigcirc_6$ | $\bigcirc_6$ |
| Opening hours | $\bigcirc_7$ | $\bigcirc_7$ |

| | (56) | (58) |
|---|---|---|
| **Branch You Visit Most Often:** | | |
| Lack of privacy to discuss personal matters | $\bigcirc_1$ | $\bigcirc_1$ |
| Staff not interested in me/in customers | $\bigcirc_2$ | $\bigcirc_2$ |
| Poor staff attitude | $\bigcirc_3$ | $\bigcirc_3$ |
| Poorly informed staff | $\bigcirc_4$ | $\bigcirc_4$ |
| Not enough counter positions open | $\bigcirc_5$ | $\bigcirc_5$ |
| Queueing to see a cashier | $\bigcirc_6$ | $\bigcirc_6$ |
| Poor access for wheelchairs and prams | $\bigcirc_7$ | $\bigcirc_7$ |

**Branch Where Your Account is Held:**

| | Have actually complained | Felt like complaining |
|---|---|---|
| | (59) | (60) |
| Statements not received when requested | $\bigcirc_1$ | $\bigcirc_1$ |
| Cheque books not received when requested | $\bigcirc_2$ | $\bigcirc_2$ |
| Instructions not carried out correctly | $\bigcirc_3$ | $\bigcirc_3$ |
| Standing orders/direct debits not processed correctly | $\bigcirc_4$ | $\bigcirc_4$ |
| Mistakes concerning charges | $\bigcirc_5$ | $\bigcirc_5$ |
| Administrative errors (letters sent to wrong address etc) | $\bigcirc_6$ | $\bigcirc_6$ |
| Loan or overdraft refused | $\bigcirc_7$ | $\bigcirc_7$ |

*(please read the important information about credit on page 6)*

| | | |
|---|---|---|
| **Others** (Please tick the circle(s) and write in details) | $\bigcirc_8$ | $\bigcirc_8$ |

| |
|---|
| |
| (61) |

I have not complained or felt like complaining in the last 6 months     $\bigcirc_1$

**ABOUT NATWEST CASH MACHINES**

**35** How often do you use cash machines outside Natwest branches?

(62)

| | |
|---|---|
| More than once a day | $\bigcirc_1$ |
| Once a day | $\bigcirc_2$ |
| 2-3 times a week | $\bigcirc_3$ |
| Once a week | $\bigcirc_4$ |
| Once a fortnight | $\bigcirc_5$ |
| Once a month | $\bigcirc_6$ |
| Less often than once a month | $\bigcirc_7$ |
| Never | $\bigcirc_8$ Go to **40** |

**36** At what time of day do you normally use NatWest cash machines outside branches?

| (a) on weekdays | | (b) on weekends | |
|---|---|---|---|
| | (63) | | (64) |
| 6.01am-9.00am | $\bigcirc_1$ | 6.01am-9.00am | $\bigcirc_1$ |
| 9.01am-12.30pm | $\bigcirc_2$ | 9.01am-12.30pm | $\bigcirc_2$ |
| 12.31-3.30pm | $\bigcirc_3$ | 12.31-3.30pm | $\bigcirc_3$ |
| 3.31-4.30pm | $\bigcirc_4$ | 3.31-5.30pm | $\bigcirc_4$ |
| 4.31-5.30pm | $\bigcirc_5$ | 5.31-8.30pm | $\bigcirc_5$ |
| 5.31-8.30pm | $\bigcirc_6$ | 8.31-11.30pm | $\bigcirc_6$ |
| 8.31-11.30pm | $\bigcirc_7$ | 11.31-6.00am | $\bigcirc_7$ |
| 11.31pm-6.00am | $\bigcirc_8$ | Don't use on weekends | $\bigcirc_8$ |
| Don't use on weekdays | $\bigcirc_9$ | | |

*Now please answer the questions on the next page.*

**37** In your opinion, how reliable are the cash machines you use outside NatWest branches?

(65)

| | |
|---|---|
| Cash machines always seem to be working | $\bigcirc_1$ |
| Cash machines are working more often than not | $\bigcirc_2$ |
| Cash machines are out of order more often than not | $\bigcirc_3$ |
| Cash machines always seem to be out of order | $\bigcirc_4$ |
| I never use NatWest cash machines | $\bigcirc_5$ |

**38** Thinking of last time you wanted to use a cash machine outside a NatWest branch, was the machine working?

(66)

Yes    $\bigcirc_1$   Go to **40**

No    $\bigcirc_2$   Go to **39**

**39** In what way was the machine not working?

(67)

| | |
|---|---|
| No cash available | $\bigcirc_1$ |
| Machine not working at all | $\bigcirc_2$ |
| Balance/receipt not available | $\bigcirc_3$ |
| Other | $\bigcirc_4$ |
| Don't know | $\bigcirc_5$ |

### ABOUT YOURSELF

Please answer the following questions about yourself. This information helps us provide the right service to all our different types of customer. It will be treated in the strictest confidence and used for statistical purposes only.

**40** Your age:

(68)

| | |
|---|---|
| 16-20 | $\bigcirc_1$ |
| 21-24 | $\bigcirc_2$ |
| 25-30 | $\bigcirc_3$ |
| 31-34 | $\bigcirc_4$ |
| 35-40 | $\bigcirc_5$ |
| 41-44 | $\bigcirc_6$ |
| 45-50 | $\bigcirc_7$ |
| 51-54 | $\bigcirc_8$ |
| 55-60 | $\bigcirc_9$ |
| 61-64 | $\bigcirc_x$ |
| 65+ | $\bigcirc_0$ |

**41** Your sex:

(69)

| | |
|---|---|
| Male | $\bigcirc_1$ |
| Female | $\bigcirc_2$ |

**42** Are you... (please tick one)

(70)

| | |
|---|---|
| Living in rented accommodation | $\bigcirc_1$ |
| An owner occupier | $\bigcirc_2$ |
| Living with parents | $\bigcirc_3$ |
| Living in some other accommodation | $\bigcirc_4$ |

**43** Do you have any children under 16?

(71)

Yes    $\bigcirc_1$

No    $\bigcirc_2$

CSM 08/93

**44** How many years have you been a customer of the National Westminster Bank (or any of the banks from which it was formed?)

(72)

| | |
|---|---|
| Less than 1 year | $\bigcirc_1$ |
| 1-5 years | $\bigcirc_2$ |
| 6-10 years | $\bigcirc_3$ |
| 11-20 years | $\bigcirc_4$ |
| 21-30 years | $\bigcirc_5$ |
| 31 years or more | $\bigcirc_6$ |

**45** Into which of these broad ranges does your income, before tax, fall?

(a) Your own annual income?
(b) Your total household annual income?

| | Own (73) | Household (74) |
|---|---|---|
| Less than £5,000 | $\bigcirc_1$ | $\bigcirc_1$ |
| £5,000 up to £9,999 | $\bigcirc_2$ | $\bigcirc_2$ |
| £10,000 up to £14,999 | $\bigcirc_3$ | $\bigcirc_3$ |
| £15,000 up to £19,999 | $\bigcirc_4$ | $\bigcirc_4$ |
| £20,000 up to £24,999 | $\bigcirc_5$ | $\bigcirc_5$ |
| £25,000 up to £34,999 | $\bigcirc_6$ | $\bigcirc_6$ |
| £35,000 or more | $\bigcirc_7$ | $\bigcirc_7$ |
| Not earning | $\bigcirc_8$ | $\bigcirc_8$ |

Do you have any other comments you would like to make about NatWest, or any suggestions for improvement to the service?

(COL 75 = 2)

*Credit is available only to persons aged over 18 and is subject to status and conditions. Credit is available from National Westminster Bank plc, of 41 Lothbury, London EC2P 2BP. A written quotation is obtainable on request from any branch.*

col 76 = 8

Thank you very much for completing this questionnaire. Your answers will be treated in the strictest confidence and your privacy respected. Please return it in the reply paid envelope provided to:

CSM
Research Resources Limited
Central House
33-66 High Street
Stratford
London E15 2YA    *No stamp is required*

PRINTED ON 100% RECYCLED PAPER

*By finding out more about you, we equip ourselves with the information we need to help you more effectively. By filling out the questionnaire, you'll be helping us in adapting our services to ensure that they meet your needs – however those needs change over time.*

*By completing the questionnaire, you will be helping us in our efforts to provide you with the services you really need – to provide for your future, to look after your family and make the most of your money.*

**Questions**  1  Explain how the answers to the questions in the questionnaire will help National Westminster Bank to market its products.

2  Comment on the nature of the questions (open/closed/easy to understand, etc.).

3  How easy (or difficult) would it be to analyse information from the questionnaire?

## Administering a questionnaire

There are three main ways of using a questionnaire:

- with a face-to-face interview
- by telephone
- through the post.

**Face-to-face** tends to be the best form of contact. It allows two-way communication between the researcher and the respondent and may allow an experienced researcher to glean more detailed and sensitive information. It is also flexible, and so gestures, facial expressions and other signs may be noted.

A questionnaire put to a person in the street is likely to be less friendly and detailed than a group discussion in a home. A street interview is brief, impersonal and uses a broadly defined sample group, whereas a home discussion can be exactly the opposite – detailed, personal and with a tightly defined sample group. One problem with face-to-face interviews is that, because of the nature of the interaction between the interviewer and the respondent, there is the risk that some of the responses may become biased.

**Telephone interviewing** is usually more appropriate for business surveys as the respondents are often busy people and unavailable for discussion. However, this method is often regarded as intrusive since it catches people unawares, especially in the home. This means that the respondent can start the interview with a negative view, which questioning will not necessarily help to overcome. However, it is a cost-effective way of reaching people, and the replies received are likely to be truthful.

The level of response to a **postal questionnaire** will vary enormously, depending on its relevance to the reader and his or her interest. Response rates are often as low as 10 per cent, so that answers are not particularly representative – they might just be representative of those who like to fill in forms! The way to avoid this outcome is to ensure that the questionnaire is brief, succinct and sent only to those for whom it is directly relevant.

### Other primary sources

Another way of obtaining primary information is through **observation** – for example, looking at how consumers behave when shopping. Information obtained like this can help to make decisions about packaging, or influence the choice of materials designed to attract the attention of shoppers.

**Discussion groups** are an inexpensive method of obtaining useful qualitative information from consumers. For example, under the guidance of a chairperson, a group of users of the same product may be invited to provide opinions upon its use.

**Opinion polls** are often used to find out about consumer awareness, opinions and attitudes. Perhaps the most famous in this field is Gallup, but there are many others. Questions are short and are designed to find out how consumers respond to issues such as image, product lines, etc.

**Electronic interviewing** is a market research technique based on an interactive system with a telecommunications network. A respondent need only be a television subscriber and will be able to respond instantly with a range of answers while a television campaign is being carried out.

## QUALITATIVE AND QUANTITATIVE DATA

The most important thing to remember is that what comes out of market research is only as good as what goes in. The structure of the questions, the sample size and type, and the nature of the questioning should all be carefully considered before any project proceeds.

The difference between qualitative and quantitative data can be broadly summarised as follows:

- qualitative information gives opinions
- quantitative information gives facts.

Qualitative information often provides the context within which the quantitative facts operate. The 'What do you think about . . . ?' approach gives people the opportunity to offer a variety of opinions, reasons, motivations and influencing factors. A group discussion allows different opinions to be offered which will frequently lead to a consensus, giving an idea of the popular view. People enjoy offering their opinions on subjects as diverse as the current political climate and the taste of a particular margarine, and what this gives the researcher is an overall view of that particular audience's reaction to a proposition. As with all research, it is vital that the audience be carefully selected to provide relevant replies. For instance, if you are sounding out large cereal farmers' opinions of their advisory body with particular reference to grain drying techniques, the sample chosen for the research should reflect that and be composed of large cereal farmers.

Frequently, however, a useful perspective is provided by a 'control' group – a second, non-target group added to the sample for comparison. This will often provide direction for the more precise quantitative research which will give depth to any particular aspect of qualitative work.

**CASE STUDY** *How British Rail researched its InterCity Business Service*

In the 1980s, British Rail carried out extensive research into its InterCity Business Service in order to improve its service and make it more competitive with major rivals. Analysis of the results of the survey revealed a need to 'reposition' the service. A major part of the research was to try to discover which features of rail travel were seen as advantages and which features as disadvantages.

To find out why people used different forms of transport, *discussion groups* were held between InterCity, car and plane users. The results of this research revealed a complicated picture of why different people used different services – what to one person was seen as an advantage, to another was unacceptable.

| Mode of transport | Benefits mentioned by users |
|---|---|
| Car | Privacy <br> Flexibility <br> Accessibility <br> Control over journey <br> Speed |
| Plane | Standard of service <br> Thrill of flying <br> Arrive fresh |
| InterCity | The space to move around <br> The ability to work while travelling <br> Centre to centre |

The major finding of this research was that, for business travellers, the key factor influencing their views of the different modes of transport was the status accompanying their choice of transport.

Having identified through customer research areas of dissatisfaction with its service, InterCity has been able to set about revitalising its business travel. InterCity has designed a package aimed at improving the facilities on business travel by rail, emphasising features such as lack of strain, the space to move around and the ability to work while travelling.

**Questions**

1  Describe how British Rail could have used (a) qualitative research and (b) quantitative research, to chart transport users' views.

2  Set up a discussion group with a small selection of rail travellers. Find out their views on the alternative forms of travel. What are their views on British Rail's service?

# ORGANISING THE DATA

When an organisation has completed the important task of gathering the information, it has to decide what to do with it. There are three stages involved:

- sorting and storing the information
- presenting the information
- making sense of the information.

Being able to construct an effective **marketing information system** is of crucial importance to the process of market research. Such a system should ensure that information flows throughout an organisation to those people responsible for making decisions. Today, the handling of marketing information has been transformed by the use of information technology. Specialist software, scanning devices and electronic data processing make it easy to deal with large volumes of information, and to present the results in several different ways for easy interpretation.

# LIMITATIONS ON COLLECTION OF DATA

Several restraining influences should be placed on the collection of information. Some are general influences such as budgetary restrictions and storage capacity. Other equally important limits are imposed by **relevance**.

Of the wealth of information held by various departments within an organisation, only some will have any value in marketing terms. It is important to be selective before data collection starts, otherwise a great deal of time and effort will go into collecting information that is never used or is not relevant.

The most restrictive limitation on internal research is its relevance. It must also be easy to **update**. It is not, therefore, simply a matter of using information as it is presented but 'translating' it to tell us what we need to know. There are limitations on how much this information, which has been collected for another purpose, can be of value to a marketing function.

External sources present much the same problem in their sheer diversity, accessibility and usability. Again, before embarking on an investigative programme the parameters must be clearly defined.

This will help to ensure that any time, money and effort allocated to the research is well used.

The same rules apply to primary research projects. The requirements should be carefully considered to ensure that the results provide valuable information concerning the relevant issues and market areas. The objectives will also usually dictate the technique adopted for conducting the research.

## COSTS OF MARKET RESEARCH

The value of research should be defined in relation to its objectives. For example, how important and potentially valuable is it for an organisation to undertake such research? If deemed to be of high value, it will more than likely justify higher expenditure.

There are many elements to costing market research which vary enormously according to the nature of the project. If a consultant or market research organisation is hired, costs will rise significantly. However, it is crucially important that cost-cutting does not affect the quality of the project undertaken as this can materially affect the results.

The danger with all research is that the planning stage is neglected. If this is the case, however much money is spent on it, the results will reflect the inadequate nature of the planning stage. It is crucial, therefore, that all aspects of the research are carefully planned and investigated before implementation.

It is important to remember that marketing is not a static process. The market needs to be constantly monitored, researched, and improvements made to the products and services on offer to customers.

The costs of meeting the company's and the customers' requirements can vary but, by knowing as much as possible about the environment in which the organisation operates, effort can be made to ensure that the marketing budget is applied cost-effectively by minimising wastage and targeting the marketing effort as precisely as possible. The budget must cover not just the research requirements but also all elements of the marketing mix.

Depending on the nature of the market being addressed, the costs are generally higher the more specialist the market. For example, on a cost-per-thousand basis, the C1C2/female/45+ group is more difficult and therefore more expensive to identify than 'all adults'. On the other hand, it is well known that the more tightly the target market is identified, the better the response will be, and the more cost-effective the expenditure.

Cost-efficiency holds the key to effective marketing, and prioritising that expenditure is important to ensure that the maximum potential benefit receives more urgent attention than other issues, all of which is part of ensuring cost-effective use of resources.

Market research reduces uncertainties and helps to lower the risks of decision-making. It is an important process which helps managers to make good use of marketing information.

# CASE STUDY

You have recently been employed by your Local Authority as a Health Education Officer. Your prime function is to promote healthy living in your area. One specific aspect which you have been asked to target is smoking and you have obtained the information illustrated below:

## Cigarette smoking by sex and socio-economic group: 1990 (percentages)

|  |  | Current cigarette smokers | Current non-smokers of cigarettes | |
|---|---|---|---|---|
|  |  |  | Ex-regular cigarette smokers | Never or only occasionally smoked cigarettes |
| Men | Professional | 16 | 33 | 51 |
|  | Employers and managers | 24 | 37 | 39 |
|  | Intermediate and junior non-manual | 25 | 30 | 45 |
|  | Skilled manual and own-account non-professional | 36 | 33 | 31 |
|  | Semi-skilled manual and personal service | 39 | 29 | 33 |
|  | Unskilled manual | 48 | 24 | 28 |
|  | **All aged 16 and over** | **31** | **32** | **37** |
| Women | Professional | 16 | 22 | 62 |
|  | Employers and managers | 23 | 21 | 55 |
|  | Intermediate and junior non-manual | 27 | 19 | 54 |
|  | Skilled manual and own-account non-professional | 32 | 20 | 48 |
|  | Semi-skilled manual and personal service | 36 | 16 | 48 |
|  | Unskilled manual | 36 | 19 | 45 |
|  | **All aged 16 and over** | **29** | **19** | **52** |

## Cigarette smoking by sex (percentages)

| | | 1982 | 1988 | 1990 |
|---|---|---|---|---|
| Men | Current cigarette smokers | | | |
| | Light (under 20 per day) | 20 | 18 | 17 |
| | Heavy (20 or more per day) | 18 | 15 | 14 |
| | Total current cigarette smokers | 38 | 33 | 31 |
| | | | | |
| | Ex-regular cigarette smokers | 30 | 32 | 32 |
| | Never or only occasionally smoked cigarettes | 32 | 35 | 37 |
| | | | | |
| Women | Current cigarette smokers | | | |
| | Light (under 20 per day) | 22 | 20 | 20 |
| | Heavy (20 or more per day) | 11 | 10 | 9 |
| | Total current cigarette smokers | 33 | 30 | 29 |
| | | | | |
| | Ex-regular cigarette smokers | 16 | 19 | 19 |
| | Never or only occasionally smoked cigarettes | 51 | 51 | 52 |

| **Average weekly consumption per smoker by sex** | **1982** | **1988** | **1990** |
|---|---|---|---|
| Men | 121 | 120 | 118 |
| Women | 98 | 99 | 97 |

**Task a** What deductions can be made from the information provided? Explain how this might help you with your project.

**Task b** Before developing your strategy you have decided to survey smokers in your district. One of the reasons for this is to find out the extent to which they reflect the figures shown nationally. Prepare a questionnaire to be administered by interviewers. In your questionnaire

- use a variety of questioning techniques
- identify the purchasing habits of smokers
- try to find out which categories of smokers 'might' be prepared to give up if targeted successfully by a campaign
- discover what help smokers might require in order to cease smoking
- identify smokers who are least likely to be influenced by a campaign
- find out the most effective way of locally influencing the actions of smokers.

**Task c** Before you administer the survey you need to identify the sampling technique which you intend to use. Choose a suitable sampling technique, explain why you have chosen it and then use it to 'pilot' your survey.

**ASSIGNMENT**   Your task in this assignment will be to design a questionnaire using the principles outlined in the chapter. Whether you go on to apply the questionnaire to obtain data will depend on your circumstances and the time available. Ask your tutor.

A class of students set out to discover whether there was a demand for a second screen at their local cinema. They needed to find out how many people went to the cinema, how often they went, what sort of people they were and the types of films they liked. This sort of information would show whether there was a large demand for a cinema, the type of people who would go most frequently, and what types of films would attract the biggest audiences.

The class had already been told by the cinema owner that age was a very important factor influencing the frequency with which people went to the cinema and the types of film they preferred to see.

The class set out to classify cinema-goers into different age groups. First they took into account their own experiences and then interviewed friends and relatives in different age groups. Using this information they were able to come up with the following groups:

5–15     16–25     26–35     36–50     51+

Having chosen their main criterion for classification, the next step was to devise a questionnaire containing all the other questions they needed to ask. The questionnaire had to be simple to use in the field and easy to read off when completed. A short section of their questionnaire is shown below:

| Age group | 5–15 | 16–25 | 26–35 | 36–50 | 51+ |
|---|---|---|---|---|---|
| How often do you go to the cinema? | | | | | |
| More than once a week<br>Once a week<br>Once a fortnight<br>Once a month<br>Hardly ever<br>Never | | | | | |
| What types of films do you like to watch? | | | | | |
| Horror<br>Adventure<br>Comedy<br>Romance<br>Other | | | | | |

Your task is to design a complete market research questionnaire to find out whether there is the demand for an additional screen at *your* local cinema. You should consider the following points:

- What will you ask?
- Who will you ask?
- When will you ask?
- How will you ask?

Alternatively, you could design a questionnaire to research the demand for a new supermarket, a new leisure centre, a new car park, or a new disco.

# The Marketing Mix

## WHAT IS THE MARKETING MIX?

The marketing mix is made up of **the four Ps**. To meet the needs of customers an organisation must:

- develop **products** to satisfy them
- charge them the right **price**
- get the goods to the right **place**
- make consumers aware of the product through **promotion**.

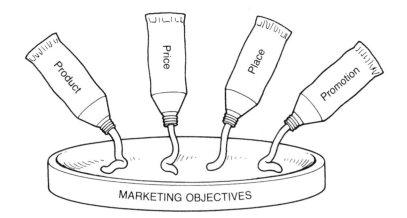

FIGURE 4.1
*Ingredients of the
marketing mix*

## MATCHING OBJECTIVES

In earlier chapters we have looked at those areas of marketing which prepare for change or for decision-making. However, marketing is not just about preparation, it is also about taking *action*. Marketing provides the energy that drives our economy and is responsible for bringing goods and services that consumers want and need into the marketplace.

The way in which organisations respond to **market signals** (such as rising demand) will reflect their **corporate objectives** and this will in turn influence the strategies and techniques they employ. These objectives give an organisation a unifying purpose and create a yardstick against which to assess achievements.

Businesses and other organisations do not simply set out to maximise profits. They have responsibilities to a variety of

**stakeholders**, who may be customers, shareholders, employees, creditors, suppliers etc. Each of these exerts some influence on the shape of corporate strategy.

The role of the marketing function is to generate a market-centred philosophy in an organisation, and to set out a plan showing how the organisation can achieve its objectives. From this plan, decisions are made on how to turn ideas into reality. These decisions involve the ingredients of the marketing mix.

## CORPORATE PLANNING

The first question that any organisation must answer is 'Where are we going?' Rather than seeking maximum profits, an organisation may seek to be the **brand leader** or otherwise to dominate a particular market – this may give it a dominant long-term position. **Corporate growth** is another common objective. Taking over other companies, diversifying and introducing new products may not help profitability, but it will provide managers with control over a large corporate unit. Other organisations take great pride in the way they are seen by the public, and may be prepared to sacrifice profit but never reputation.

At the heart of corporate planning lies the need to match marketing objectives with corporate objectives (see Figure 4.2). Doing so directs an organisation's activities towards satisfying the wishes of the consumer and enables it to achieve its goals.

FIGURE 4.2
*Matching objectives*

## CASE STUDY  *British Airways*

British Airways is not only the world's largest airline, but also one of the most profitable. It has always maintained a leading position in the world airline

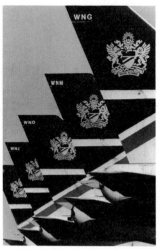

*Courtesy British Airways*

industry. For example, it operated the world's first daily scheduled international air service, the first jet passenger flight and the first commercial supersonic aircraft.

Today BA seeks to continue to set the trends that the rest of the industry follows. Its objective is to maintain corporate growth and to take advantage of the anticipated global expansion of the industry. To achieve this objective BA believes in the need to expand traditional markets by increasing activities in regional British cities and outside Britain.

As air travel becomes more common and more frequent for many people, expectations grow. For those involved in marketing at BA, the objective is to provide better quality goods and services and good value for money in every market segment in which it operates as rivals seek to achieve a competitive edge. This involves maintaining quality, innovation and service, whilst constantly responding to the requirements, preferences and aspirations of customers.

**Questions**

1   Consider carefully both the corporate and the marketing objectives mentioned in the case study. Describe how achieving the marketing objectives will enable British Airways to reach its corporate goals.

2   Suggest three alternative courses of action which the BA marketing team could adopt to work towards its objectives.

3   In 1993, BA received a lot of bad publicity for a 'dirty tricks' campaign it waged against Virgin Airways. This involved, for example, ringing up Virgin's customers to offer them alternative flights on British Airways. How might such tactics be counter-productive for BA?

# MARKET SEGMENTATION

Customers are not all the same. However, groups of consumers can be divided into discrete **segments**, in the same way that we divide an orange up into separate segments. For example, Levi sells jeans, but the jeans market is split into a number of segments all catered for by Levi. One way of segmenting the market is by sex, another way is by the type of jeans – e.g. loose-fit, regular-fit, stone-washed, pre-wash (see Figure 4.3).

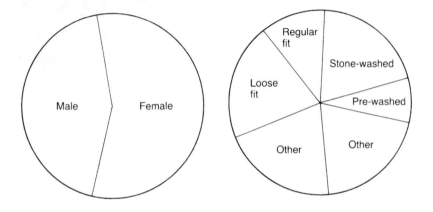

FIGURE 4.3
*Two ways of dividing up (segmenting) the jeans market*

---

Segmentation can be defined as the strategy whereby a firm partitions the market into sub-markets (segments) which will respond in similar ways to marketing inputs.

---

Segmentation can be contrasted with market **aggregation**, where the firm treats the whole market as an undifferentiated mass (hence 'mass marketing'). Some products are aimed at a mass market in which there is no clear division between segments – for example, Saxo table salt in this country is aimed to sell to nearly everyone. However, when we look at most products we can see that they are aimed at particular groups of consumers. This is true even of toilet rolls (up-market or down-market brands), sugar (ordinary consumer or health-conscious), and televisions (ranging from standard to luxury sets).

There are a number of ways of segmenting markets. We shall look at four ways: geographic, demographic, psychographic, and behaviouristic.

## Geographic segmentation

This is a simple form of market segmentation. Certain countries, regions, etc. are assumed to have common characteristics which influence buying attitudes. In international marketing it makes sense to analyse particular market segments in terms of such characteristics as population, income per head, trade carried out by the country, as well as tastes, and the nature of competition in the market.

Figure 4.4 gives some useful indicators for businesses looking at the markets of western European countries.

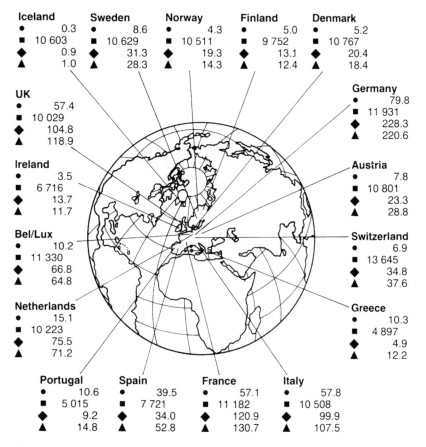

**Iceland**
- 0.3
■ 10 603
◆ 0.9
▲ 1.0

**Sweden**
- 8.6
■ 10 629
◆ 31.3
▲ 28.3

**Norway**
- 4.3
■ 10 511
◆ 19.3
▲ 14.3

**Finland**
- 5.0
■ 9 752
◆ 13.1
▲ 12.4

**Denmark**
- 5.2
■ 10 767
◆ 20.4
▲ 18.4

**UK**
- 57.4
■ 10 029
◆ 104.8
▲ 118.9

**Germany**
- 79.8
■ 11 931
◆ 228.3
▲ 220.6

**Ireland**
- 3.5
■ 6 716
◆ 13.7
▲ 11.7

**Austria**
- 7.8
■ 10 801
◆ 23.3
▲ 28.8

**Bel/Lux**
- 10.2
■ 11 330
◆ 66.8
▲ 64.8

**Switzerland**
- 6.9
■ 13 645
◆ 34.8
▲ 37.6

**Netherlands**
- 15.1
■ 10 223
◆ 75.5
▲ 71.2

**Greece**
- 10.3
■ 4 897
◆ 4.9
▲ 12.2

**Portugal**
- 10.6
■ 5 015
◆ 9.2
▲ 14.8

**Spain**
- 39.5
■ 7 721
◆ 34.0
▲ 52.8

**France**
- 57.1
■ 11 182
◆ 120.9
▲ 130.7

**Italy**
- 57.8
■ 10 508
◆ 99.9
▲ 107.5

FIGURE 4.4
*The markets of western Europe in 1992 (Source: OECD)*

**Key**
- Population (millions)
■ GDP per capita (£s)
◆ Exports total (£ billion)
▲ Imports total

## Demographic segmentation

This involves dividing the population into discrete segments either by age (e.g. for clothes retailing), or by sex (e.g. for the sale of cosmetics), or by family size (e.g. for selling different sizes of breakfast cereals), or by income group (e.g. in selling own-brand and manufacturers' brands in a supermarket), or by occupation (e.g. in selling life insurance to teachers or stunt drivers), or in any other way.

### Psychographic segmentation

This is concerned with identifying personality traits and distinguishing characteristics in groups of the population. Examples are young and outgoing (for the sale of new forms of music) or grey and conservative (for classical and 60s music).

### Behaviouristic segmentation

This looks at consumer behaviour patterns – frequent/infrequent purchase, loyalty to a product etc. For example, one segment of the market may always purchase your product while another is made up of people who switch frequently between brands. An experienced drinker may stick with Guinness, while an inexperienced one may try out a range of beers and stouts.

Usage rate is an important factor to consider when segmenting a market. A small number of consumers may be responsible for the bulk of the purchases of a particular product.

## POSITIONING

It is important to build up a clear consumer profile of the sorts of people or groups that we are targeting our products at. What do they think and feel? What do they want to look like? What are their ambitions? How much money do they have to spend? What factors influence their buying decisions? If we get a clear picture of these things we will be able to provide the benefits that they seek in a product. Furthermore we will be able to target our marketing activities at their requirements.

An important decision for a marketer is where to **position** a good or service in the market. A choice that needs to be made frequently is between 'up-market', 'middle-market' and 'down-market'. Once a position has been chosen it is difficult to change later. For example, a 'down-market' clothes shop will find it difficult to change its image to sell high-priced fashion items. Positioning means the way in which a firm and its products are viewed by consumers in terms of the criteria that these consumers see as being important for them – value for money, 'greenness', the superior lifestyle associated with the product, functionality, etc.

## CASE STUDY  *Positioning a new hairdressing business*

There are currently four hairdressing salons in Midtown. Angelo's is the top-of-the-range salon charging high prices and giving a high-quality service in luxurious premises. Belinda's charges a highish price but offers a more functional service. Maria's places an emphasis on service but charges a relatively low price. Tony's is the most down-market of all the salons and charges a low price for a quick turnover.

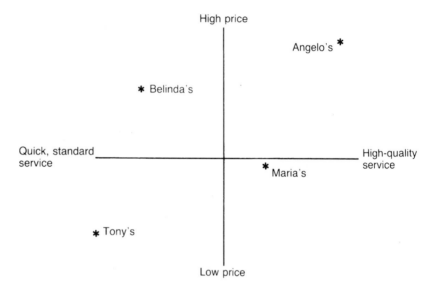

**Questions**
1  What factors would the owners of each of these businesses have considered in positioning their products?
2  What factors would have limited their ability to choose where to position their products?
3  If you were going to open up a new hairdressing business in competition with these four, which market segment would you choose, and why?

## CHOOSING A MARKETING STRATEGY

**Undifferentiated marketing** (see Figure 4.5) is where a single marketing mix is offered to the total market. This is unlikely to be

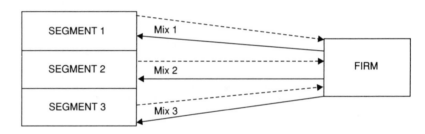

FIGURE 4.5
*Undifferentiated
marketing*

successful because most markets consist of different types of buyers
with different wants and needs.

**Differentiated marketing** (see Figure 4.6) is the process of attacking
the market by tailoring separate product and marketing strategies to
different segments of the market. For example, the car market may
be divided into an economy segment, a luxury segment, a
performance segment, etc.

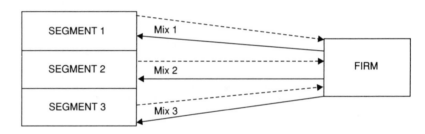

FIGURE 4.6
*Differentiated
marketing*

**Concentrated marketing** (see Figure 4.7) is often the best strategy
for the smaller firm. This involves choosing to compete in one
segment and developing the most effective mix for this sub-market.
Jaguar, for example, concentrates on the luxury segment of the car
market.

FIGURE 4.7
*Concentrated
marketing*

Although companies will try to select and dominate certain market
segments, they will find that rivals are engaged in similar strategies.
They will therefore try to create a differential advantage over rivals.
The *positioning strategy* of a business relates to selecting a market
segment and creating a differential advantage over rivals in that
area. For example, Porsche is positioned in the prestige section of the

car market with a differential advantage based upon technical performance.

## CASE STUDY  *Segmentation of the tea market*

Tea is Britain's traditional drink. It accounts for just under 50 per cent of everything we drink (excluding plain water) and tops the drinks table as number one.

In the hot beverage market, tea is perceived to be as British as fish and chips or a pint in the pub. It has heritage and tradition and is associated with a morning cuppa, as a mealtime drink or as afternoon refreshment. It is drunk by almost everyone, no matter what their background or occupation.

There are three major players in the tea market: Lyons Tetley, Brooke Bond and Premier Brands. These account for more than 50 per cent of total tea sales in the UK. The market can be divided into the segments shown in the figure.

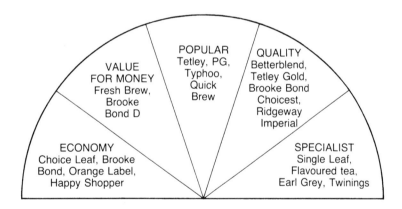

As well as divisions in the market according to the segments shown, there are also variations according to buying behaviour. For example, Tetley traditionally performs well in the north of England, whereas PG performs well in the south.

Tetley teas are manufactured by Lyons Tetley, which belongs to the food division of Allied Lyons. The group's key strengths lie in the following:

- building brands
- meeting changing consumer needs through new product development
- international thinking and operation

- having the financial resources and quality of staff to meet these objectives.

Tetley's Greenford factory produces over 100 different packet styles and around 30 different blends of tea. Styles of pack range from loose tea in cartons to tea bags in plastic boxes.

Tetley's advertising agency is DMB&B whose main function is to develop and produce advertising for Lyons Tetley. At the same time, it also provides other specialist agency services, such as public relations and sales promotions. The advertising agency has to become an authority on the market it is handling. By placing itself in this position, it is able to produce advertising that is attention-grabbing and entertaining by communicating a message that is not just relevant to the brand, but which also addresses competitive activity in the market at that point in time. As a result the client–agency relationship is a close one, though there are some areas of overlap between the functions and expertise of each.

Tetley tea advertising involves communicating different messages as the market situation develops. Its key feature is its ability to be memorable and amusing. For example, the Tea Folk have supported the brand since 1973 and have given Tetley an identifiable trademark. As well as projecting the qualities of the brand, they have reflected major product innovations, such as the round tea bag designed to maintain and develop Lyons Tetley's market share.

**Questions**

1 As there are three major players in the tea market, what sort of competitive activity would you expect?

2 Comment generally on the consumer profile of a tea drinker. Mention: factors affecting demand; consumer needs; the image of tea; socio-economic groupings; life-style.

3 How would a knowledge of this consumer profile affect the way in which tea is marketed?

4 Look at the different market segments for tea. Explain how a promotion for the popular sector would differ from a promotion for the specialist sector.

5 Explain why the group Allied Lyons identifies one of its strengths as 'meeting changing consumer needs through new product development'.

6 What is the role of an advertising agency (you may need to do some research)?

7 Explain why the marketing process must be a dynamic and progressive activity.

# THE ELEMENTS OF THE MARKETING MIX

The **marketing mix** is made up of a complex set of variables which an organisation can combine in order to ensure that marketing and corporate objectives are achieved. It will include strategic, tactical and operational elements and techniques.

'Mix' is an appropriate word to describe the marketing process. A mix is a composition of ingredients blended together to fulfil a common purpose. Every ingredient is vitally important and each depends upon the others for its contribution. Just as with a cake, each ingredient is not sufficient on its own but with all blended together it is possible to produce something very special. In the same way that there are a variety of cakes to suit various tastes, a marketing mix can be designed to suit the precise requirements of a market.

As a result the marketing mix must have:

- **A time-scale** – An organisation must have a plan which indicates when it expects to achieve its objectives. Some objectives will be set to be attained in the near future. Others might be medium-term (one to five years) and others might be visionary objectives for attainment in the longer term.

- **Strategic elements** – These will involve the overall strategy of the organisation. They require considerable use of judgement and expertise and are only decided by senior managers. Such decisions might involve the development of a new product or a new market strategy.

- **Tactical or medium-term elements** – The business environment has to be constantly monitored and decisions have to be taken according to whatever changes take place. External events might affect pricing strategies, product modifications or amendments to marketing plans.

- **Short-term operational elements** – These involve predictable everyday decisions such as contacts with customers, analysis of advertising copy and minor decisions about packaging.

The commitment and support of a programme of planning with sufficient resources will underlie the manipulation of the marketing mix and will ultimately determine how capable an organisation is of achieving its objectives.

## CASE STUDY *The Sony Video Walkman*

In the early 1990s, Sony launched its revolutionary Video Walkman, backed by its biggest corporate advertising campaign, costing £10 million. The Video Walkman is a full-feature video recorder and television combined to make an item only slightly larger than a Filofax. The starting price was £799, but now there is a cheaper play-only version. Its 8mm format allows it to use videotapes the size of an audio cassette.

As part of the launch, Sony spent £1 million on 8mm software for the UK market. Initially these videos were sold by retailers placing telephone orders with Sony – 'only to order' selling. However, with the growth of sales some retailers now stock the films themselves.

**Questions**

1 Identify each of the four ingredients of the marketing mix illustrated in this case study.

2 Comment on how each of these ingredients might be varied in the future in order to reach a mass market.

3 Which segment of the market was the product originally aimed at?

### The product

The product is the central point on which all marketing energies must converge. The product is more fully discussed in Chapter 5. Finding out how to make the product, setting up the production line, providing the finance and manufacturing the product are not the responsibility of the marketing function. However, it is concerned with what the product means to the customer. People buy goods and services for a variety of reasons and a wide range of characteristics will influence their decision to buy.

- *Appearance* – Often the way a product looks is considered to be as important as what it can do. Carpets, furniture and jewellery are goods which must be designed to appeal to the tastes of the customer.
- *Function* – Consumers will want to know what a product can do and how well it can do it. When you buy a car you might want it to accelerate quickly or last a long time. The functions of a car which are necessary to a taxi driver may be radically different from the functions for a motorist who wants a vehicle for recreational use.
- *Status* – Consumers often associate products with a particular life-style. Organisations then try to emphasise the association to create an image for the product. For example, certain car

badges and designer labels encourage consumers to make the purchase because of the status they portray. Red Stripe, the premium lager brand marketed by HP Bulmer, was successful because of its cult status.

*Courtesy HP Bulmer*

The product range and how it is used is a function of the marketing mix. The range may be broadened or a brand may be extended for tactical reasons, such as matching competition or catering for seasonal fluctuations. Alternatively, a product may be **repositioned** to make it more acceptable for a new group of consumers as part of a long-term strategic plan.

Today many UK companies that have moved into wider European markets have had to consider how they need to change production processes. This has involved:

- reviewing the effects on capacity of planned expansions in sales
- assessing the impact on processes of changes in technical standards required by the European Union in order to make required changes
- assessing the impact on processes of changes in (and complying with) European standards on products
- assessing the implications of changes in certification, testing and inspection requirements and responding when required.

## The price

Of all the aspects of the marketing mix, price is the one which creates sales revenue – all the others are costs. The price of an item is clearly an important determinant of the value of sales made (see Chapter 6). In theory, price is really determined by the discovery of what customers perceive is the value of the item on sale. Researching consumers' opinion about pricing is important as it indicates how they value what they are looking for as well as what they want to pay. An organisation's pricing policy will vary according to time and circumstances. Crudely speaking, the value of water in the Lake District will be considerably different from the value of water in a desert.

## The place

Though figures vary widely from product to product, roughly a fifth of the cost of a product goes on getting it to the customer. 'Place' is concerned with various methods of transporting and storing goods, and then making them available for the customer. Getting the right product to the right place at the right time involves the distribution system (see Chapter 7). The choice of distribution method will depend on a variety of circumstances. It will be more convenient for some manufacturers to sell to wholesalers who then sell to retailers, while others will prefer to sell directly to retailers or customers.

As the distribution system is constantly changing, organisations need to update their plans frequently. The type of distribution network chosen for each product should be compatible with other elements in the mix and will help to reinforce the overall nature of the marketing mix.

## The promotion

Promotion is the business of communicating with customers. It will provide information that will assist them in making a decision to purchase a product or service (see Chapter 8). The razzmatazz, pace and creativity of some promotional activities are almost alien to normal business activities.

The cost associated with promotion or advertising goods and services often represents a sizeable proportion of the overall cost of producing an item. However, successful promotion increases sales so that advertising and other costs are spread over a larger output. Though increased promotional activity is often a sign of a response to a problem such as competitive activity, it enables an organisation to develop and build up a succession of messages and can be extremely cost-effective.

## The importance of the mix

The marketing mix is a carefully constructed combination of techniques, resources and tactics which form the basis of a marketing plan geared to achieve and match both marketing and corporate objectives. Whenever objectives or external influences change, so the blend of ingredients will have to be varied. The effective solution to any problem will involve the careful scrutiny of every element. Changes to the mix have to be carefully considered and implications have to be assessed. Often timing is of crucial importance.

A *ratio* can be used to relate the effectiveness of a change in a component in the mix to its cost. A successful change would be one where the ratio of effectiveness to cost is high.

No two mixes, even between similar types of organisations, will ever be the same. Each will represent a unique approach to developing a strategy for the resources they have available.

## SUR/PETITION

Edward de Bono has coined the term **sur/petition** to signify a situation in which business organisations concentrate on providing a range of **integrated values** for consumers.

The word 'competition' comes from the Latin and literally means 'seeking together' or 'choosing to run in the same race'. Sur/petition means 'seeking above'. Sur/petition would take place even if there were no competition – the business seeks to beat its previous values.

Edward de Bono argues that there have been three phases of business philosophy:

- Phase 1 was product-driven – you strove simply to provide a good or service.
- Phase 2 involved competition – you sought to beat your rivals.
- Phase 3 now involves sur/petition. In this phase, businesses creatively seek to provide a range of integrated values for consumers. Purchasers don't simply want to buy a car, they will also need to drive the car, to park it, to insure it, etc.

Sur/petition involves creating integrated solutions. De Bono talks about creating value monopolies resulting from **valufacture** – that is, the creation and formation of values. The marketing mix should therefore be directed at valufacture. Businesses that take sur/petition to heart will create value monopolies. These are in no way illegal – they are successful simply because they are the best.

## THE CUSTOMER IS ALWAYS RIGHT

In their book *The One to One Future: Building Relationships One Customer at a Time*, Don Peppers and Martha Rogers urge businesses to form impregnable relationships with individual customers. They argue that even the mass marketer can strike up these relationships. This involves gathering as much information as possible about individual customers and then organising your organisation to meet these individual needs. We can refer to this as **customer segmentation** (which is a step forward from product segmentation).

Peppers and Rogers illustrate this point by reference to a service that could be offered by mail-order catalogue operators:

- The customer could order gifts for friends and relatives several months in advance.
- The company would then schedule delivery of the gifts on the right days.
- You would be charged for each gift two days before delivery.
- You would receive a reminder postcard 10 days before each gift was sent.
- When you received your annual catalogue you would receive a reminder form of last year's gifts and addresses.

The same logic can be applied to a variety of other situations and products. The business develops an individual relationship with customers for their lifetime purchasing requirements. The customer thus becomes more disposed to buy, leading to increased sales, and lower unit costs of production. The authors talk about the marketing department becoming a 'customer management organisation' designed around portfolios of customers. Customer loyalty would be the key to the success of the proposal.

## CASE STUDY  *Mass customisation*

In an article in the journal *European Management* in 1993, Roy Westbrook and Peter Williamson identified the latest stage of industrial revolution emerging from Japan as that of 'mass customisation'. Mass customisation makes it possible to increase the variety of products available to consumers whilst continuing to reduce unit costs of production.

Westbrook and Williamson identify the mid-1970s to the mid-1980s as being a period known as 'market in' in Japan. While introducing cost savings through component and process design, manufacturers added additional features to standard products in order to stimulate increased demand.

However, by the late 1980s Japanese customers were again reaching saturation: 'They not only had most types of products, they now had a range of each. Worse still, the gadgets, bells and whistles were losing their novelty.' Product life-cycles were shortened.

A new strategy was therefore required for the 1990s – to personalise the product for each customer. This has involved responsive marketing to find out what customers need and coupling it with highly responsive and flexible production methods.

Westbrook and Williamson quote the example of the Melbo company which makes customised suits with a lead time of just three days:

> What you will not find are the usual acres of racks, crammed with stock and occupying lots of phenomenally expensive Tokyo real estate. Instead the entire store carries less than a hundred suits, with a floor space requirement only a fraction of that needed by competitors. Melbo's customers do not come to fit themselves into a suit on the rack because the company's 'Ready-Made Order System' will guarantee that a suit designed by houses like Givenchy, Daniel Hechter, or Nina Ricci, but individually cut and sewn to fit them, with a choice of over a hundred fabrics, will arrive at their home or office within the week.

**Questions**

1 What do you understand by the term 'mass customisation'?

2 How is it likely to (a) meet the requirements of consumers, (b) benefit producers, (c) lead to a more dynamic economy?

3 How is mass customisation likely to involve and influence the elements of the marketing mix?

4 Is mass customisation a way forward for all business organisations?

**Task** Complete the table below.

| Product | Market | Segment |
|---|---|---|
| Persil washing-up liquid | Washing-up liquid | Premium, concentrated |
| Porsche | | |
| Andrex tissue | | |
| The Sun | | |
| Harrods | | |
| Diet Coke | | |

**ASSIGNMENT** Imagine that you are responsible for the launch of a new Vauxhall car. Work in small groups to complete the following tasks:

**Task** a Describe the features of this new car.

**Task** b What sort of customers would it appeal to?

**Task** **c** Analyse the segmentation and targeting of this car.

**Task** **d** Comment on each of the elements of its marketing mix.

**Task** **e** What unique selling points (USPs) does it have?

As a group, present your findings back to the other groups.

# The Product

At some stage in their life most people come up with an idea for a new product. We have all met people with wild and wonderful ideas – 'a device for winding in electric fences on sheep farms', 'toothbrushes that play nursery rhymes when they are wet', 'automatic golf-ball finders' and many more. None of these have ever gone beyond the stage of 'the idea' – yet!

Hickory–Dickory–Dock

**Production** involves going beyond the loose idea, into market and product research to provide a **marketable product**. A product offers the purchaser a range of benefits. It will be composed of several elements.

On the surface there are often clear **tangible benefits** – things you can touch and see. Tangible features of a product include:

- shape
- colour
- size
- design
- packaging

The **intangible features** are not so obvious. These include the reputation of a firm ('You can be sure of Shell') or the corporate or brand image (like the Shell logo).

There are extra features to be considered such as:

- after-sales service
- availability of spare parts
- customer-care policy
- guarantees.
  - What else can you think of?

A product is made up of a range of features which serve to meet customer requirements. A customer buying a new car may not just want a family saloon – additional requirements may be things like:

- a blue car
- four doors
- a well known name
- a long guarantee
- credit facilities
- after-sale free servicing
- low petrol consumption
- a proven safety record.

In fact, a survey of 1720 car drivers in early 1994 (the annual Lex survey) showed that while 41 per cent looked mainly for security and 37 per cent for safety, only 6 per cent were mostly interested in the top speed and 14 per cent in acceleration. Environmental concerns featured prominently with 27 per cent expressing this as their main interest. The survey pointed out that environmental worries are not yet sufficiently strong to induce people to switch from car travel to other modes of transport, but could nevertheless influence the type of car that people would prefer to buy. The Lex survey thus indicated that the days are long gone when motorists sought principally speed and acceleration when choosing a car. The motorists identified that they would like the following improvements in their next car:

| | | | |
|---|---|---|---|
| Security | 41% | Acceleration | 14% |
| Safety | 37% | Ease of driving | 11% |
| Fuel efficiency | 32% | Styling of car | 10% |
| Driver comfort | 16% | Top speed | 6% |
| Reliability | 15% | | |

# PRODUCT CONCEPT

Have you ever thought about why you buy products? At a simple level you may buy a coat to keep you warm or a newspaper to read. However, consumer buying behaviour is a complex process. We all have a range of different motives for making the buying decisions which we do. For example, think about the sort of clothes you wear and then contrast them with the sort of clothes you would definitely not want to wear! A product for many of us is not simply a way of keeping warm or just having something to read, it is more than this. It is something which fits in with our perception or self-image. Products are not simply purchased to meet a single need; the ownership and use of a product involves a whole range of factors that make up the **product concept**.

For example, it may appear that a couple choose to holiday in the West Indies because they are attracted by the sand, sun and surf. However, when questioned further, it may come to light that they are more concerned with the 'image' which they present – friends, associates and other 'significant others' will become aware that they are able to afford to holiday in the West Indies. Holidaying in the West Indies is associated with a particular life-style. In the public imagination it may represent being rich and able to afford exotic things.

The purchaser of an expensive modern car will probably be interested in the quality and reliability of the vehicle. He or she may be attracted by the 'state of the art' technology and many other features of the car. However, a significant part of the product concept may also involve the ingredient of showing the world that 'they have arrived'.

In a similar way, you may like to purchase a second-hand trench coat from Oxfam not just because it will keep you warm and cost relatively little – in addition, you may believe that it gives you an 'arty image'.

The reason I wear it is because it keeps me warm

# PRODUCT DIMENSIONS

Product benefits can be broken down into a number of important *dimensions*. These include:

- generic dimensions
- sensual dimensions
- extended dimensions.

**Generic dimensions** are the key benefits of a particular item. Shoe polish cleans shoes. Freezers store frozen food. Deck-chairs provide a comfortable seat on a sunny day. Hairdressers cut and style hair.

The **sensual dimensions** of a product are those that have an effect on the senses – design, colour, taste, smell and texture. A ring doughnut has a shape, appearance, texture, taste and smell all of its own. The sensual benefits of products are frequently highlighted by advertisers. This is clearly the case when advertising food and drinks – 'smooth and creamy', 'the amber nectar', and so on.

The **extended dimensions** of a product include a wide range of additional benefits. Examples are servicing arrangements, credit facilities, guarantees, maintenance contracts, and so on.

---

# THE PRODUCT LIFE-CYCLE

Central to the planning process will be decisions which have to be taken about the portfolio of products on offer. Answers will be needed to questions such as:

- When shall we launch product A?
- What would we realistically expect the performance of each of our products to be?
- Which products will require support?
- Which products would we expect to do well/badly?

To find the answers an organisation will use a series of tools to aid the planning process. One such tool will be the **product life-cycle**.

### The classic life-cycle

Markets are in a constant state of change. Over a period of time tastes and fashions alter and the technology used to produce goods and services will move on. As a result, there will always be demand for new products and old products will become redundant.

Which of the following (if any) have you seen recently:

- a black and white television
- a radiogram
- a reel-to-reel tape-recorder
- an instamatic camera
- a Ford Anglia
- a twin-tub washing machine?

The product life-cycle is a useful mechanism for planning changes in marketing activities. *It recognises that products have a finite market life and charts this through various phases*. The sales performance of any product introduced to a market will rise from nothing, reach a peak and then, at some stage, start to decline. The life-cycle can be further broken down into distinct phases, as illustrated in Figure 5.1.

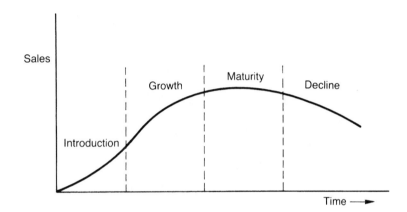

FIGURE 5.1
*The classic life-cycle*

- *The introductory phase* – During this period it is necessary to create demand. Growth is slow and volume is low because of limited awareness of the product's existence.

- *The growth phase* – Sales then rise more quickly. It is during this phase that the profit per unit sold usually reaches a maximum. Towards the end of this phase, competitors enter the market which reduces the rate of growth.

- *Maturity* – In this period most of the potential customers have been reached. However, there will still be plenty of scope for repeat purchases. Competition from sellers in the market becomes stronger and new firms enter the market.

- *Decline* – The product becomes 'old' and sales start to fall. Perhaps a new or improved product will have entered the market.

The concept of the product life-cycle is perhaps best understood when related to real products and current developments.

## CASE STUDY  *Album sales*

In September 1989, sales of long-play records (LPs) accounted for over a quarter of all album sales in the UK. By September 1992 the figure had fallen to just over 6 per cent. While total sales in the market had fallen, the sale of compact discs (CDs) had almost doubled.

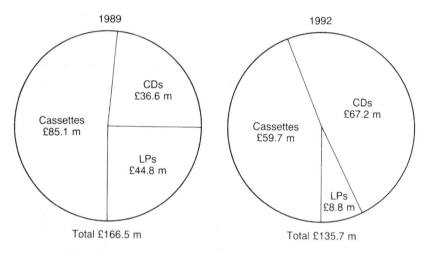

In terms of product life-cycles we could say that:

- LPs are in decline
- cassettes are between maturity and decline
- CDs are between growth and maturity.

The market for albums exemplifies the importance of applying the concept of the product life-cycle to real situations. While LPs were the staple diet for many British consumers in the 1960s, 70s and 80s, they have rapidly declined in sales in the face of the onslaught of new sound technology. In fact, more recently the pace of change has quickened. Two new products were launched late in 1992 which may or may not represent the shape of things to come.

The *MiniDisc* is like a CD but only a third of the size. It can make recordings and is shockproof. If, while jogging, you trip over a molehill, the laser scanner may jump, but an electronic memory will keep the music going until the laser finds it place again. The MiniDisc was launched as a high-quality out-and-about system and is intended to replace the tape-recorder.

The *Digital Compact Cassette* has been promoted hard through glossy magazines. It has near CD quality, records digitally and will play the old analogue tapes. It is also seen as the replacement for the standard tape-recorder.

Neither product is expected to make massive sales immediately. Initial sales during the introductory period of the life-cycle are what the industry calls 'adopters'. Adopters reflect a premium which consumers are prepared to pay at the cutting edge of consumerism. However, in a rapidly changing marketplace it is difficult to predict the future for such products.

**Questions**

1  Which of the two new products seems to be currently making the most headway in the market?
2  What factors might affect the lengths of their life-cycles?
3  Why do many modern products have a relatively short life-span?
4  Identify two products which you consider to be in each of the different stages of the classic product life-cycle.

### Injecting life into the product life-cycle

The life-cycle of a product may last for a few months or for hundreds of years. To prolong the life-cycle of a brand or a product, an organisation may inject new life into the growth period by readjusting the ingredients of its marketing mix (see Figure 5.2).

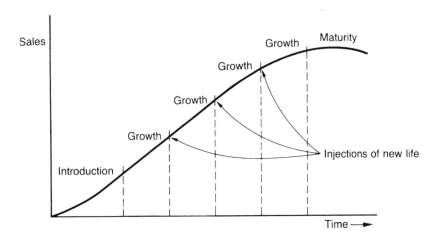

FIGURE 5.2
*Injecting new life into
a product*

A readjustment of the marketing mix might involve one or several of the following activities:

● Change or modify the product, to keep up with or ahead of the competition. For example, in 1992 Mars took the unprecedented step of slightly altering the ingredients of the Mars Bar, as well as changing the shape of the bar. In 1990, Rowntree brought out their 'Blue Smartie' to improve their competitiveness against M&Ms, and in 1992 they brought out the 'Gruesome Greens'.

- Alter distribution patterns, to provide a more suitable place for consumers to make a purchase. For example, Next started catalogue trading in 1989.

- Change prices to reflect competitive activities. For example, the price of home computers has been slashed in the mid-1990s as more similar products become available.

- Have a promotional campaign. The Guinness campaigns have helped to extend the life of a well-established product.

### Alternative product life-cycles

To a large extent the classic life-cycle of a product is a gross simplification. There are, in fact, many alternative explanations which help to illustrate the life-cycles of products.

In their French text on business, *Economie D'Entreprise*, J.L. Cordon and J.P. Raybaud suggest a series of different life-cycles as illustrated in Figure 5.3.

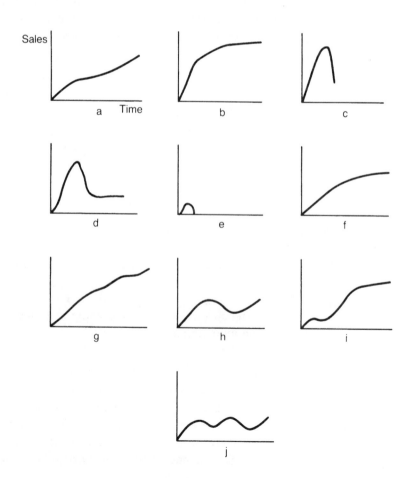

FIGURE 5.3
*A series of possible product life-cycles*

**a** *Apprentissage long* (long introductory period) – For example, some novels are available in bookshops for a long period before the public starts to buy them in significant numbers.

**b** *Pas d'apprentissage* (virtually no introductory period) – Some new 'wonderdrugs' become stars straight away.

**c** *Feu de paille* (straw on fire) – These are products that rise quickly in popularity and are burnt out quickly in a very short period. This is the case with some children's toys, such as trolls. Some pop groups are 'one-hit wonders'.

**d** *Feu de paille avec marché résiduel* (straw on fire but with a reasonable residual market) – Some products boom quickly but in decline still leave a sizeable market. Though the skateboard craze came and went you will see some skateboards in the shops. There is usually scope for some of the more efficient firms to stay in the market.

**e** *Echec* (flop) – Many new products flop. Oft-quoted is Clive Sinclair's C5 road vehicle (a sort of motorised tricycle).

**f** *Cycle long* (long cycle) – Many products continue to go from strength to strength, such as potato crisps and chocolate bars.

**g** *Relances successives* (periodic rejuvenations) – Many products are frequently injected with new life.

**h** *Nouveau départ* (relaunch) – Some products need to be relaunched to bring them out of decline. To do this a product may need to be redesigned or have its image substantially altered. For example, in recent years the Babycham drink has been relaunched because of declining sales over a number of years.

**i** *Introduction manquée* (false start) – Sometimes the launch and introductory phase of a product fails to catch the public imagination. Seven Up was launched with six different names before Seven Up took off!

**j** *Mode* (fashion) – Some products have booms and slumps in sales according to fashion or season. The sales of swimwear and fireworks are examples.

Try to identify one extra product to match each of the life-cycle alternatives suggested by Cordon and Raybaud.

## Consumers and the life-cycle

Looking at the life-cycle from the angle of consumers provides important insights into changes in a market and their influence upon strategies. For example, in the introductory phase of the life-cycle 'early adopters' try products. As the product moves into growth, more consumers become adopters. As the life-cycle of the product moves on, competition will intensify. The number of competitors operating in the market will increase as it nears maturity. Organisations will fight to retain their market share and this might lead to product diversification and price-cutting. Consumers will become more selective about their purchases. During maturity, suppliers will depend on repeat purchases. Usage will fall during decline (see Figure 5.4).

| Stage | Users/buyers |
| --- | --- |
| Development | Few trial or early adopters |
| Growth | Growing number of adopters |
| Shakeout | Growing selectivity of purchase |
| Maturity | Saturation of users, repeat purchase reliance |
| Decline | Drop off in usage |

FIGURE 5.4
*The consumer and the life-cycle*

## Product portfolios

Businesses with a single product are always likely to be vulnerable to variations in the marketplace. By spreading investment across a **range of products**, an organisation reduces its risks.

Most companies produce a range of products, each of which has its own life-cycle. By using life-cycles, companies can plan when to introduce new lines as old products go into decline. The collection of products that a company produces is known as a **portfolio**.

In Figure 5.5, $T_1$ represents a point in time. At that point product 1 is in decline, product 2 is in maturity, product 3 is in growth and product 4 has recently been introduced. This helps to avoid serious fluctuations in overall profit level and ensures that the most profitable products provide support for those which have not yet

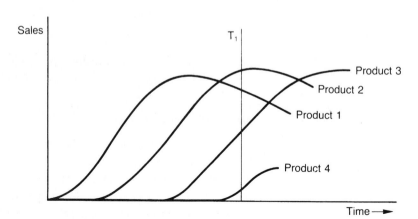

FIGURE 5.5
*A product portfolio*

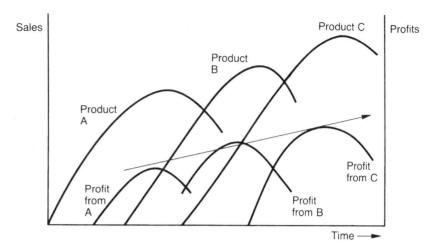

become quite so profitable. Figure 5.6 indicates how the portfolio can be managed to develop profitable growth.

Any organisation does well to bear in mind the simple principle known as **Pareto's rule**. This suggests that 20 per cent of time and effort put in tends to produce 80 per cent of the results. An extension of this idea is that 20 per cent of customers can account for 80 per cent of a firm's sales. This is a useful 'rule' to remember when trying to work out which products are the real breadwinners in a particular situation. The implication for international marketing is that a small number of markets may yield most of the best results. The question is, then, whether you should concentrate on developing new markets or concentrate on your best existing markets.

### Different stages in international development

In international marketing the marketer needs to be aware that some countries will be more developed and have sophisticated consumer requirements. Consumers might have a higher standard of living and therefore require up-market products. In some international markets there will be more competition than in others. An organisation might therefore find that whilst the demand for a particular product is in decline in its home market, it is at the growth stage in other countries.

The firm can then transfer its marketing efforts to emerging markets. For example, in the 1990s it is possible to transfer the sales of some products from western European to eastern European markets.

# RESEARCH AND DEVELOPMENT OF PRODUCTS

Many people associate the **research and development** (R&D) function of a company with the invention of new products. Whilst this is very important, the development of existing products is of equal significance because consumer preferences are continually changing. The task of product research and development is to come up with the goods and services that will meet the needs of tomorrow's customers.

In any well-run company, research and development have strictly commercial functions – to further the company's business objectives by creating better products, to improve operational processes and to provide expert advice to the rest of the company and to customers.

Some research is not expected to pay for itself within a foreseeable time span. Large companies may allocate as much as one-tenth of their research budget to so-called **blue-sky** investigations whose most likely contribution is to the development of new products and a possible pay-off in the distant future.

Within an organisation anybody who is directly working on a project and affected either up or down the line by your work is considered to be an internal customer. If there is no internal customer for work from any area of the organisation then the research project is unlikely to fit into the development process and will fail.

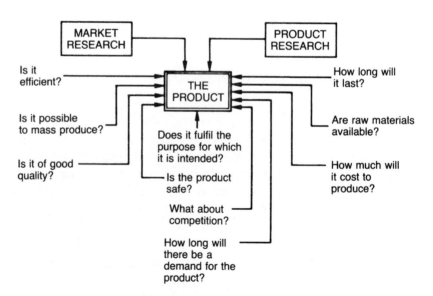

FIGURE 5.7
*Key questions about
the product*

Product research and development goes hand in hand with market research and development. Considerable liaison is required between these two areas, and processes need to be standardised. Setting up a production process or a new line can involve considerable cost, and careful work in the early stages will help to ensure that profits are made. Product researchers and marketing managers attempt to investigate all the questions indicated in Figure 5.7 before a decision is made finally to go into production.

---

**CASE STUDY** *Walls' Tangle Twister*

Many product advances are made possible by breakthroughs in production techniques. Twenty years ago lollies were little more than tapered blocks of ice on a stick. The technology – pouring juice into a straightforward rigid metal mould – restricted a company like Walls to simplicity. Then the lolly embraced rubber technology: by casting ice in a flexible rubber mould the lollies could be shaped more intricately because the mould could be peeled off.

More recently the Tangle Twister hit the high-street freezers. This was made possible by an ingenious invention from Walls' design engineers. They came up with a nozzle that could make a lolly by twisting together three separate flavours of ice. The innovation represented a quantum leap in lolly technology.

Such ideas are dependent on the combination of research and development, production engineering, investment funds, investment in people, and the key edge of information technology.

**Questions**
1 What do you understand by the term 'technology'?
2 How does new technology enable the development of new products?
3 List six new products that have developed from new technology in recent years.
4 What is the impact of new technology on the life-cycles of existing products?
5 How does the case study show that a number of integrated elements are required for new technologies to come to the fore?

### Product researchers

Researchers use marketing information to help them to develop products or services and choose suitable **designs**. Design is simply the art of making things of quality that people want, and/or packaging or presenting them in an attractive way. The layout of a bookshop, for example, has to be designed – a customer must be able to find quickly what he or she wants. In this case the right use and allocation of space is vital to ensure profitability. So is the concept of service: many retail shops have been investing heavily in technology so as to benefit from point-of-sale data capture.

Product researchers must also consider production costs, ease of manufacture and selling prices.

A company might be reluctant to change an earlier design, particularly if it provides status (e.g. the radiator grill on a BMW car). Conversely, small ('cosmetic') changes may be made to products to bring them up-to-date – for example, in 1993 Shell updated its logo to give it a 'modern feel'.

Once a design has been completed the product researchers will build a prototype which can then be tested. Some prototypes will be discarded while others may be modified and improved. When a product has been tested and thought to be successful, and all the marketing and production questions have been answered, the firm will need to 'tool up' its production line. This is summarised in Figure 5.8.

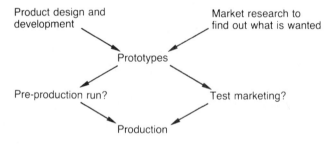

FIGURE 5.8
*Between design and production*

## Built-in obsolescence

Many products feature **built-in obsolescence**. Fashion clothes are designed to last for a season, and cars are built to last for only a few years before repairs are necessary. Manufacturers are able to sustain long-term market demand by limiting the life-spans of products. The opinion of some is that this leads to a huge waste of resources, but others see it as boosting demand, employment and output in the economy.

# ECONOMIC ANALYSIS OF A PRODUCT VENTURE

An economic analysis of a product venture will need to take place as part of the process of research and development. The analysis will be based on estimations of future costs and revenues.

## Cash flows

A large quantity of information related to outputs, prices, costs, taxes and royalties to be paid will need to be collected and assessed. When all this information is available for reliable estimates to be made, the net cash flow over a period can be calculated. This is the total amount of cash coming into the company, based on expected volumes of product sales after allowing for the project expenditure.

At this stage the most uncertain assumption often relates to the product price. Some companies do not try to forecast the future price but assume instead a price that is prudent and realistic and test the economic viability of a new project against that price.

One example of a business' net cash flow over more than 10 years is illustrated in Figure 5.9. For the first years the cash flow is *negative* while the project is being investigated and there is expenditure on R&D, plant, materials, etc. Then the cash flow becomes *positive* after the product has been launched.

The positive cash flow of the venture should be sufficient for the repayment of, and profit on, the investment, after taking into account the loss of purchasing power of money due to *inflation*. The

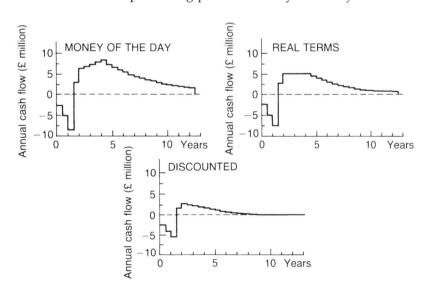

FIGURE 5.9
*Forecasted cash flows*

cash flow must therefore produce a sufficient return in terms of the *money of the day* to offset this loss of purchasing power. To take account of likely future inflation, a **real-terms cash flow** – expressed in terms of money with a constant value – is calculated from the cash flow in terms of money of the day (see Figure 5.9).

The likely **return on the investment**, taking account of the risks inherent in the venture (and hence its economic acceptability), is examined by calculating a **discounted cash flow**. The risks are many and varied, and include technical and commercial risks, the risks of significant increases in technical costs, amongst other external factors (e.g. a change in tax structures).

It is extremely difficult to anticipate such possibilities in detail and, consequently, some companies prefer to test the economic acceptability of a project at a discount rate appropriate to an assumed level of risk. Such a discount rate is called the **project screening rate** and is usually in the range 5–20 per cent. A company is not completely free to choose what it feels to be an appropriate rate, since it must compete with others in the market.

A useful way of understanding the future economic performance of a project is to examine the **cumulative cash flow**. This is the progressive sum of the annual cash flows. An example is given in Figure 5.10. From this a number of important measures of the **economic acceptability** of the venture are immediately apparent, such as the 'pay-out time', the 'maximum exposure' and the 'ultimate cash surplus'. The economic acceptability can now be judged according to the project's ability to meet the requirement that the cumulative cash surplus discounted at the project screening rate is positive and sufficient to justify the risks taken.

It is helpful to relate the time it takes to recover the investment in a project to the life-cycle of the product. In Figure 5.11, for example, there will be an ongoing drain on resources up to the point of launch. The investment can then be recovered through the revenue from sales until the point at which the investment is finally recovered (in the diagram this takes place during the growth stage).

---

# FORECASTING PRODUCT SUCCESS

Earlier in this chapter we looked at the life-cycle of a product based on consumer demand. However, it is also important to look at

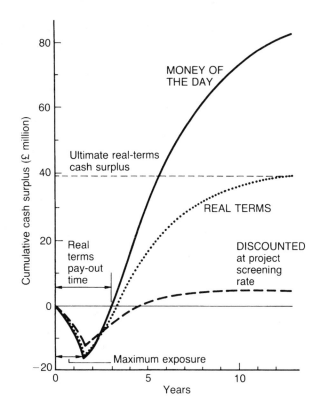

FIGURE 5.10
*Cumulative cash flow
from Figure 5.9*

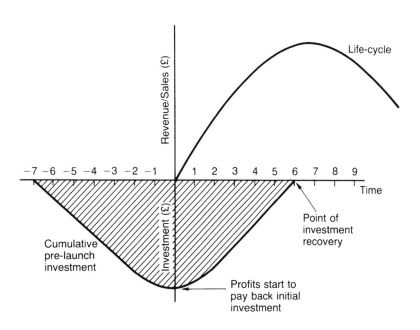

FIGURE 5.11
*The investment
recovery process during
the product life-cycle*

111

*restrictions imposed from the production side.* We can illustrate this point by looking at the exploration of oil-fields.

Interest in an area may be triggered by a geologist's curiosity, a news item, or by an invitation from a government to bid for exploration rights. Before this can be developed further a realistic assessment must be made about:

- the probability of finding economic fields
- the contract terms that might be applicable
- economic aspects such as the production and transportation costs.

These assessments are made to establish whether an exploration programme is justified – that is, whether anticipated benefits exceed expected costs.

An initial estimate of the reserves contained in a prospective area can be expressed in the form of an **expectation curve** (see Figure 5.12). Expectation curves highlight the uncertainty associated with exploration (or any other form of production) particularly at an early stage.

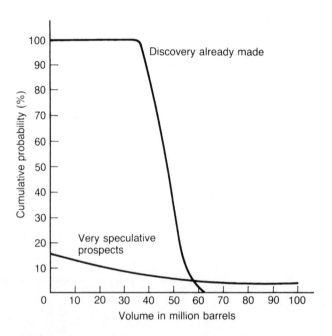

FIGURE 5.12
*Expectation curves*

Based on an analysis of the geological information, expectation curves show the probabilities of finding reserves of a certain magnitude in the area. In a well defined area with a history of discoveries, for instance, there may be a high degree of certainty about the current reserves, but little chance of finding major additions. A speculative venture in a little known area, on the other hand, means that the chances of finding any hydrocarbons at all may be low – but there is an outside chance of making a very large discovery (e.g. the discoveries of oil in the mid-1990s off the Falkland Islands).

As with all new major products developed by a large company, several steps of evaluation will take place before the final 'go ahead' is given. The activities involved in an exploration programme are aimed at defining the geological structures as accurately as possible (see Figure 5.13).

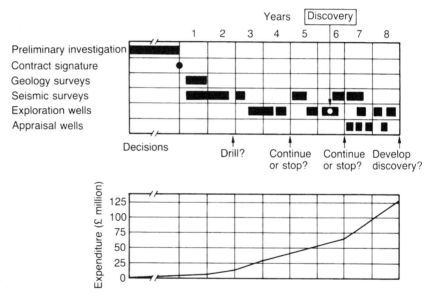

FIGURE 5.13
*A typical exploration programme*

A preliminary investigation will identify whether there is any possibility of discovering oil. On the basis of this information contracts will be signed with the landowners to provide the basis for the right to develop the field. A geological survey will then be carried out, and periodic seismic studies will take place throughout the development stage. Exploration wells will be drilled to locate a point of extraction. Only after this has been done is it possible to determine whether oil and gas is trapped and whether the geological assumptions are valid. A cycle of further surveys and appraisal wells is undertaken to reduce the geological uncertainties and to provide an increasingly accurate estimate of oil and gas reserves.

Information obtained from these activities is used in planning the field development. With each cycle the costs of the exploration programme increase significantly. An efficient exploration is therefore one which obtains the maximum information with the minimum effort.

## PRODUCT PLANNING

In the exploitation of oil reserves, a given company will have a range of interests under review at any one moment in time. Some old fields will be drying up, others will be close to maturity, whilst newer fields will be flourishing, or still in the process of early development. **Product planning** *involves devising methods to evaluate the performance of a portfolio of products, developing processes to extend the lives of some, to add bits to others, and planning the development of new initiatives*. An oil company will usually have a wide range of interests including gas and chemicals. The purpose of product planning is to make sure that you produce a mix which is compatible with company strategy.

### The product mix

The product mix is the complete range of products produced by a company. Some business organisations try to **diversify** their range of products, because by doing so they spread the risks. However, in the last decade of the twentieth century we are seeing another trend amongst a number of large companies – they are simplifying operations to concentrate on their **core strengths.**

## CASE STUDY  *Blue Circle Industries plc*

For generations the name of Blue Circle has been associated with cement. Though cement is still very much a part of the business today, over the last few years Blue Circle has become a company very different from the one-product organisation of the past.

The acquisitions of Armitage Shanks (1980), Birmid Qualcast (1988) and Myson (1990) brought a whole new range of products, production techniques and people to the group. For example, Blue Circle's Home Products Division owns New World, the UK's leading manufacturer of gas cookers; Armitage Shanks, the UK's biggest sanitary ware manufacturer; Qualcast, one of Britain's best known brands of lawnmower; and Potterton, the manufacturer of boilers and central heating equipment. The company has also developed its interests in the USA, and in waste management, brick manufacture and property.

The main driving force behind these changes has been the need to diversify – to reduce the company's dependence on one product and to make full use of its resources.

These diverse businesses are organised into five divisions: Cement, Home Products, Enterprises, Holdings, and Overseas. They operate under the parent company, Blue Circle Industries plc, based in London.

Each division comprises businesses which, by virtue of their product or location, work well together. The launching of new products and the introduction of new initiatives help to make sure that the businesses are able to compete successfully in their own fields.

**Questions**
1 Explain why the Blue Circle businesses are organised into five divisions.
2 Set out a diagram to illustrate the different products that make up the product mix of the Blue Circle group.
3 How does Blue Circle benefit from having a mix of products?
4 What disadvantages might there be to an organisation from having such a diverse product mix? Why in recent years have many companies reduced their mix of products to concentrate on core lines?

### Portfolio analysis

Perhaps the best-known method of analysing a product portfolio to see its balance was devised by the **Boston Consultancy Group**. The technique is based on the 'experience curve' which shows that the unit costs of adding value fall as cumulative production increases (see Figure 5.14).

Gains in efficiency stem from greater experience. The Boston Consultancy Group argued that the principle had general currency,

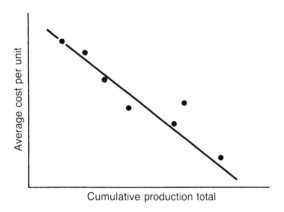

FIGURE 5.14
*An 'experience curve'*

and that, as a rough rule, average cost per unit fell by 20–30 per cent with each doubling of experience. Greater experience stems from:

- economies of scale
- the elimination of less efficient factors of production
- increased productivity stemming from technical changes and learning effects
- improvements in product design.

The key lesson to be learnt is that the benefits of experience do not just arise – they need to be *engineered*. Companies must act to ensure that these benefits are reaped. They will result from active managerial policies.

An important implication of the work of the Boston Consultancy Group is that 'experience' is a key asset. Companies which have a high market share should be able to accumulate more experience. Therefore companies should strive for a high market share. The best indicator of market share is relative – that is, the ratio of a company's market share to that of its largest competitor:

$$\text{Relative market share of A} = \frac{\text{Market share of company A}}{\text{Market share of nearest competitor}}$$

This indicator gives a clear measure of comparative strengths. The Boston Consultancy Group used statistical evidence to argue that a ratio of 2:1 would give a 20 per cent cost advantage.

### Product portfolio and market growth

The Boston Consultancy Group argued that the faster the growth of a particular market the greater the costs necessary to maintain market position. In a rapidly growing market, considerable expenditure will be required on investment in product lines, and to combat the threat posed by new firms and brands.

To summarise, the Boston Consultancy Group identified two key elements in the analysis of a product portfolio:

- The greater the cumulative experience, the greater the cost advantage.
- The faster the growth of a market, the greater the cost of maintaining market position.

On the basis of these two general rules, BCG devised a portfolio matrix which is illustrated in Figure 5.15.

| Market growth \ Relative market share | High | Low |
|---|---|---|
| High | Prospects | Question marks |
| Low | Yielders | Dogs |

FIGURE 5.15
*Product portfolio matrix*

The matrix identifies four main types of products:

- **Prospects** are those classes of products which compete in rapidly expanding markets. They take up large sums of cash for investment purposes. However, they also yield high cash returns. On balance they provide a neutral cash flow – but generally, they will go on to be the yielders of the future.
- **Yielders** have a high market share in markets which are no longer rapidly expanding. Because the market is relatively static they require few fresh injections of capital. Advertising and promotion will be required to inject fresh life from time to time. However, the net effect is of a positive cash flow. Yielders provide the bread and butter of a company in the form of profits at the end of the day. Yielders are often referred to as **cash cows**.
- **Question marks** have won a relatively low market share in fast-growing markets. Can these be turned into market leaders? What needs to be done to improve their performance? These are just some of the key questions which will help to determine the viability of such products. The company knows that such products may go on to be powerful earners, but at the same time they may prove to be a drain on resources. What should be done with the question marks?
- **Dogs** are products with a low market share in a low-growth market. Because of the importance of experience these are products which are relatively poor competitors. As such they will generate a negative cash flow.

In terms of cash flow, the product portfolio matrix of Figure 5.15 can be redrawn as in Figure 5.16. Cash generated by the yielders is used to help in the development of the question marks. The purpose of this is to increase the market share of the question marks in order to move them into the prospect category, with the expectation that eventually they will become yielders (Figure 5.17).

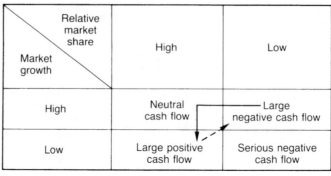

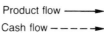

FIGURE 5.16
*A cash flow and product flow*

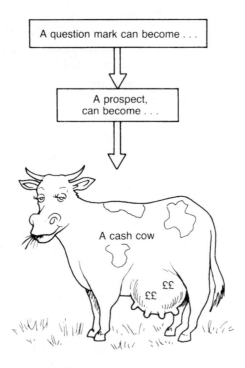

FIGURE 5.17
*The development of a cash cow*

In order to manage the development of product success effectively, it is important to have a balanced portfolio of products at any moment in time. A company will require a number of yielders to provide the bread and butter of the organisation. At the same time it is important to develop the cash cows of the future by investing in the prospects (sometimes referred to as **stars**). Fortunately the prospects will pay their own way. You therefore need to prop up your question marks and cut out your dogs.

In international marketing, national markets may take on the roles of cash cow, star, dog, etc.

## Replacement/extension of existing products/markets

What happens when a question mark fails to become a star? What happens when a cash cow goes into decline? These are questions which require constant review by a marketing department. It is necessary to re-evaluate the performance of products constantly.

There are a number of ways of assessing performance:

- *Expected sales and profits* – A product's performance can be evaluated against its previous performance. Once these indicators start to dip, then it is clear that remedial action needs to be taken.

- *Relative market share* – Relative market share is always important because once it starts to *fall* the product becomes endangered by losing its competitive edge. Once it starts to lose impact in the public imagination it is in danger of becoming an 'also ran'.

- *Threats* – The development of threats in the marketplace needs to be carefully monitored. Threats range from the emergence of new technology, the arrival of competition, changes in consumer expenditure patterns and so on.

Each product line within a company product portfolio claims a given share of scarce resources. These resources can be used in different ways – and there is an **opportunity cost** to be considered. If a product can be transformed from a declining position to one of high profitability, then it will merit its position in the portfolio. If it is a drain on resources then it detracts from other products. At this time, it is important to prune weak areas, to replace declining products by new potential winners.

### *Ansoff's product–market matrix*

Another way of analysing a product strategy is by using **Ansoff's product–market matrix**. This theory was developed by H. Igor Ansoff. It looks not just at the management of the product portfolio but also more widely at market developments and opportunities. Ansoff's matrix matches existing and new product strategies with existing and new markets (see Figure 5.18). In doing so his matrix suggests five alternative market strategies which hinge upon whether the product is new or existing or whether the market is new or existing.

- **Consolidation** implies a positive and active defence of existing products in existing markets.

119

|  | Existing products | New products |
|---|---|---|
| Existing markets | Consolidation Market penetration | Product development |
| New markets | Market development | Diversification |

FIGURE 5.18
*Ansoff's product–
market matrix*

- **Market penetration** suggests a further penetration of existing markets with existing products. This will involve a strategy of increasing market share within existing segments and markets.
- **Product development** involves developing new products for existing markets.
- **Market development** will use existing products and find new markets for them. These new markets will be identified by better customer targeting, market research and further segmentation.
- **Diversification** will lead to a movement away from core activities. This might involve some form of integration or diversification into related activities.

## THE LAUNCH OF A NEW PRODUCT

The **launch** is the most spectacular day in the life of a product (although a launch may be spread over several weeks). It is the time when a product is finally revealed to the critical scrutiny of the customer in the marketplace. In recent years the launching of products has become an art. At one time there was considerable secrecy associated with the launch. Today a common marketing technique is to provide sneak glimpses, and to provide leaked information to whet the appetite of the market. Previews and exposures to the press have become as common in marketing as in politics.

The major part of the advertising budget on a new product will normally be spent in the pre-launch and launch period. If the money invested in the launch is not to be wasted, then it is important to blast off with dramatic effect. Champagne receptions for the press and chosen market contacts are standard practice in many consumer durable markets, coupled with extravagant sideshows.

For other consumer goods, expensive television and press advertising campaigns have become routine. Promotional pricing, trial offers, and free gifts are also effective ploys.

The launch should either make potential consumers widely aware of the new product or make them want to find out more about the product. Whilst new product development is an important activity for companies, it is one that has a high degree of risk associated with it; hence, a large majority of new products that are launched either fail to be accepted by the market, or do not meet the financial criteria expected of them.

One result is that a number of companies try to reduce the risks associated with product development, either by modifying existing products, or by copying competitors. Even with this latter strategy there is no guarantee of success. What is important is that market opportunities are studied carefully and related to the strengths and weaknesses of the firm.

A useful classification of new product development is based on the contrast between **offensive** and **defensive**. Offensive product development occurs with the application of new technology as well as by responding positively to new patterns of consumer demand. Defensiveness is a reaction to competition in your area of business.

## ASSIGNMENT

Toyota is attempting to coax executives away from their traditional Jaguars and BMWs. In the early 1990s it launched its Lexus LS400 at an initial price of £34 250.

Toyota hopes to repeat the four-litre car's success in the United States, where 24 000 models were sold in the first year after the launch. Toyota expects that sales of the car will initially be small in Britain but sees it as a way into the European executive saloon market.

Powered by a V8 engine, the Lexus has gained a reputation for having 150mph performance without sacrificing quietness and a smooth ride. Features include anti-lock brakes, air-conditioning, leather upholstery and a compact disc player with seven speakers.

Toyota recognised that its biggest problem was in creating a separate identity for the Lexus in an expensive status-conscious market. The Lexus therefore has a separate badge and the name Toyota does not appear on the car.

A special dealership network has been established among Toyota distributors, while a 'Club Lexus' warranty scheme, including hotel bills in the event of breakdown, is provided for three years.

**Task a** Identify the target market for the Lexus. What are the best ways of reaching this market? Who are the main competitors?

**Task b** If you had been given the responsibility for launching the Lexus, what steps would you have taken?

**Task c** In terms of the Boston Consultancy Group matrix, where would you place the Lexus in the Toyota portfolio? How can Toyota try to ensure that the Lexus performs well within the portfolio?

**Task d** What techniques have Toyota employed to ensure the success of the Lexus? Are these measures effective? What else needs to be done?

# ASSIGNMENT

**Task a** What factors are likely to make up the product concept for:
- someone who buys *The European* newspaper
- someone who wears an expensive but 'state of the art' fashion garment
- a student who buys a folder that is to contain a coursework assignment?

**Task b** Identify an existing product which is commonly used by students (e.g. a chocolate bar, a type of crisps, a make of ballpoint pen). This will be the focus for your task.

1 Identify what 'the product concept' is for the product you have chosen.

2 Identify the 'generic dimensions', the 'sensual dimensions' and the 'extended dimensions' of your chosen product.

3 Make a comparison between these product dimensions and those of three major competing products.

4 Highlight the major weaknesses and strengths of your product when compared with the competition. To carry out this task you may need to research the views of a sample of consumers of the chosen product type.

5 Prepare a 15-minute presentation. This should first outline your findings and then go on to identify ways in which the company could improve the product and its image in order to give it a competitive edge over rivals. In the presentation you should use three overhead transparencies.

# CHAPTER

# 6

# Pricing

In January 1994, Eurotunnel announced the prices it would charge in 1994 for its Le Shuttle service. They were as shown in Figure 6.1.

|  | **Standard** | **Five-day** |
|---|---|---|
| May–June | £280 | not available |
| July–August (Sun–Thur) | £280 | not available |
| July–August (Fri–Sat) | £310 | not available |
| September–October | £260 | £160 |
| November–December | £220 | £130 |

FIGURE 6.1
*Eurotunnel's return fares Dover to Calais*

The decision on what prices to charge took a lot of thought. There were many factors influencing the prices that could be charged. The costs of running the service and paying back the capital costs of the project were a major consideration. A particularly important factor in this case was the prices charged by competitors (ferries and hovercrafts mainly). Other factors include taxes that need to be paid to governments, and the demand and supply conditions in the marketplace (see Figure 6.2).

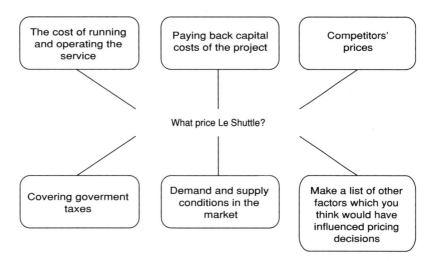

FIGURE 6.2
*What price Le Shuttle?*

In this chapter we set out to find out what exactly we mean by price and how pricing decisions are made.

123

# DEFINING PRICE

The Oxford English Dictionary defines prices as the *'sum or consideration or sacrifice for which a thing may be bought or attained'*.

However, to produce a watertight definition of pricing which gives a clear indication of its importance in the marketing mix is like trying to define the length of a piece of string. In some situations, a particular definition will be appropriate, in others it will not.

A major problem stems from the fact that 'price' has different meanings for different groups of people:

- *Buyers* – For buyers, price may be regarded as an unwelcome cost. Price involves sacrificing the next-best alternative that could be bought (this is sometimes referred to as **opportunity cost**). Price can also be used as a measure of the value of a particular item.
- *Sellers* – For sellers, price is a key element in the marketing mix. It is an important selling point. Getting the price 'right' is an important tactical decision and as such it is a key factor influencing revenue and profit. We all know of a business that sold wonderful products which were just a little too expensive – it went bust. We also know of businesses which sold themselves too cheaply, so not enough revenue was generated to cover costs adequately.
- *Government* – The price of individual products is an influence on the general price level – and hence votes!

We also need to be aware of the international impact of prices. The prices of a country's products alter with the **exchange rate**. When the price of the pound increases against other currencies then British goods become less competitive in other countries. Fewer goods will be sold abroad, leading to falling order books at home.

These contrasting viewpoints about prices often conflict. Each perspective needs to be considered in setting prices.

---

**CASE STUDY** *A competitive price for Le Shuttle?*

The prices charged by Eurotunnel and its competitors are closely related to each other because they offer a similar product – that is, a short journey linking France to the United Kingdom. In early 1994 the prices of standard fares between Dover and Calais were as shown below.

|  | Winter off-peak | Summer off-peak | Summer peak weekend |
|---|---|---|---|
| Le Shuttle (car and unlimited passengers) | £220 | £280 | £310 |
| Stena Sealink (car and up to 5 passengers) | £126 | £220 | £320 |
| P&O (car and up to 8 passengers) | £139 | £139–221 | £289–320 |
| Hoverspeed | £142 | £297 | £338 |

Eurotunnel is hoping to capture 50 per cent of the cross-channel market by 1996. Indeed, it needs to capture such a high share of the market if it is to pay back the money it has borrowed for massive construction costs.

Eurotunnel in effect offers a 'no frills attached' product at a competitive price. The prices it charges will be considerably more than competitors in the winter when it hopes that the prospect of faster journeys will capture the custom of many motorists. It is essential for Eurotunnel to be seen to be the quicker service. The journey time is 35 minutes, the same as for the hovercraft, but 40 minutes quicker than the ferry.

However, ferries require cars to arrive at least 20 minutes before the ferry departs, and with 10 minutes extra to disembark the time taken in a crossing is more like 105 minutes from motorway to motorway, compared with an hour by tunnel.

A number of national newspapers have summed up the advantages of the two methods in the following way:

|  | Le Shuttle | Car ferry |
|---|---|---|
| Winter price | Substantially more expensive | Relatively cheap |
| Summer price | A little bit more expensive | Relatively cheap |
| Time taken | About one hour | Nearer two hours |
| Comfort | Own car seat | Passenger lounges |
| Sea view | None | Yes |
| Frequency | Up to 4 per hour | Every 90 minutes |
| Reliability | Weatherproof | Uncomfortable in bad seas |
| Booked trips | No | Yes |
| Restaurants | No | Yes |
| Shopping | No | Yes |

Of course these advantages and disadvantages will vary. Passengers may find that they are faced with unforeseen delays when using either service. Travelling in your own car has the advantage (if you see it that way) that you don't have to mix with other people, but then again some passengers may prefer to travel in a well-equipped boat with plenty of recreational activities and opportunities to spend money.

As a new venture, Eurotunnel is reluctant to get involved in a *price war* with its rivals. This could have disadvantages for all involved. Instead Eurotunnel will focus on some of the major *non-price advantages*, such as missing unpleasant weather conditions and a no-booking system. Eurotunnel wants its service to be seen as a kind of rolling motorway linking Britain and France.

Eurotunnel has moved into a very profitable market in which the rival ferry companies have been making healthy profits. It seems likely that profit margins will be cut back and that some cross-channel operators will link together. Already Sealink and P&O are hoping that the Office of Fair Trading will allow them to provide a combined service offering two sailings per hour.

**Questions**  **1**  What factors do you think are most likely to give Le Shuttle a competitive advantage in the cross-channel market?

**2**  What factors are most likely to give it a competitive disadvantage?

**3**  Why did it set its prices at the levels shown in early 1994?

**4**  Why did Eurotunnel not want to start a price war with its rivals?

**5**  What has subsequently happened to the pricing strategy of Eurotunnel, and the pricing strategy of its rivals? Explain changes that have occurred. What are likely to be the effects of these changes?

---

## HOW IMPORTANT IS PRICE IN THE MARKETING MIX?

Selecting the right price is one of the most critical decisions to be taken in the marketing mix. If Eurotunnel has set its price too high or too low then Le Shuttle may prove to be a very expensive failure.

The importance of price within the marketing mix varies from one market to another and between different segments in the same market. In low-cost non-fashion markets, price can be critical (e.g. in the sale of white emulsion and gloss paint for decorating). In fashion markets, such as fashion clothing, it can be one of the least relevant factors. Certain products are designed to suit a particular price segment (e.g. economy family cars) whilst others perform a specific function regardless of cost (e.g. sports cars). For consumers with limited budgets, price is a key purchasing criterion, whilst for others for whom 'money is no object', price is less important.

The price of products in international markets is crucial. The price that you charge needs to be:

- competitive with the prices of similar products in international markets
- set in such a way that you will not lose out dramatically as a result of small (or sometimes large) changes in international exchange rates.

*When the price of the £ falls*, this makes the value of British goods more competitive. However, if it falls too much then exporters will find it difficult to cover costs. *If the price of the £ rises*, then exporters will make a larger return on each sale that they make. However, if the price of the £ rises too much then foreigners will stop buying our goods. There is thus an acceptable *margin* for changes in the price of the £, but very large rises or falls harm exporters (see Figure 6.3).

£ rises too much. Exporters find that sales fall off considerably, cutting into or destroying profits

£ rises by an acceptable amount – export sales begin to fall

£ keeps its value

£ falls by an acceptable amount – export sales rise in volume but fall in value

£ falls too much. Exporters find that the volume of their sales increase considerably – but the money received from sales is barely enough to cover production and sales costs

FIGURE 6.3
*The effects of changes in the exchange rate*

## PRICING DECISIONS

A number of situations can be identified in which pricing decisions have to be made. The most important of these are:

- *when a price needs to be set for the first time* – This can happen when a new product is launched on the market, when new outlets are used, when new contracts are made, or when businesses move into new international markets.

- *When it becomes necessary to make a change in the pricing structure* – This may be because of the development of competition (e.g. European Union competitors selling in the UK after the creation of the Single Market), or a movement along the product life-cycle, or a change in demand or cost conditions.

What steps should a firm take in selecting an appropriate price in one of these situations? The firm will need to consider **objectives**, **strategies** and **techniques** (see Figure 6.4).

FIGURE 6.4
*Objectives, strategies
and techniques*

```
┌─────────────────────────────────┐
│          OBJECTIVES             │
│    (e.g. to maximise profits)   │
│                                 │
│               ↑                 │
│                                 │
│          STRATEGIES             │
│    (e.g. to charge a low price) │
│                                 │
│               ↑                 │
│                                 │
│          TECHNIQUES             │
│    (e.g. to charge a very low   │
│     mark-up cost, which will    │
│       maximise unit sales)      │
└─────────────────────────────────┘
```

## PRICING OBJECTIVES

The starting point in pricing is to be clear about your goal or **objective**. Some possible objectives are as follows:

### Profit maximisation

A key assumption of many business theories is that profit maximisation is the most important pricing target. While it is true that unless businesses can make profits in the long run their futures will be uncertain, studies of actual business behaviour reveal a wide range of alternative objectives rather than simple short-term profit maximisation.

### Price competition

A competitive price is one that gives a competitive edge in the marketplace. It is not necessarily one that is lower than that of a rival because other elements of the marketing mix add to the competitive edge. For example, it is possible for the manufacturer of Gillette razor blades to argue that they are better quality than those of rivals, giving scope to charge a higher yet more competitive price than those applying to other blades (see Figure 6.5).

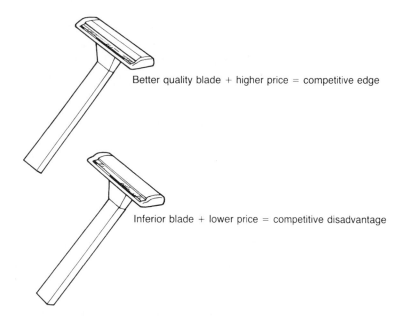

Better quality blade + higher price = competitive edge

Inferior blade + lower price = competitive disadvantage

FIGURE 6.5
*The combination of
higher price and other
benefits can lead to a
competitive advantage*

The Rolls Royce car is another good example of a relatively expensive product which maintains its competitive edge in international markets because of its combination of benefits.

A further element of competitive pricing is to set a price that *deters new entrants* in a particular market. Large firms with some degree of monopoly power may be inclined to keep prices relatively low in order to secure their long-term market dominance. From time to time in business you will hear the owner of a small company say: 'Of course we would like to diversify into producing *x* but we simply couldn't compete with the prices offered by the big fish.'

### Yield on investment

Any money that is allocated to a particular use bears an opportunity cost. Could this money be spent in a better way? What are the alternatives that are sacrificed? Investors usually have expectations of what they regard to be an appropriate rate of return on investment. This yield will then be an important factor in determining pricing decisions. Investors will quickly make their feelings known to managers if they feel that the wrong pricing decisions are made.

### Sales maximisation

If you generate a lot of sales then you can produce on a large scale. High sales also give you a good profile in a particular market.

Sometimes organisations (or parts of organisations) set out to generate high sales figures because it makes them look good. The sales manager who sells a lot will need to lead a large sales team, thus enhancing his or her own position and salary and bonus.

However, sales should be related to *the cost of making those sales*. For example, a sales division may be able to generate sales in Europe, Asia, North and South America and Australasia, but the cost of physically distributing goods and organising sales in all these areas may be prohibitive.

## Satisficing

H. A. Simon put forward the view that businesses might want to **'satisfice'** – that is, to achieve given targets for market share and profits from sales which may not maximise profits but would instead inflate boardroom egos. This can arise when the managers of a company are clearly different from the owners. If the managers can provide sufficient profits to keep the shareholders satisfied, then a proportion of profits can be diverted to provide more perks for managers and larger departments.

*Satisficing policies* are most likely to be associated with industries where there is only a limited degree of competition. *Satisficing objectives* are fairly common in many organisations ranging from schools to oil companies. Managers will readily produce long lists of achievements which do not always relate to a profit margin at the bottom line. In large organisations it is often difficult to relate activities to financial statistics, and managers with the ability to make a lot of noise can give the impression of being effective. (If you do not believe this, ask your college lecturer for their view on the subject!)

## Other objectives

There are many other possible objectives in establishing prices. For example, a company may want to maximise sales to create brand leadership, or it may want to establish a high price in order to establish a reputation for quality.

In setting the objectives outlined above, it is essential to remember that it is not only customers that may respond unfavourably. Other groups that need to be considered include:

- *competitors*, who may choose to match price cuts or not to match price increases

- *distributors*, who may insist on high margins and thus resist price-cutting
- *employees*, who may ask for wage increases (wages are often one of the most important component costs)
- *government bodies*, who may withhold contracts, certificates or grants
- *shareholders*, by seeking higher dividends.

## PRICING STRATEGIES

Once a pricing objective has been established, it is necessary to establish an appropriate strategy. Three broad pricing strategies can be considered: 'high-price', 'market-price' and 'low-price'. Before going on to look at each of these in turn, it is helpful to say a few words about the relationship between price and sales.

### Demand curves

*A demand curve shows the quantity of items of a product that consumers will be willing to buy at different prices.*

Common sense seems to tell us that more of a product will be bought at a cheaper price than at a higher price. For example, market research on the number of adults who would use weekly a new swimming pool produced these results for different prices:

| | |
|---|---|
| £4 | 100 |
| £3 | 150 |
| £2 | 250 |
| £1 | 800 |
| 75p | 1200 |
| 50p | 1400 |
| 40p | 1500 |
| 30p | 1600 |

The demand for a product is commonly shown graphically by means of a **demand curve**. Figure 6.6 plots the demand curve for the swimming pool.

An individual demand curve can be likened to a snapshot taken at a particular moment in time showing how much of a product would be bought at different prices. At that moment in time, price is seen to be the only variable that can be altered which will influence the quantity purchased.

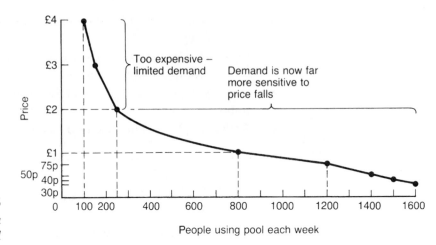

FIGURE 6.6
*The demand curve at a
swimming pool*

Most demand curves drawn from real situations will have a shape
which is more of a squiggle than a straight line. However, the
common factor of nearly all demand curves is that they slope down
to the right, indicating that – assuming conditions of demand remain
the same – more units will be bought at a lower price than at a
higher price. Therefore, in this chapter we will simplify demand
curves into *straight lines*.

Most businesses need to consider carefully the effect of increasing
their sales. If they want to sell only a small number of items (e.g.
designer jeans) in the marketplace, they will probably be able to do
so at a high price. However, if they want to sell a lot of items then
they will only be able to do so at a relatively lower price (see Figure
6.7).

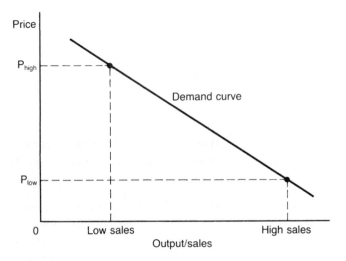

FIGURE 6.7
*A 'trade-off' between
price and quantity
demanded*

It is, however, possible to increase sales or keep sales constant without lowering the price. This can be done by raising the **demand** for the product. An increase in demand for a product leads to a shift in the demand curve to the right, as in Figure 6.8.

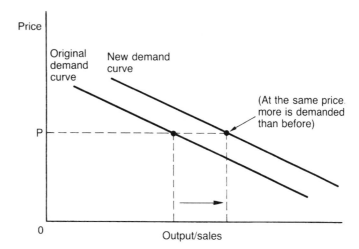

FIGURE 6.8
*A shift to the right in the demand curve for a product*

Factors which might cause an increase in the demand for a product include:

- an increase in the number of people (population) available in the market (a way of increasing population in international marketing is to sell your product in new countries)
- a change in tastes in favour of your product
- an increase in the price of competing products
- an increase in the incomes of people making up your market (for example, today many businesses are focusing their marketing operations on the rapidly growing Pacific Rim markets in China, Malaysia, Singapore etc. where people's disposable incomes are rising very quickly).

The demand curve for most products is continuously shifting as a result of pressures such as changes in tastes and fashion. Most businesses can influence and shape these external factors by a careful use of the marketing mix (e.g. by changing the product, by advertising, and by sales promotion as well as adjustments in price).

## Low-price strategy

A low-price strategy should be considered when consumers respond very positively to small downward changes in price.

In technical terms we can measure this response by calculating the **elasticity of demand**. This is the measure of changes in quantities purchased as a response to price changes. Demand is said to be 'elastic' if the change in quantity demanded is of a greater *proportion* than the change in price that initiated it. If the price of a particular brand of washing powder is lowered by 10 per cent and there is an increase in sales of 20 per cent, then the demand for the product is said to be elastic because the change in price leads to a more than proportionate response in quantity demanded.

Price elasticity of demand can be measured by the formula:

$$\frac{\text{Percentage change in quantity demanded of product A}}{\text{Percentage change in price of product A}}$$

In the washing powder example, price elasticity of demand is 20 per cent divided by 10 per cent, which is 2.0.

The key consideration in lowering price is to *increase revenue*. If the percentage increase in quantity demanded is proportionately higher than the percentage change in price that triggered the rise in demand, then revenue will increase. Products with an elasticity value greater than 1.0 are said to have elastic demand.

However, it must be remembered that elastic demand does not always mean that a firm will benefit from price reductions. If a firm in a price-sensitive market lowers it price, then there will be a strong chance that other competing firms will follow suit.

Another consideration is *cost*. If a firm lowers the price of a product, and sells more, it will usually have to pay out more in expenses and other costs ('the cost of sales').

A low-price strategy is important when it is easy for consumers to compare competitors' prices. For example, brands of washing powder sit side-by-side on the shelves of a supermarket, so there is a strong incentive to charge a low price.

This is also true when the product cannot be classed as a **necessity**. Necessities tend to have low price elasticities of demand compared with luxury items. It is therefore possible to charge a relatively higher price for necessities in the knowledge that the consumer 'needs' to buy the product.

When the product is in plentiful supply it would also be a mistake to charge a high price – because the product is readily available from competitors.

In the situations outlined above, in which price cuts may lead to large increases in turnover, then a low-price strategy may well strengthen a company's position, for example when selling to supermarket customers. Price in these situations plays a crucial role in the marketing mix.

---

**CASE STUDY** *Aldi supermarkets*

Aldi supermarkets are a good example of an organisation exporting its low-price strategy to more and more markets. Initially the company operated in its home base of Germany using a formula of concentrating on a small range of high-turnover non-perishable items in very basic shops with no frills attached. This formula gave Aldi a dominant position in the German discount market.

The company concentrated on roughly 500 fast-selling lines such as canned and packaged groceries, dairy products and fruits and vegetables. Most of these products were Aldi exclusive lines developed for them by manufacturers and based on high-quality standards. Because there were so few lines the items were not price-marked – checkout staff were expected to remember the prices of all items or consult a list. Each supermarket had a very small staff.

Market research showed that three-quarters of all German householders shopped for some items at Aldi, and the company had a market share of over 20 per cent for canned vegetables, canned meat, canned milk, margarine, sherry, tea and spirits.

From the power base of its existing home market, Aldi has been able to spread out progressively into new international markets. In the early 1990s it had a strong presence in several neighbouring European states, with 102 stores in Denmark, 220 in Belgium, 270 in the Netherlands., 104 in Austria, 16 in north-east France as well as 225 in mid-western United States. In the 1990s it has also moved increasingly into the UK market, and its presence has had a considerable impact here. It now seriously threatens the big retail groups including Sainsbury, Tesco, Dee Corporation/Gateway, Argyll/Safeway, Asda and the Co-ops.

In the 1990s the UK is seeing the increasing spread of new forms of low-cost stores, such as Kwik Save, Safeway's Lo Cost stores, the Co-op's Pioneer shops and more recently Costco from the United States. These are all essentially no-nonsense discount stores along the Aldi lines.

**Questions**
1   Describe the main ingredients of the Aldi marketing mix.
2   What are the main strengths and weaknesses of its emphasis on low prices?
3   How does the emphasis on low prices limit its scope for competing in terms of the other Ps of the marketing mix?
4   How effective have low-cost discount stores been in the UK in recent years?
5   How have UK supermarket stores responded to the Aldi challenge?
6   What are likely to be the long-term effects of low-price competition in the UK supermarket sector?

## Market-price strategy

There are situations where one or more of the following conditions exist:

- products are bought frequently
- competitive products are highly similar
- a few large companies dominate supply in a specific industry.

In any of these situations, firms could quickly lose all their business if they set prices above the competition. Conversely, if they lower prices their competitors may be forced to follow. Firms tend to set prices at market-price level and the role of price is therefore *neutral*.

**Neutral pricing** will often exist for many standard products at supermarket chains. For example, in January 1994 a survey by the Consumers Association showed the following prices being charged by some supermarket stores:

| | Asda | Gateway | Tesco | Sainsbury |
|---|---|---|---|---|
| Persil E3 washing powder | £1.79 | £1.79 | £1.79 | £1.69 |
| Heineken 4-pack lager | £2.69 | £2.99 | £2.69 | £2.69 |
| Ski 4-pack yoghurt | £1.05 | £1.19 | £1.19 | £1.19 |

The same survey, however, also indicated that shoppers could save up to 25 per cent on their weekly shopping bills if they bought own-brand products from supermarkets. However, chains of supermarkets often match each others' prices in own-brand sales.

### High-price strategy

This can be either a long-term or a short-term policy. A long-term policy will mean that the firm seeks to sell a high-quality product to a select market. This is true of international car sales where Jaguars, Rolls Royces and Lamborghinis are sold at exclusive prices. High prices are an essential feature of up-market products – it is essential to maintain an exclusive *image*, to be reflected by the price.

A short-term policy is based on advantages gained by a patented product, a heavy investment in new equipment, or some other form of barrier to entry to a market by competitors. In these circumstances price has a negative role in the marketing mix.

When an appropriate strategy has been determined a suitable pricing technique can be chosen.

## PRICING TECHNIQUES

How are prices set in practice? Important influences on pricing techniques include:

- cost
- demand
- competitors' prices.

Practical pricing involves elements of all three. We next explore some commonly used pricing techniques.

### Costs as a key element of pricing

The quantity of product sold (the **sales volume**) is a critical factor in the success of any kind of business. The reason is that every business has to pay two different kinds of costs associated with sales: fixed costs and variable costs.

**Fixed costs** are so-called because they remain the same no matter how many units of product are sold. For instance, a shop has to pay the same rent, rates, heating and lighting, wages, insurance and much else no matter how large or small its sales are in a particular month. The same applies to a factory, or any other kind of business.

**Variable costs** are those that vary according to the number of units sold. For instance, if a shop sells confectionery, the more confectionery sold to customers, the more has to be bought from the wholesaler. If a factory makes furniture, the more furniture sold the more wood and other materials have to be bought from the supplier. In other words, *these costs vary directly with the number of units that are sold*.

## What is the 'margin'?

The difference between the *variable costs* of each unit of product and the price paid by the customer is called the **margin**. So, clearly, the ratio of variable costs to the margin remains the same no matter how many units are sold.

However, the ratio of *fixed costs* to the margin changes with the number of units sold. For instance, if your fixed costs are £1000 a year and you sell 100 units, then each unit has to 'carry' £10 of fixed costs. If the margin is £20, then the fixed costs represent 50 per cent of the margin. If, on the other hand, you sell 500 units, then each unit has to carry only £2 of fixed costs – which is 10 per cent of the margin.

### Fixed and variable costs: an example

Let us use the example of a service station to illustrate the nature of costs.

- Fixed costs at a service station include staffing, insurance, heat/ light, security, and office costs.
- Variable costs are the price paid by the service station to the refinery for bulk supplies of petrol, diesel and lubricants; plus items such as stationery and sales promotion.

Figure 6.9 shows typical values for the total fixed and variable costs of a service station. Both lists have been greatly simplified for the sake of clarity.

To recover total fixed costs of £62 thousand, a service station selling half a million litres a year must add 12.4p per litre (£62 000 divided by 500 000) to the variable cost.

A similar-sized but more successful service station selling 3 million litres a year would have to add only 2.06p per litre. In other words, *the minimum price per litre* (before profit) that the lower volume station must charge its customers is 42.88p (30.48 + 12.4); whereas the higher volume station can cover all its costs, both fixed and variable, by charging 32.54p (30.48 + 2.06). The higher volume station can afford to charge less per litre, and still make a bigger margin – to be used for further investment and distribution to shareholders.

| **Fixed costs** (£000) | | **Variable costs** (pence per litre) | |
|---|---|---|---|
| Staff | 35.0 | Fuel | 30.00 |
| Insurance | 2.0 | Bank charges | 0.30 |
| Heat/light/power | 5.5 | Sales promotion and advertising | 0.15 |
| Security | 1.5 | Postage and stationery | 0.03 |
| Local business tax | 6.0 | | |
| Maintenance and repair | 2.0 | | |
| Office | 6.5 | | |
| Depreciation | 3.5 | | |
| Totals | 62.0 | | 30.48 |

FIGURE 6.9

*Typical costs for a petrol service station*

We can illustrate this point graphically by using an example related to the three pie charts in Figure 6.10. Assume:

- Each unit of sales has a retail price of £1.00.
- Variable costs per unit are 60p in each case.
- Fixed costs are £50 000 per annum in each case.
- Each of the three retail outlets has the same fixed costs (rents, local business taxes, staff, depreciation, etc.).

The pie charts show how the per-unit ratio between fixed costs and variable costs changes with the number of units sold. The more units sold, the lower the *proportion* of the unit price taken by fixed costs.

- Each unit sold by retail outlet no. 1 must carry 60p variable costs and 33p fixed costs, leaving a margin of 7p.
- Each unit sold by retail outlet no. 2 must carry 60p variable costs and 25p fixed costs, leaving a margin of 15p.
- Each unit sold by retail outlet no. 3 must carry 60p variable costs and 10p fixed costs, leaving a margin of 30p.

Retail outlet no. 3 therefore makes the most efficient use of its fixed costs. As a result it will have the financial resources to invest in

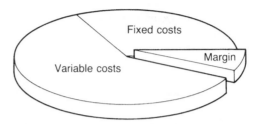

Retail outlet no. 1 sells 150 000 units per annum

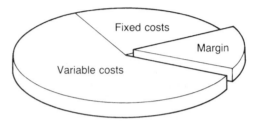

Retail outlet no. 2 sells 200 000 units per annum

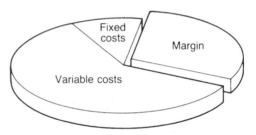

*FIGURE 6.10*
*Cost and margins per*
*unit sold*

Retail outlet no. 3 sells 500 000 units per annum

improved premises and equipment, and thus improve its own efficiency, the quality of its service to customers and its profitability.

### Cost-plus pricing

Any study of how firms price products in the real world inevitably reveals a very high proportion of businesses using no other basis than a **mark-up** on the cost of providing the product or service concerned. Information about costs is usually easier to piece together than information about other variables such as likely revenue. Firms will often therefore simply add a margin to the **unit cost**.

The unit cost is the average cost of each item produced. If a firm produces 800 units at a total cost of £24 000, the unit cost will be £30.

Talk to many owners of small businesses and they will tell you that they 'cost out' each hour worked and then add a margin for profits; or they will simply mark-up each item sold by a certain percentage. For example, fashion clothes are frequently marked up by between 100 and 200 per cent.

The process of cost-plus pricing can best be illustrated in relation to large firms where **economies of scale** can be spread over a considerable range of output.

For a large firm, unit costs will fall rapidly at first as the overheads are spread over a larger output. Unit cost then becomes relatively stable over a considerable quantity of output. It is therefore a relatively simple calculation to add a fixed margin (e.g. 20 per cent) to the unit cost. The firm is able to select an output to produce and to set a price that will be 20 per cent higher than the unit cost of production (see Figure 6.11).

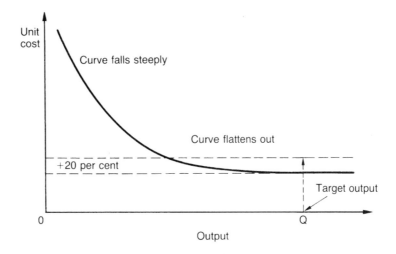

FIGURE 6.11

*Select a target output 0Q and then add 20 per cent to the unit cost to get price*

Whilst cost–plus pricing is very popular, there are many dangers associated with it. If the price is set too high, sales may fall short of expectations; and if the price is set too low, then potential revenue is sacrificed. However, the greatest danger of cost-based pricing is that it indicates a *production-orientated approach to the market*. Emphasis on costs leads to tunnel vision that looks inwards at the company's product rather than outwards to the customers' perception of the product.

Firms that operate in international markets may favour cost-plus pricing because it involves using a simple formula rather than having to calculate the relative strength of demand in lots of quite different markets.

However, if an international business applies this method of pricing too rigidly, this can cause problems in the marketplace. If demand is lower than expected, for example, unit costs may be slightly higher. In this situation the company accountant may press for price increases. This will make it even more difficult to make sales. If, on the other hand, demand is higher than expected, unit costs may fall slightly, demanding a price reduction. This may lead to a loss of potential revenue.

## Contribution pricing

**Contribution pricing** involves separating out the different products that make up a company's portfolio, in order to charge individual prices appropriate to a product's share in total costs. In international markets a business will also separate out the different product markets in order to assess the contribution of each regional or national market.

We have already identified two broad categories of costs: variable (direct) costs vary directly with the quantity of output produced or sold; fixed (indirect) costs have to be paid, irrespective of the level of output or sales.

When a firm produces a range of individual items or products, or sells products in a variety of international markets, it is easy to determine direct costs, but not indirect costs. For example, in a food processing plant producing 100 different recipe dishes it is easy to work out how much goes on each line in terms of raw materials, labour input, and other direct costs. However, the same process cannot be applied to indirect costs – the salary of the managing director, the business rates paid on the factory building, and so on.

---

**Contribution** is the sum remaining after the direct costs of producing individual products have been subtracted from revenues.

---

When the contributions of all the individual products that a firm produces have been added together they should more than cover the firm's indirect costs.

There are strong arguments in favour of contribution pricing because of the way it separates out the individual products and analyses them *in terms of their ability to cover the direct costs which can be attributed to them.* A new product may be brought 'on stream' because it can be shown that it will cover its direct costs and make a contribution to covering the company's total indirect costs.

In contrast, if we were to analyse individual products in terms of the relationship between their total revenue and total costs, calculations might show a loss. For example, if two products used the same distribution facilities, it would not make sense to expect both products to cover their own distribution costs individually. Contribution pricing enables a more rational analysis of individual products. Prices can be set in relation to each product's own direct costs (see Figure 6.12).

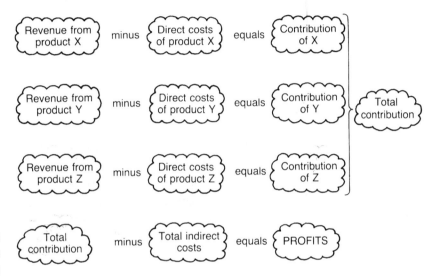

FIGURE 6.12
*Calculating profits using contributions*

Contribution is an excellent way of pricing for firms selling to a range of international markets which share a common fixed cost base. However, whilst contribution pricing is possible in many situations, it is not so easy in others.

We can illustrate this by using the example of oil-based products. Oil product prices are set by a variety of market and other influences, both national and international, so crude oil costs are only one element. Any cost allocated to a specific product must, by the nature of the production process, be an arbitrary one. This is because a barrel of crude oil is refined to produce the full range of petroleum products required by consumers, in varying quantities depending on the nature of the crude, the refining processes employed, and the pattern of demand at the time (see Figure 6.13).

As with a butcher, who produces many different cuts of meat from one animal, there is no way, other than by arbitrary choice, of establishing what share of the raw materials costs should be allocated to the product. It is competition in the marketplace which establishes what the butcher can charge for each cut of meat, and which sets the prices an oil company can obtain for its products. The

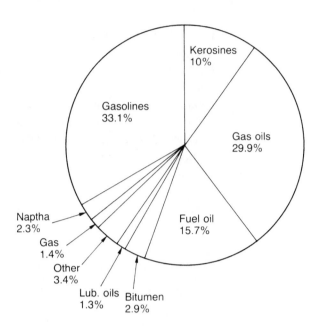

company's objective is that these prices will add up to more than its overall costs and produce a profit for its shareholders that provides an adequate return on their investment.

## Demand-orientated pricing

Market research is essential to establish and monitor consumers' perceptions of price. **Demand-orientated pricing** involves reacting to the intensity of demand for a product, so that high demand leads to high prices and weak demand to low prices, even though unit costs are similar.

When a firm can split up the market in which it operates into different sections, it can carry out a policy of **price discrimination**. This involves selling at high prices in a section of the market where demand is intense (where demand is *inelastic*), and at relatively low prices where demand is elastic – where there is a more than proportionate response in quantity demanded as a result of a fall in price. Price discrimination can be carried out in a number of situations (Figure 6.14).

### Customer-orientated discrimination

Some customers may have an intense demand for a product while others only have a weak demand. Discrimination would involve selling the same type of product to the first type of customer at a high price and to the second at a lower price. However, you can

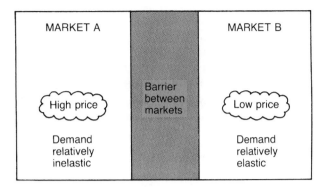

FIGURE 6.14
*Price discrimination*

only do this if you can physically divide up your market so that the customer with the intense demand cannot get hold of the lower-priced item. It is common practice to introduce some products at a higher price and then later to reduce the price. For example, many books are initially sold in hardback at a high price. When that segment of customers has been satisfied the cheaper paperback is produced.

### Product-orientated discrimination

Slight modifications can be made to a product to allow high and low price strategies. For example, many car models have additional extras (the two- or the four-door version, with or without sunroof, etc.). Customers have the choice of the cheaper or more expensive version. In a similar way, you can purchase cheaper or more expensive versions of the same sewing machine, depending on whether you are prepared to pay for the additional facilities associated with the more expensive version.

### Time-orientated discrimination

Sellers are able to discriminate when demand varies by season or time of day. In high season, a product can be sold at a high price. At other times, prices will need to be reduced. This applies to a wide range of items from fashion clothes to river cruises. Some products experience varying intensities of demand during the course of a single day – for example, telephone calls are charged at a higher rate during certain hours of the day.

### Situation-orientated discrimination

This applies to houses – the same type of house may sell for one price in the centre of town and for another price in a quiet suburban area. House prices also vary widely from one region to another. Cinema and theatre seats may be priced according to their proximity to the screen or stage. Although production costs are similar, demand varies with the situation.

There is frequently price discrimination between different countries, which have different average incomes and other factors influencing demand. Products will therefore be sold at different prices according to elasticities of demand in various countries, and regions within a country. For example, cars are cheaper in continental Europe than in the UK.

International marketers need to be aware that it is usually illegal to 'dump' cheap goods in foreign markets. You cannot offload large quantities of goods that you cannot or do not want to sell in your domestic market at knock-down prices in foreign markets.

### Perceived value for money

In general, customers have views about what constitutes value for money. If prices are too high, customers might not consider that they are getting value for money. If prices are too low, they will begin to question the quality of a product.

From the consumers' point of view, therefore, value for money is a key ingredient when weighing up prices. Research carried out by *Marketing* in the early 1990s on over 800 shoppers confirmed this view. It was possible to argue that superior value in a shop will overcome disadvantages in location, to some degree. Customers will beat a longer path to a superior outlet.

In the survey, reasons given for choosing where to shop varied by region, with southerners giving more weight to 'quality' in the value equation. Northerners rated their reasons like this:

1   Prices/value for money
2   Nearest to home
3   Variety of goods
4   Convenient/handy
5   Know layout

Southerners' ratings were slightly different:

1   Prices/value for money
2   Easy parking
3   Convenient/handy
4   Good-quality products
5   Know layout

Low-prices/value-for-money was thus the outstanding reason for choice of store. Other questions in the research confirmed that consumers carefully weighed prices versus quality, in reaching a value judgement. Only a minority bought on price alone: 9 per cent 'always checked and chose the cheapest', and 13 per cent always bought things on special offer even if they were not needed on that occasion. By monitoring customer perceptions of price, a seller realises that the appropriate price band for a sale is, in fact, fairly limited (see Figure 6.15).

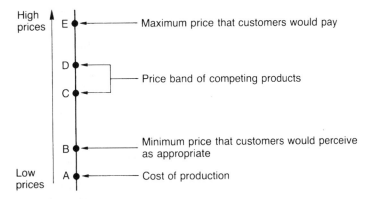

FIGURE 6.15
*Customer perception of price*

Assume that a product costs £A to produce. The business cannot sell the product for less than £B without its quality being questioned (How can it be sold for such a low price? Is there something wrong with it?). Competing products are selling for prices between £C and £D, and the maximum chargeable price would be £E.

If the product is 'nothing special' in terms of customer perception, then the price should be pitched between £B and £D. However, if the product is really exciting, and captures the imagination of consumers, it can be pitched anywhere between £C and £E. In selling for the first time to a new overseas market, it may be necessary to pitch the price between £B and £C in order to compete with existing national brands.

## Competition-orientated pricing

In extremely competitive situations, costs have to be treated as a secondary consideration in short-term price determination. This is particularly true when competing products are almost identical, customers are well informed and there are few suppliers.

The nature and extent of competition is frequently an important influence on price. If a product is faced by direct competition, then it will compete against other very similar products in the marketplace.

This will constrain pricing decisions so that price setting will need to be kept closely in line with rivals' actions. In contrast, when a product is faced by indirect competition (i.e. competition with products in different sectors of the market) then there will be more scope to vary price. This opens up the possibility for a number of strategies. For example, a firm might choose a high-price strategy to give a product a 'quality' feel. In contrast, it might charge a low price so that consumers see the product as a 'bargain'.

An individual firm might try to insulate itself against price sensitivity by differentiating its products from those of rivals. Markets are sometimes classified according to the level of competition that applies. An extreme level of competition is termed **perfect competition** (it exists in theory rather than practice). The other extreme is **monopoly** where a single firm dominates a market. In the real world, most markets lie between these extremes and involve some level of imperfection:

> Perfect competition → Imperfect competition → Monopoly
>
> *Decreasing levels of competition*

If a perfect market could exist there would be no limitations to new firms entering the market, and buyers would know exactly what was on offer and would incur no costs in buying from one seller rather than another. Products would be almost identical. In a monopoly situation, only one firm exists and barriers prevent new firms from entering the market (e.g. a very high cost of setting up, the existence of patent and copyright restrictions, and other barriers). The seller has considerable powers to control the market.

In imperfect markets as we know them, there may be few or many sellers. Products are usually **differentiated** and consumers do not have perfect information about the differences between products.

In the real world, businesses do strive to give themselves the protection of monopolistic powers. They seek to reduce competition, and they seek to make their products seem 'better' than those offered by rivals. Monopolistic powers enable firms to push up prices and hence make larger profits. However, larger profits should not always be viewed as a cost to consumers. Profits can be ploughed into research and development, into advanced technology and the production of large outputs at lower average costs.

In today's global economy, large multinational companies have the ability to move quickly into new markets and into the production of new products. The reduction in world trading *restrictions* and the creation of new larger internal markets have helped to reduce monopolistic power in domestic markets. In the Single Market of the European Union we are experiencing increasing competition in many areas. We are seeing the development of European-wide competition between firms each with a strong base within their own country. Each of these firms is having to 'think European' – that is, to consider the whole of the European Economic Area as being its domestic market.

The level of competition is a key determinant of price. Where there are many close competitors, there is little or no scope to charge a price which is above the market price. In a situation where there is no competition, the seller can often charge a relatively high price. However, the seller cannot charge more than the consumer is prepared to pay. At the end of the day consumers can spend their income on alternative products. Between these two extremes, we find hundreds of different markets. In some the consumer has more power, in others it is the seller.

## Short-term pricing policies

Pricing can be used as an incisive tool to pursue short-term marketing and selling targets for a company. Typical attack-based policies include:

- skimming pricing
- destroyer pricing
- penetration pricing
- promotional pricing.

### *Skimming pricing*

At the launch of a new product, there will frequently be little competition in the market, so that demand for the product may be somewhat inelastic. Consumers will have little knowledge of the product. **Skimming** involves setting a reasonably high initial price in order to yield high initial returns from those consumers willing to buy the new product. Once the first group of customers has been satisfied, the seller can then lower prices in order to make sales to new groups of customers. This process can be continued until a larger section of the total market has been catered for. By operating in this way the business removes the risk of underpricing the product.

The name 'skimming' comes from the process of skimming the cream from the top of a milk product (see Figure 6.16).

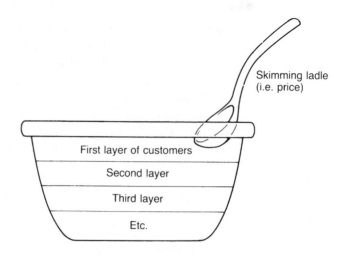

FIGURE 6.16
*Skimming*

## Penetration pricing

Whilst skimming may be an appropriate policy when a seller is not sure of the elasticity of demand for the product, **penetration pricing** is appropriate when the seller knows that demand is likely to be elastic. A low price is therefore required to attract consumers to the product. Penetration pricing is normally associated with the launch of a new product for which the market needs to be penetrated (see Figure 6.17). Because price starts low, the product may initially make a loss until consumer awareness is increased.

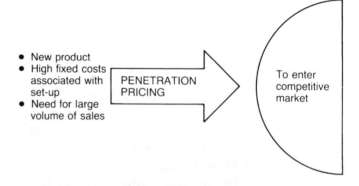

FIGURE 6.17
*Environment appropriate for penetration pricing*

A typical example would be that of a new breakfast cereal or a product being launched in a new overseas market. Initially it would be launched with a relatively low price, coupled with discounts and special offers. As the product rapidly penetrates the market, sales and profitability increase. Prices can then creep upwards.

Penetration pricing is particularly appropriate for products where economies of scale can be employed to produce large volumes at low unit costs. Products which are produced on a large scale are initially burdened by high fixed costs for research, development and purchases of plant and equipment. It is important to spread these fixed costs quickly over a large volume of output. Penetration pricing is also common when there is a strong possibility of competition from rival products.

### Destroyer pricing

A policy of **destroyer pricing** can be used to undermine the sales of rivals or to warn potential new rivals not to enter a particular market. Destroyer pricing involves reducing the price of an existing product or selling a new product at an artificially low price in order to destroy competitors' sales (see Figure 6.18). For example, when in late 1993 the new Costco stores entered the UK market, British supermarkets in the localities of the Costco stores slashed their prices to loss-making levels in an attempt to beat off the new American rivals.

This type of policy is based on long-term considerations and is likely to lead to short-term losses. The policy is most likely to be successful when the company that initiates it has lower costs than its competitors or potential rivals. However, it cannot be sustained in the long term because it will erode the profit base required to initiate research and development projects.

FIGURE 6.18
*Destroyer pricing*

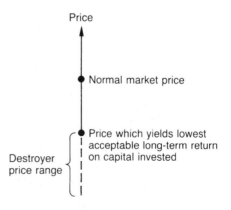

### Promotional pricing

Prices can be lowered from time to time to promote a product. **Promotional pricing** can be used to inject fresh life into an existing product or to create interest in a new product. Promotional pricing can be employed to increase the rate at which a product turns over. This can be used to reduce levels of stock or to increase the rate of activity of a business.

A form of promotional pricing is the use of **loss-leaders**. Supermarkets frequently use loss-leaders to boost sales. A loss-leader is a good which is sold at little or no profit or even at a loss. Only a small number of the items sold by supermarkets are loss-leaders. The aim of selling in this way is to give the impression that all items in the shop are cheap – a shopper seeing that cornflakes are 10p cheaper in one supermarket may falsely expect all prices to be cheaper in that store. Another use of loss-leaders is to attract new customers, who will then spend on other, profitable items.

## PRICING AND THE MARKETING MIX

In this chapter we have concentrated on the importance of pricing decisions. However, pricing is used to complement other elements in the marketing mix. The marketing department will carefully consider how it can use price to complement *place*, *promotion* and *product*.

Pricing decisions need to be accompanied by:

- product differentiation to produce the required benefits for customers
- careful segmentation, so that benefits are promoted to those who appreciate them most
- development of valid non-product features, such as better delivery, and after-sales service
- improvement of product strengths
- attention to company and product image.

## QUOTING PRICES IN NATIONAL AND INTERNATIONAL MARKETS

With the removal of national barriers to trade, the European market should be seen as an *enlarged domestic market* for UK producers. When quoting prices in this market there are only two real alternatives: either **ex-works** or **delivered**.

Selling 'delivered' means arranging transport, insurance and customs clearance, bearing the costs, and not treating the order as completed when it leaves the factory gates but only when the customer has received the goods. Selling 'delivered' also helps the exporter to know and control the transport costs.

The term 'ex-works' means that the *buyer* is responsible for arranging the transport, insurance and customs duties and other features of buying goods.

Choosing which of these pricing methods to adopt should involve finding out what the customers prefer and what the competition offers. In western Europe there seems to be a preference for quoting full delivery prices.

### What currency should be quoted?

An exporter should find out what type of currency the buyers prefer to use for purchases. Most customers in western Europe like to pay in their own currencies. This means that the seller may have to take on the risk of changes in the exchange rate between the time of quotation and the time of actual payment.

At some stage in the future it is possible that European traders will be able to quote in **ecus** (European Currency Units).

Before sending goods overseas it is important to check that they can and will be paid for. Major banks and other specialist **status reference agencies** can provide reports on the **creditworthiness** of potential customers. Insurance can be taken out against non-payment – this is called 'credit insurance'. Such insurance can be obtained from banks, insurance companies, and the government's Export Credit Guarantee Department.

When a company sells goods abroad it will not be paid immediately. There are three main ways of financing exports:

- *A bank finance scheme* – Most large banks offer export finance, including credit insurance.
- *Factoring* – This involves *selling your invoices* for money owed to you to a factoring company (often owned by a major bank). The factoring company immediately pays you about 80 per cent of the debt. The factoring company will then collect the money owed to you when it is due – you then receive the balance owing to you minus the factor's commission.
- *Selling through an export house* – This also gives rapid payment. The export house buys goods from you on its own account and supplies the customer.

### Payment terms

Thirty days is a common credit period in the European Union, but businesses still need to negotiate a credit period when making deals.

Seventy per cent of UK exports are sold on an open-account basis – payment is made by settling up within a given credit period through a bank payment. About 20 per cent of UK exports are sold using bankers' **letters of credit**, whereby a reputable bank guarantees to make the payment at the end of the credit period. Letters of credit guarantee that customers get the goods they want and that the exporter is paid promptly. Exporters must give proof of delivery by submitting certain documents, and if these documents are accurate then payment will be made within a couple of days.

# ASSIGNMENT

**Task** **a** A UK company decides to *reduce* the price of its products in Germany and France by 10 per cent. It estimates that this will lead to an immediate increase in sales in Germany of 15 per cent and in France of 20 per cent. Will this pricing decision necessarily increase the profits from sales in these two countries? State all your assumptions clearly.

**Task** **b** Swedish railways found that most of its commuter trains were substantially under-used, some carriages running with 90 per cent of the seats empty. It therefore decided to halve its railway fares. This led to an increase in demand of 400 per cent for commuter rail journeys.

　　**1** What factors would determine whether this was a sound pricing decision or not?

　　**2** Would it be sensible for British Rail to halve its fares?

# ASSIGNMENT

You are asked to produce and justify a pricing strategy for Eurotunnel cross-channel services between Dover and Calais up to the year 2000.

**Task** **a** Identify the major competitors in the cross-channel ferry market.

**Task** **b** Outline the current prices that they charge for different services (e.g. winter, summer peak, etc.).

**Task** **c** Show how prices have altered over the last year.

**Task** **d** Identify the major competitive strengths and weaknesses of each service.

**Task** **e** Produce a pricing strategy for Eurotennel for the next few years that will enable them to gain and maintain a competitive advantage.

**Task** **f** Show how this pricing strategy is integrated with other elements of the marketing mix (place, promotion and particularly product).

**g**   Produce a written report and back it up with a 10-minute presentation to the Marketing Manager at Eurotunnel explaining why and how you have chosen your particular pricing strategy.

Information about prices and services may be obtained from:

North Sea Ferries, King George Dock, Hull HU9 5QA

Hoverspeed, International Hoverport, Ramsgate CT12 5HS

Brittany Ferries, 84 Baker Street, London W1

Sealink UK Ltd, Eversholt House, Eversholt Street, London W1

P&O, 220 Tottenham Court Road, London W1P 9AF

Eurotunnel plc,
Le Shuttle Customer Service Centre,
PO Box 300, Dept. 302, Cheriton Parc,
Folkestone, CT19 4QD

# Distribution

Distribution (or **place** in the four Ps of the marketing mix) is the process of making goods or services available for those who want to buy them. It will include:

- the process of moving goods and services to the places where they are wanted
- the channels through which the products are available (e.g. shops, mail-order, wholesalers).

FIGURE 7.1
*Distribution makes products available for customers*

Distribution may involve a single step, or any number of steps. For example, a local baker may make the bread and then supply it direct to his or her customers. In contrast, a furniture store may supply chairs and tables that have been manufactured in Scandinavia, which have passed through a number of hands and been stored two or three times before arriving at their final destination.

A number of key decisions have to be made about distribution. Managers will try to ensure that goods are moved efficiently to meet customer needs on time. They will also be concerned about choosing the best **channel of distribution** so that efficiency and sales can be maximised. Such decisions should never be under-rated. Many organisations such as Avon and Reader's Digest, and many more, have built and developed their successes on their ability to use this element of the marketing mix to reach customers and satisfy their needs.

One important element in distribution is **timing**. Many goods are seasonal and it is important that products reach customers when they require them. For example, fireworks which reached retailers on 6 November would be of little use. In fact, any distributor which sends goods late or at a time when customer needs have already been satisfied will be at a competitive disadvantage. Establishing an efficient distribution system is particularly important for perishable products.

In international markets, distribution systems may be extremely complex. The international marketer has to deal with transporting products over larger distances, with many more choices of transport, often with significantly higher costs. It is also necessary to deal with distribution systems which reflect different economic, social and cultural developments, influencing the ways in which customers are reached through the market. Such distribution systems may be completely different from those marketers are used to in the home market.

# PHYSICAL DISTRIBUTION MANAGEMENT

Physical distribution includes all the activities concerned with moving products, both inwards to manufacturer or outwards towards customers. Physical distribution management (**PDM**) describes the role of managers in developing, administering and operating systems to control the movement of raw materials and finished goods.

Physical distribution management is an important part of the marketing mix. It helps an organisation to meet customer needs profitably and efficiently. In doing so it enables manufacturers to provide goods for customers at the right time, in the right place and in the condition required. It may also reduce the **lead-time** – from when a customer first makes an order until the time when that order is delivered.

There are many different aspects to physical distribution, most of which are integrated and should be designed to work together as a whole. For example, if this book were not available on the shelf of your local bookshop, what processes would be put into operation if you placed an order? They would probably look something like Figure 7.2.

Think of all the different stages that have been brought into play to ensure that the need of the customer ordering a book has been met. Firstly, the customer used a bookshop. He or she knew where to obtain the book or order it. The bookshop then used some form of **communication system** to inform the publisher of this need. The publisher processed the order, again using some form of communication system or **information technology**. Copies of the book were stored in a **warehouse** where stocks were held and

157

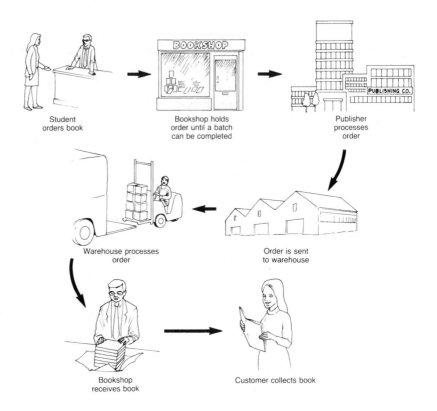

FIGURE 7.2
*Distributing a single
copy of a book*

inventories monitored. The book was **transported** to the bookshop,
to be picked up by the customer.

**Costs** are an important element in each stage of the distribution
process. The stages are interdependent, so if one breaks down or
causes a delay, the customer need is not met as well as it should be.
For physical distribution to work, therefore, each of the stages
should work efficiently.

## Transport

Transport is a key component in physical distribution. Choosing the
'best' possible transport system involves weighing up and trading
off a number of key components. What forms of transport should be
used (road, rail, air, sea etc.)? Can these forms of transport be
integrated? What are the best possible routes? Do you use your own
fleet or outside carriers? How do you maximise safety? How do you
minimise costs? How do you make sure that the products arrive on
time and in the best possible condition?

Different forms of transport have their own distinctive advantages
and disadvantages. Pipelines are expensive to construct, cheap to
run, and expensive to repair. Roads give door-to-door delivery, are

fast over short and some long distances, and make it possible to use your own fleet relatively cheaply. However, road travel is subject to traffic delays and breakdowns, and drivers are limited to working only so many hours in a day. Rail transport is cheap and quick over long distances, particularly between major cities. However, it is not always appropriate for reaching out-of-the-way destinations and is costly for guaranteed speedy deliveries. Air is very fast between countries, provided the ultimate destination is not off the beaten track. Air is generally used for carrying important, urgent, relatively light and expensive loads. Sea transport is a cheap way of carrying high-volume bulky loads.

**Containerisation** of loads has made possible the integration of these different forms of transport. Routes and services have been simplified to cut out wasteful duplication. Special types of vehicles have been designed to carry special loads. Direct motorway connections between cities have proved to be of major importance in determining location decisions, as have fast intercity rail services and air links.

Different methods of transport may prove to be more or less cost-effective in different situations depending on the cost of transport relative to the type of good being transported, the price of the good, or the speed with which it is needed. Heavy bulky items may be sent by road, rail or sea depending on the distances involved. Urgent items such as first-class post or important medical supplies may be sent by air.

---

## CASE STUDY  *Reducing transport costs at Shell*

Greater cost-effectiveness is a worthwhile target. Over the last few years Shell Transport has reduced the cost of oil product transported by £2 per tonne (a 20 per cent reduction).

The increased efficiency is based on a number of factors:

- the UK's improved road system
- larger, more efficient road tankers
- non-rush-hour deliveries
- better planning systems (to translate hundreds of thousands of orders a year into sensible delivery schedules)
- better information systems (details of backlogs of orders to be delivered, and other information, such as every order from the distribution terminals, is now available on the PC of everyone who needs the information)
- more efficient handling of customer orders and payments
- investment in depots
- use of contracts
- use of salaried drivers
- maintenance of safety at all times
- working closely with refineries.

**Questions**

1   Which of the benefits outlined above are (a) internal economies of scale (i.e. economies resulting from the expansion of Shell Transport itself), and (b) external economies (resulting from growth outside of Shell).

2   What are the costs of using larger delivery vehicles (a) to Shell and (b) to groups and individuals external to Shell?

3   What future developments can you foresee which will affect distribution costs of petrol? Explain what the effects will be.

### Transporting overseas

When transporting overseas a number of documents are used to aid the transportation process.

A **bill of lading** is a transport document used for goods transported by sea. It has three separate functions. Firstly, it *evidences the contract of carriage* between the shipper and the exporter or foreign buyer to transport the goods by sea. Secondly, it is used as a *receipt* for goods taken on board ship and provides details of the goods. Finally, it is a document of *title*, which means that the holder of the bill has the right to possess the goods.

An **air waybill** is for goods transported by air. This is both a receipt and a contract for carriage but is not a document of title.

A **road consignment note** or **truck receipt** is an acknowledgement issued by the carrier of the goods to the effect that the goods are to be transported by road. It specifies the name and address of the consignee, the place of delivery and the place and date of taking the load by the carrier. It acts as both a receipt and a delivery note.

The Simpler Trade Procedures Board (SITPRO) has made efforts over recent years to standardise the layout of documents used for international trade.

---

**CASE STUDY** *Sales distribution*

In Nestlé Grocery and Nestlé Food there are sales teams for each of the key areas: supermarket chains, the Co-operative movement and the wholesale and independent grocery trade. Nestlé Food also has teams specialising in the sale of chilled foods and frozen foods, as well as its own temperature-controlled storage and distribution systems.

Orders for the various divisions are received and processed by sales teams in Croydon, York, Chepstow and Warrington. These offices also handle the day-to-day questions and problems posed by customers.

Deliveries to customers are made in a variety of ways. Large orders to major customers are often sent direct from factories, or in the case of confectionery, from a large finished-goods store. Smaller deliveries are handled through a national network of depots fitted with the most modern equipment designed to hold and handle the wide range of different products and packs.

A fleet of trucking vehicles carries finished goods from factories either direct to customers or into the distribution stores and depots. Storage and distribution are very important. For example, chilled foods have a short life and must be moved swiftly from the factory to the grocery store. Frozen foods must be stored in refrigerated warehouses before being transported in temperature-controlled vehicles.

All movements of vehicles are controlled by a computerised national scheduling system. All sites have computers linked to the powerful head office systems. Applications range from straightforward automation of clerical and secretarial work, through normal commercial systems such as stock control and invoicing, to more sophisticated order picking and load planning systems.

**Questions**  1  Make a list of all the ingredients of an efficient distribution system for a large organisation such as Nestlé.

2  What problems might arise if a distribution system was not as efficient as the one illustrated in the case study?

### Trading off costs against service

The physical distribution system balances the need for customer service against the need to minimise costs. Maximising customer service potential may imply a lot of stock and warehousing space, a considerable number of distribution staff, and rapid transport. However, minimising costs implies the reverse – minimum stock, limited storage space, skeleton staff and slow transport. Designing a physical distribution system therefore involves trading off costs against service, or inputs against outputs.

**Inputs** include all the distribution costs – that is, freight costs plus inventory costs plus warehousing costs plus other service costs. It is important to take a detailed look at these costs and to assess how they can be controlled to minimise *waste*. It is essential to know the distribution cost of every product dealt with. This involves a detailed analysis of how much labour time, transport time and other factors are spent on each product (see Figure 7.3).

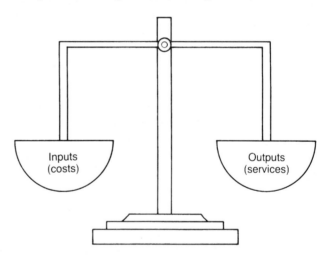

FIGURE 7.3
*Balancing inputs
against outputs*

**Outputs** can primarily be measured in terms of the value of services to customers. Distribution can give a clear competitive benefit in meeting customer needs, for example for a quick, prompt and efficient service. Every business must decide whether it is going to give a distribution service that is better than, the same as or worse than those of its competitors. Weaknesses in distribution will clearly need to be compensated for by strengths in other areas of the marketing mix.

The system that you come up with will depend largely on the scale of your operations and the size of the market you work in. If you operate from a single plant, you may try to locate in a central market position, or you may choose the spot with the best transport and communication links. For example, a business handling a lot of international mail from customers overseas may choose to locate near to an airport.

A business that wants to maximise customer service will have the highest **inventory costs**, because it needs to hold stock to meet all foreseeable requirements. The key inventory decisions are when to order and how much to order. The danger of keeping too little in stock is that you may lose custom because of dissatisfaction with the quality of your service. In contrast, too much stock adds to the cost and wastage through goods becoming soiled or out of date.

Quite clearly distribution is a key area of marketing. It should be seen as a very important part of meeting customer needs and requirements. Responsibility for physical distribution is often shared between the Sales Manager, Inventory Control Manager, and Transport Manager. It is imperative, however, that these functions are centrally coordinated through the marketing function.

# EVALUATING DISTRIBUTION CHANNEL ALTERNATIVES

The **channel of distribution** is the system through which goods are transferred from producer to end-user. Every business must constantly appraise its existing channels and from time to time they will need to be reorganised.

When looking at how to develop a channel to reach customers it is important to establish the major **objectives**. It is also necessary to explore any **constraints** in achieving these objectives and examine possible alternatives. The alternatives will then need to be evaluated before a decision can be made as to how to plan the channels (see Figure 7.4).

The distribution channel is the route to the customers. In defining the objectives it is necessary to consider:

- the customers' needs
- the nature of the competition
- the nature of the other services (**middlemen**) involved.

For example, if the overriding objective is to supply customers the day after a product has been manufactured, for the lowest price on the market, it will be necessary to discover the quickest and most effective channels with the least delays, and how the rivals are operating and what they are offering.

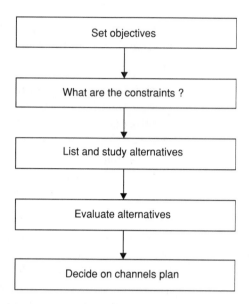

FIGURE 7.4
*Planning channels*

Some alternative channels are shown in Figure 7.5. To reach a mass market a product may be distributed through more than one channel. Alternatively, a company may give exclusive rights to certain dealers or middlemen. It is essential to specify who does what at each stage of the distribution map. If a particular channel of distribution looks as if it may cause problems it may have to be scrapped in favour of another channel.

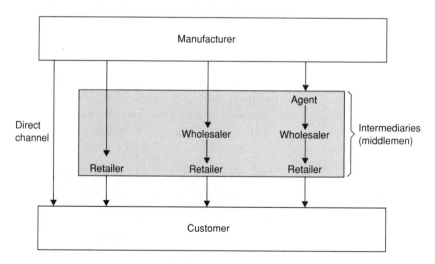

FIGURE 7.5
*Some channels of distribution*

Three main criteria can be used in evaluating channel alternatives. These are:

- economic
- control
- adaptive.

164

In evaluating the **economic performance** of alternative routes, costs must be weighed against revenues in order to make profit calculations. **Control** is also a major consideration because customers will often blame the producer for breakdowns and problems in distribution. A distribution channel should also be capable of being **adapted** to changing circumstances.

A business operating a single plant and selling in several scattered markets can choose whether to distribute directly from the plant or through a range of localised intermediaries. On the other hand, a firm with several plants and several markets must weigh up a range of distribution channels. Does it use the same distribution channels for all its products, or does it set up specialist routes? Clearly, in this situation choosing the correct channels of distribution is very important.

Industrial products (machines, bulldozers, expensive computer systems etc.) are commonly sold by the maker direct to the user. Consumer goods (clothes, food, games, sports equipment etc.) are more usually distributed through retail shops. In this case the maker can supply the shops directly, and this sometimes happens; but to do this the company might need a large salesforce. An alternative is to use **wholesalers** who buy in bulk and who can be served by a smaller salesforce. The wholesaler is part of the chain of distribution and is a link between the manufacturer and the retailer, as shown in Figure 7.6.

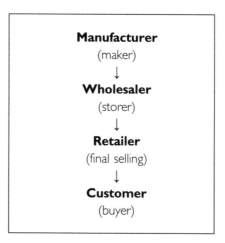

FIGURE 7.6
*The traditional
channel of
distribution*

The choice of distribution channel can have a marked effect upon other areas of the marketing mix, such as price, promotion or product. For example, if it is decided to distribute through a chain of readily accessible cut-price stores, this will have obvious implications for the public perception of the product.

Some manufacturers require very tight distribution schedules. Nowhere is this more true than in the distribution of fresh food, and this limits the number of intermediaries who can sensibly be involved in the distribution process. Therefore it is important for any organisation to analyse who will be involved in each of the stages of distribution and identify the number of stages. Does it really need to use a wholesaler or would it be possible to market products direct to customers? Many companies prefer to concentrate on their core functions and allow others to sell their goods to final users on their behalf.

Though it is usual to accept one of the available distribution arrangements, in certain markets it is possible to set up a new one from scratch, such as the door-to-door selling used by Tupperware or Avon.

### Other types of channel flows

As we have seen, physical distribution is about getting the product or service to the consumer. Of course, several other flows take place at the same time. For example, the **title of ownership** of goods will need to go to the purchaser, and this may be in the form of a receipt or invoice. **Payment** will flow from the purchaser to the seller.

**Information** will need to flow both ways between the buyer and the seller. The seller must make clear what the terms of the offer are,

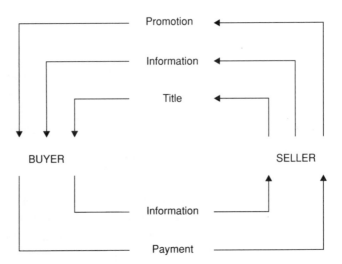

FIGURE 7.7
*Other types of channel flow*

and the buyer needs to specify his or her requirements. To start all this off, the seller **promotes** the product to the buyer (Figure 7.7).

Nowadays it is common practice for producers to try to **integrate** these flows. For example, promotional materials for other products may accompany the invoice, receipt or delivery of the product.

## Why use intermediaries in distribution?

Manufacturers may lack the financial resources to carry out their own expensive direct marketing operations. By contracting out the process of distribution they can concentrate on their core functions.

In addition, the expense of direct marketing often requires that several similar or complementary products are promoted at the same time, to spread the cost between the products.

The intermediary is also a **specialist**. When a company sells its products in this way it benefits from the specialist's expertise in a wide range of areas – such as packaging, pricing and where to sell. The author of a book may be able to produce a very good end-product but will lack the time, know-how, contacts and money required to promote the book to bookstores.

## Overseas market channel structures

The choice of channel structure for an overseas market may be much more complicated simply because the available distribution systems vary. As a result the international marketer has to research the distribution systems relevant to a product before entering each market.

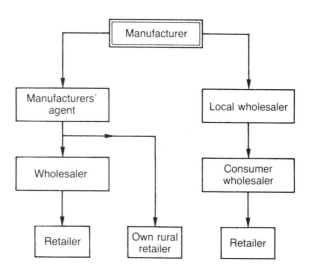

FIGURE 7.8
*Typical distribution patterns in India*

167

For example, when exporting to India one must choose between a local wholesaler or a manufacturers' agent. The local wholesaler sells on to a consumer wholesaler who then sells on to a retailer. On the other hand, a manufacturers' agent either sells to a rural retailer or to another wholesaler (see Figure 7.8).

A number of factors influence what sort of channel the international marketer will seek to use. These may include the geographical location of the market, the type of product, the number of intermediaries, and any legal restrictions imposed by host nations.

## THE ROLES OF A WHOLESALER

Some people argue that intermediaries add to a producer's costs by taking a commission for their services, and that this increases prices. It is also possible to argue that the wholesaler provides many valuable functions.

### Advantages of wholesalers

#### *Breaking bulk*

Manufacturers produce goods in bulk for sale but they might not want to store the goods themselves. They want to be paid as quickly as possible. A number of wholesalers buy the stock from them and generally payment is prompt. The wholesaler then stocks these goods, along with others bought from other manufacturers, on their premises, ready for purchase by retailers.

#### *Simplifying the distribution process*

The chain of distribution without the wholesaler would look something like Figure 7.9. Manufacturer 1 has to carry out four journeys to supply retailers 1, 2, 3 and 4, and has to send out four sets of business documents, and handle four sets of accounts. The same situation applies to each of the manufacturers, so that in total 16 journeys are made and 16 sets of paperwork are required. (This is a simplification, because in the real world thousands of different transactions might be involved.)

The wholesaler can simplify the costs and processes of distribution in the following ways:

- by cutting down on journeys, fuel and other costs
- by cutting down on paperwork – invoicing, administration etc.

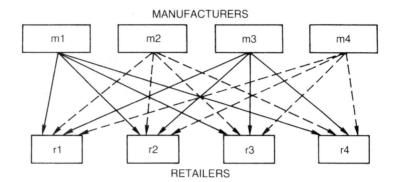

FIGURE 7.9
*The distribution chain
without the wholesaler*

The chain of distribution with the wholesaler would look something like Figure 7.10. With the wholesaler everything is simplified.

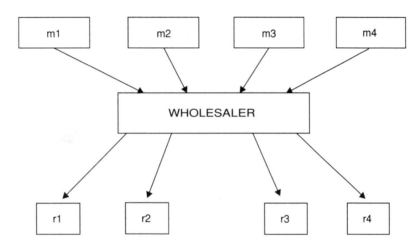

FIGURE 7.10
*The distribution chain
with the wholesaler*

### Storage

Most retailers have only a limited amount of storage space. The wholesaler can be looked upon as a huge storage cupboard for the retailer. Provided the retailer agrees to take supplies at regular intervals, the wholesaler will perform this important storage function. With the growth of cash-and-carry facilities (see below), it has become easier for the retailer to stock up on supplies that are running down.

### Packing and labelling

The wholesaler will sometimes finish off the packaging and labelling of goods, perhaps putting price tags on goods or brand labels for supermarkets.

169

## *Offering advice*

Being in the middle of the process of distribution, wholesalers have a lot of market information at their fingertips. In particular, wholesalers know what goods are selling well. With this in mind they can advise retailers on what and what not to buy and manufacturers on what and what not to make.

## Types of wholesalers

Some wholesalers handle a wide range of general merchandise, but the majority specialise in particular lines (tobacco, steel, etc.). Many outlets are small and operate within a limited geographical area. In contrast, a number (particularly in the grocery trade) are large and have regional and even national distribution capabilities.

The largest single unit in the British wholesale trade is the Co-operative Wholesale Society (CWS). The CWS also manufactures many lines of its own, owns interests overseas (e.g. tea estates in India), and owns its own shipping and transport fleet.

The last twenty years have seen the growth in size and importance of cash-and-carry warehouses, and voluntary groups, in wholesaling.

## *Cash-and-carry warehouses*

Most small retailers buy a large proportion of their stock from a **cash-and-carry** warehouse. Retailers are responsible for transporting the selected goods from the wholesale warehouse to their premises, and they are able to buy the goods at a 'trade discount'.

The inside of a cash-and-carry premises is very similar to that of a large supermarket, except that goods are packed in bulk and the buildings are sparsely decorated.

## *Voluntary groups*

Some wholesalers have set up **voluntary groups**. A voluntary group is made up largely of small retailers (the VG stores in Figure 7.11) who have agreed to buy most of their stock from the group wholesaler. For example, the retailers might be contracted to purchase at least 70 per cent of their supplies from the group wholesaler. The group wholesaler buys goods in bulk from manufacturers at discount prices.

The voluntary group movement was a reaction to the growth in power and influence of chains of supermarkets that were undercutting the small corner shop from the mid-1960s onwards.

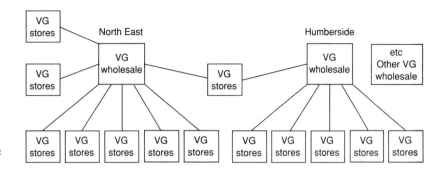

FIGURE 7.11
*Voluntary groups*

Some well-known small shops operate under the voluntary group system – for example, Late Shop, Happy Shopper, VG, Spar, Mace and Wavyline.

## RETAILING

The French word *retailler* means to cut again. We have already seen that the wholesaler breaks down bulk supplies from the manufacturer. The retailer then cuts the bulk once again to sell individual items to consumers.

We can identify a number of categories associated with retailing which can be used in any classification system.

### Ownership

Who owns the retail unit? Is it independently owned by a sole trader? Is it owned by a large multiple with shareholders? Is it a cooperative or is it a franchise outlet?

### Range of merchandise

Does the retail outlet specialise in a narrow range of goods or does it have a spread of interests? Examples of specialist outlets include ice-cream parlours, furniture stores and fast food outlets. Woolworths is an example of a more general outlet. Harrods at one time claimed to sell everything from 'a pin to an elephant'. In some of the large French supermarkets you can purchase a cement mixer within yards of the cheese counter.

### Pricing policy

Some retail outlets concentrate at the bottom of the price range. They offer discounts and low prices. They buy in bulk and sell large

171

quantities. The early policy of Jack Cohen, founder of Tesco, was 'pile them high, sell them cheap'. In contrast, other retail outlets aim for an up-market price image. This is true of exclusive fashion shops, clothing and jewellery stores. Here, even if turnover is low, mark-up is several hundred per cent for many items.

In between these two extremes there are retail outlets with mid-market pricing strategies as discussed in Chapter 6.

### Location

Low-price stores frequently choose locations where business rates and other site costs are minimised. In contrast, large multiples and department stores need a town centre location, or a situation near a major road. Small ('corner') shops need a healthy volume of local custom for their livelihood – their strength rests in local convenience.

### Size

Many variety stores are now over 50 000 square feet, but superstores and hypermarkets have areas from 25 000 to 100 000 sq ft.

---

## CASE STUDY  *Costco: will it work?*

In December 1993 the first grocery warehouse club – Costco – opened its doors to the public in Thurrock, Essex. It has 35 tills, employs 350 staff and has 749 parking spaces. Dubbed 'The Silent Enemy', warehouse clubs are believed to be the lowest-cost form of retail distribution in existence.

Only members can shop in warehouse clubs, for which they pay an annual subscription. In the USA, the home of these clubs, they cover anything from 100 000 to 250 000 sq ft. Their format is cheap. No advertising takes place and goods are displayed in cut cases. The range of 3500 to 4500 lines

compares with 16 000 usually found in a supermarket. The motto for warehouse clubs in the USA has been 'stack it high and watch it fly!'

Costco has blasted like an Exocet missile on to the British retailing scene. Many feel that the mere existence of Costco will help to push prices down. The company has used no promotional support at all and thinks a lot of its notoriety is due to other supermarkets trying to stop their planning application in Thurrock.

On the day the Thurrock Costco opened, 6000 members paying between £17 and £22 for membership had already signed up. The Costco philosophy is clear – use low prices to pull in those with an eye for a bargain and with deep pockets, and then try to get them to buy on impulse.

**Questions**
1   Given that Costco has many trade customers, would you describe it as a wholesaler or a retailer?
2   Why are many of the big supermarket chains worried about the introduction of warehouse clubs?
3   How could supermarkets react to the introduction of such clubs?
4   Comment on your feelings about the Costco form of retailing. What are the advantages and disadvantages for customers using a Costco warehouse store?
5   Do you think that the Costco form of retailing will work? Could it spread to areas other than groceries?

## Types of retailers

### Independent traders

The *Census of Distribution* classifies an **independent trader** as a retail organisation with fewer than ten branches. The average number is one or two branches. The market share and number of independent traders have been declining, particularly in food.

Many small shops in this country are owned by one person whose business interests are confined to a single shop. These small retailers often set up in business by putting their savings into starting up the shop. They then buy their stock by borrowing money from the bank and paying it back when they have sold their goods. There are of course advantages and disadvantages to being a small operator (see Figure 7.12).

| Advantages | Disadvantages |
|---|---|
| Personal relationship with customers | Price competition from multiples who are aided by buying economies and scale of operations |
| They are convenient for shoppers, providing a local 'round the corner' service | |
| Can buy in stock to meet personal requirements of customers | The owner needs to be a 'Jack of all trades' frequently lacking specialist retailing knowledge |
| Can work longer hours | Lack of capital to expand or improve business |
| Low overheads, low site costs | Located away from high-volume sales areas |
| Benefits from joining voluntary group | |
| Can offer personal credit facilities to shoppers | Growth of use of cars has led to one-stop shopping in large shopping centres |
| Can do home deliveries | |

FIGURE 7.12
*Advantages and disadvantages of small retail outlets*

The number of independent retailers has declined throughout the last few decades of the twentieth century (see Figure 7.13). Joining a voluntary group (as described earlier in this chapter) has proved to be the best route to survival for many independent shop owners. Niche operations have also provided opportunities, as for example independent stores selling 'vegetarian food'.

FIGURE 7.13
*The British retail grocery trade 1971–1992*

| | Number of shops | | Shares of all commodity turnover (%) | |
|---|---|---|---|---|
| | 1971 | 1992 | 1971 | 1992 |
| Cooperatives | 7 745 | 2 481 | 13.2 | 10.4 |
| Multiples | 10 973 | 4 577 | 44.3 | 77.8 |
| Independents | 86 565 | 32 662 | 42.5 | 11.8 |
| All grocers | 105 283 | 39 720 | 100.0 | 100.0 |

## Multiple chains

**Multiple chains** are organised as joint stock companies, with a high degree of control being exercised by professional managers. The definition given by the *Census of Distribution* is that a multiple store has more than ten branches. Some multiples are classified as specialist stores, concentrating on a narrow range of items such as clothing (e.g. Dorothy Perkins, Top Man, Austin Reed). Others are variety chains like Marks & Spencer and Boots.

Some key features of a 'multiple' are:

- Centralised buying (in bulk at a discount).
- Concentration of fast-moving lines. They frequently sell products which are brand leaders or sell their own store labels.
- Merchandise is widely known, often through national advertising.
- Located in 'busy' shopping areas, clustered together with other well-known multiples (usually high street and shopping centre locations).
- Prices usually relatively low. Volume sales are made.
- Shops project a strong corporate image. Easily recognised shop signs, distinctive colours and logos and uniform store fittings all project a unified image. (For example, Laura Ashley has its own central department for decorating and furnishing new stores and revamping existing ones. Stores have distinctive layouts, decor and furnishings.)
- Many key functions are centralised – for example, accounting, advertising, recruitment, public relations, training and operating policies.

Most multiples are members of the Multiple Shops Federation. This is a combined pressure group and sounding-board for ideas from many of the well-known multiples.

Multiples are continuing to expand in importance. During the late 1980s, many new multiples developed in particular areas of the retailing maket, in the wake of the success of the Body Shop. Many of these were then particularly badly hit by the recession in the early 1990s.

### Supermarkets

A **supermarket** is defined as a store with at least 2000 square feet (or about 200 square metres) of selling area, using mostly self-service methods and having at least three checkout points. The layout of a store is designed to speed customer flow and reduce time spent shopping.

Supermarkets are a key feature of shopping in the 1990s. New and large supermarkets continue to be developed in most areas of population growth.

Supermarkets have thrived with the development of brand names, the increasing number of working women with less time for shopping, and consumer preferences for easy shopping at low prices. They have high turnovers at a low mark-up – by maximising sales, they are able to spread their operating costs over a large output in order to minimise unit costs.

In recent years, supermarkets have been able to meet consumer demands for green and organic products by using their considerable clout to influence producers. Because the supermarket business is highly competitive, it is also responsive to consumer preference changes.

## CASE STUDY  *Sainsbury*

Sainsbury has over 80 branches within the M25 area, each requiring several deliveries daily. Average traffic speeds in London have fallen to 11 mph as traffic densities have increased over the last decade.

Since the 1960s, Sainsbury has consolidated supplies into fewer, larger loads for final delivery. The use of 38 tonne vehicles (compared with the 7.5 ton vehicles used in the 1960s) enables more goods to be delivered in fewer vehicles, reducing delivery costs, carbon dioxide emissions and congestion.

As far as possible, supplies are made between 10 pm and 6 am to reduce congestion.

'Just in time' delivery scheduling also reduces the time that goods are held in the warehouse. The requirements of the branches are relayed to the depots via head-office computers. Some product lines are ordered on a 24-hour cycle (ordered today for delivery tomorrow), while other lines may be ordered only once or twice a week for delivery 48 hours later.

A reliable distribution system can make an important contribution to the marketing of a product. Economies of scale in the way that deliveries are made, coupled with the frequency of deliveries, helps Sainsbury to market its food for quality, freshness and price.

**Questions**

1  What problems might Sainsbury encounter delivering within the M25 area?

2  How does it attempt to overcome such problems?

3  To what extent will the solutions to these problems benefit (a) Sainsbury's customers, and (b) its position in the marketplace?

## Hypermarkets

**Hypermarkets** are simply large supermarkets. They have a massive selling area and offer a very wide range of household goods at discount prices. As well as food and clothing, they stock lines as diverse as DIY equipment, motoring accessories, cosmetics, children's toys and hardware.

They aim to provide cheaply for all the basic shopping needs of an average household. They may also contain restaurant facilities and stock consumer durables like television sets at a discount. They are usually located on the outskirts of towns where building land is cheaper.

## Department stores

The definition of a **department store**, as used by the *Census of Distribution*, is a store with a large number of departments and employing more than 25 people. Department stores are to be found on 'prime sites' in high streets in most towns and cities.

A department store is divided into separate departments, each with a departmental manager and staff. It provides a very wide range of services so that customers can do all of their shopping under one roof.

The store generally provides a high standard of service and comfort, with carpeted floors, pictures on the walls, a café, art galleries, exhibitions and displays.

A department store might charge slightly higher prices for quality goods. However, whilst it is true that department stores have an up-market image, they can also use their advantages, created by bulk buying and large scale, to offer discount prices on many items.

Department stores continue to be a force in the marketplace with their reputation for quality and service and the added incentive of credit accounts. They include many famous names such as Debenhams, House of Fraser, John Lewis Partnership and Owen Owen.

In the last decade they have moved increasingly towards customer self-selection. They have also operated with a policy of 'leasing' shopping space to other retail names with a compatible image – this makes for better use of space and is an added attraction to customers.

### Discount stores

Today, specialist companies like Argos and Comet concentrate on selling large quantities of consumer durables at **discount** prices. The aim of these stores is to produce a high level of total profit by means of a very high turnover of stock. As the name implies, they attract custom by the discounts they offer. In recent years, these stores have moved away from the original warehouse-like service, and have increasingly begun to offer credit facilities.

Discount stores tend to be located at edge-of-town positions. They are well-stocked with a wide range of models. Recent examples which have become popular in the 1990s are discount toy sellers and discount pet food sellers. These are located in large centres of population where demand is constant and high.

### Cooperative retail societies

Today there are fewer than thirty **cooperative retail societies** operating in various parts of the United Kingdom. There used to be several hundred, but over the years many of the smaller societies have joined together. The largest one is called the CRS (which in the 1990s is likely to merge its operations with the Co-operative Wholesale Society).

The Co-ops have always tried to do more than just run a shopping business. They set out to serve the local community in a variety of ways. For example, a Co-op might support a local education service for members, subsidise health care and other social activities, or finance cooperative theatre ventures and recreational facilities.

To understand the basis of cooperation, it is helpful to look back to the origins of Co-ops. The first retail cooperative was set up in 1844 by a group of twenty-eight weavers in Rochdale, Lancashire. They were fed up with being paid low wages in tokens which they could only exchange in company-owned shops, where prices were high.

They clubbed together to buy foodstuffs from a wholesaler which were then sold to members. Profits were shared out amongst members in the form of a dividend, according to how much each had spent in the shop.

To become a shareholder in a modern cooperative retail society you need only buy a £1 share. Shareholders are entitled to attend meetings, to have a say in policy-making, and to elect the officers of a local society.

For many years the Co-ops tended to share out their profits by giving a dividend to members, often by issuing stamps to shoppers with every purchase. These stamps were stuck in books and could be traded in for cash or used to make further purchases. Today, only a few societies issue stamps. Instead, the Co-ops tend to plough back their profits into improving their stores. The CRS, for example, has opened up a number of 'Leo' hypermarkets in various parts of the country.

The Co-ops are preparing for the twenty-first century by making their stores bright and attractive and by selling a very wide selection of goods. Although they have closed down many small shops, the twin aims of the Co-op are still to provide profits and to serve the local community.

## Mail-order firms

**Mail-order firms** sell goods either through agents or by members of the public ordering from a free catalogue. A mail-order agent will receive a commission of about 10 per cent of the sales made. Some firms have their own delivery service, whilst others use the Post Office, or other carriers. Many goods sold by mail-order are paid for on credit terms.

Mail-order firms cut out the middleman and so have the opportunity to sell goods at competitive prices. They are also able to use computerised methods for handling orders and stocks and sell from large warehouses situated in locations where rates are cheap and communication links efficient.

## Franchising

In the USA, one-third of all retail sales are made through firms operating under the **franchise system**. It is a method of selling that is becoming increasingly popular in the UK.

A franchise is a permission to market a product in a specified area. The person taking out the franchise puts up a sum of money as capital and is issued with equipment by the franchising company to sell or manufacture the product in which the franchise company deals. The firm that sells a franchise is called a **franchiser** and a person taking out a franchise is called a **franchisee**. The person taking out a franchise has the sole right of operating in a particular area. Franchising is common in 'fast foods', examples being McDonald's and Spud-U-Like.

FIGURE 7.14
*Advantages of the franchising system*

| Advantages to the franchisee | Advantages to the franchiser |
|---|---|
| Trades under a well-known name | Franchiser does not risk own capital |
| Has a local monopoly | Supplies equipment and training courses, which are tax-deductible |
| Works for him or herself, and receives most of the profits | Takes a percentage of profits |
| Is supplied with equipment and conception | Has people working indirectly for them who will work long hours because they are also working for themselves |
| Receives training | |

## Direct selling

The most commonly quoted examples of **direct selling** are mail-order and direct-response advertising, but these more often than not involve some form of intermediary. Mail-order firms usually buy the commodities they sell through their catalogues in bulk from manufacturers. Direct-response advertisers – such as firms that advertise in newspapers, in leaflets delivered through letterboxes, and in television advertisements giving the name and address of the firm – are often wholesalers who buy in bulk from manufacturers. It is therefore probably more accurate to say that direct selling means simplifying the chain of distribution to miss out the retailer.

Manufacturers can themselves cut out middlemen by owning their own retail units. Examples of this are breweries which own their own public houses, oil companies with their own petrol stations, and textile manufacturers with their own factory shops.

Television selling is already big business in the United States, Australia and other countries and has recently been introduced in the UK. In the USA, the Homes Shopping Network is a 24-hour viewing business, which became a huge success story in the late 1980s. The typical format is for each product to have a four-minute slot, during which time viewers can phone through on one of 200 freephone lines, order something and pay by quoting their credit card number. The products sold are mainly brand names presented in an entertaining and informative way.

### Other forms of retailing

There are other forms of retailing, accounting for small elements of sales. These include door-to-door selling, mobile shops, street trading, automatic vending and kiosks.

**CASE STUDY** *Body Shop is ready to take on Avon*

Body Shop International is ready to expand its business beyond the high street and into the home, with a complete change of operations and the establishment of a home shopping division. To improve the selling capacity of the group, it is hoped that direct selling will work alongside the stores and target people who find it difficult to shop at their leisure.

Body Shop is conducting small tests in the North East, the Midlands and the South, using consultants in the home to demonstrate the use of make-up and skin and haircare products. The hope is that, by selling direct to customers, Body Shop can increase sales to attract a wider range of people to its products.

**Questions**   1   What are the benefits to Body Shop from selling direct to customers?
2   Describe one other alternative method that Body Shop could use to increase its sales.

## THE ROLE OF AUTOMATIC IDENTIFICATION IN RETAILING

**Automatic identification** is one of the fastest growing, but least known, sectors of the high technology industry. It enables users to collect identifying information about large numbers of items without manual keystrokes and to feed data into a computer.

The **auto ID sector**, as it is commonly called, originated in the early 1970s with the advent of bar-coding on a small scale in the retailing, wholesaling and distribution industries. It took off in the late 1970s and early 1980s when supermarkets invested heavily in checkout scanners.

The essential parts of an auto ID system are a means of encoding the identifying information and applying it to the item in question, a machine to read the code, and software to feed the encoded data into a computer for analysis.

**Bar-codes**, familiar through their use on grocery packaging, account for about 70 per cent of auto ID. The scanner passes a small laser beam across the printed code and detects the distribution bars and spaces. A computer then converts the pattern into a number for processing.

The bar-codes used today are entirely numeric (i.e. all numbers, no letters). The system used for retailing in Europe, the European Article Number (EAN), gives each item a number of up to 13 digits.

The suppliers of retail goods increasingly include a bar-code on the outside of each item or its packaging. This is universal practice in the supermarket and grocery sector and has also become so in many other industries such as books and newspapers.

Increasingly, bar-code printers are combined with automatic labelling machines, or even with laminators to produce self-adhesive labels encapsulated in a clear protective coating. Bar-code readers are steadily becoming smaller, lighter, more powerful and more durable. A new generation of portable scanners, linked to powerful hand-held computers, is extending auto ID to new applications. Will the shopper of the future simply scan their product requirements with a portable bar-code reader?

At the same time, **fixed scanners** are being developed to read labels at greater distances and faster speeds – up to 400 scans per second while making fewer than one error in a million scans.

**Optical character recognition** (OCR), another widely-used auto ID technique, also depends on printed symbols. Here the scanner converts letters and numbers into computer code. An obvious advantage of OCR is that the symbols can also be read by human beings, while a bar-code only makes sense to the machine reader.

The most familiar non-optical technique for auto ID is the **magnetic stripe** applied to credit cards and other plastic cards and used for personal identification and financial transactions. A magnetic stripe can store more information than a bar-code and can easily be rewritten with new data, but it cannot be read at a distance and cannot be printed on cheaply. Most large retailing and wholesaling premises today have specialised equipment which deals quickly with credit card and cheque transactions. This means that customers do not cause hold-ups at checkout points.

Far larger amounts of data can be stored on **smart cards** with embedded computer chips. However, as yet, these have little value in retailing.

For automatic identification at greater distances or in harsher environments than bar-codes can cope with, **radio frequency** (RF) **tags** come into their own. These tags, which may be as small as a grain of rice, are embedded into a product – if necessary beneath a layer of protective material. They contain a transponder, a tiny receiver/transmitter which sends out identifying data when activated by the system's interrogating antenna. RF tags can be read at a distance of up to one metre from the antenna and do not need a direct line of site. RF is used for identifying moving vehicles to speed up traffic flow at high-security installations and in car parks. Automatic road tolls are another application – tagged vehicles can pass a toll point without stopping to pay, after which the toll is electronically collected from the driver's account.

## ASSIGNMENT

You are asked to help with the planning of a delivery system. The system has to take into account many factors – geography, population, distribution, sales patterns, location of supply sources, road usage patterns (to avoid rush hours), available means of communication, competitive activities, availability of finance. All these factors are liable to change at short notice or with no notice!

Choosing a distribution network means taking a number of relevant factors into consideration and attempting to weigh them up in relation to each other. Sometimes, a ranking technique can be fed into a computer program to give appropriate weights to relevant factors. Factors affecting distribution are assigned weights relative to their importance, and each channel is examined and ranked in terms of each factor. When ranks have been multiplied by the weighting factor and the scores totalled, the desirability of routes can be compared.

In the example shown here, the rank attached to the relative importance of each factor for each location (rank 1 being the highest) appears in the top left-hand corner of each cell and the rank multiplied by weight appears underneath the diagonal.

If you have access to a spreadsheet program, feed the data in the chart into it. Otherwise, use a calculator to answer the questions that follow.

| Factor | Weight | Alternative locations A | B | C | D |
|---|---|---|---|---|---|
| Supply location | 7 | 1 / 7 | 2 / 14 | 3 / 21 | 4 / 28 |
| Geography | 2 | 4 / 8 | 3 / 6 | 1 / 2 | 2 / 4 |
| Road usage patterns | 4 | 1 / 4 | 4 / 16 | 2 / 8 | 3 / 12 |
| Competitive activities | 2 | 1 / 2 | 2 / 4 | 3 / 6 | 4 / 8 |
| Population distribution | 3 | 2 / 6 | 3 / 9 | 1 / 3 | 4 / 12 |
| Sales pattern | 6 | 4 / 24 | 3 / 18 | 2 / 12 | 1 / 6 |
| Available communications | 2 | 2 / 4 | 1 / 2 | 4 / 8 | 3 / 6 |
| Totals | | | | | |

**Task a** Which is the most desirable location, A, B, C or D?

**Task b** What would be the most desirable location if the weighting of supply location was reduced from 7 to 1?

**Task c** If the ranking of locations in terms of geography were altered to A = 1, B = 2, C = 3, D = 4, the ranking of sales pattern was altered so that D became 2 whilst C became 1, the weight of competitive activities was raised to 3 and population distribution reduced to 2, what would be the outcome?

**Task d** Why might the supply location (i) have its weight reduced, (ii) have its weight increased?

**Task e** Why is population distribution an important weighting factor?

**Task f** Which of the factors listed influencing distribution routes are (i) largely within the control of an oil company, (ii) largely beyond the control of an oil company?

**Task g** In what circumstances is a computer program a good way of planning distribution routes?

**Task h** In what circumstances would computer programs be ineffective for planning distribution routes?

# Promotion

## THE PROCESS OF COMMUNICATION

Since early days, individuals have used hand signals, vocal patterns, symbolic drawings and facial expressions for the purpose of communicating some form of message to one another. Today, the exchange of information takes place through sophisticated media such as interconnecting computers, fax machines, telephones and an endless variety of other methods in order to accomplish the same goal. An efficient network of communications is essential for successful promotional activity. It enables an organisation not only to communicate with its customers but also to build up an image with the world at large. Such an image will help others to form a judgement about what the organisation stands for and will influence their dealings with it.

PROMOTIONAL ACTIVITY

FIGURE 8.1
*Promotion – a process of communication*

For marketing purposes, communication of products and services contributes to the persuasion process to encourage consumers to avail themselves of whatever is on offer. As all promotional activity involves an element of communication, an understanding of communication theory at this point is useful.

The process of communication involves sending **messages** to consumers through various channels or media in order to create **awareness** and **understanding** of why they might wish to buy particular products or services.

Organisations are the **senders** in the communication process and consumers are the **receivers**. A sender will put information in a form that a receiver can understand. This might involve using oral, visual, verbal or written messages to transmit the ideas. This process is called **encoding**. The sender will also choose a particular **medium** to use to send the message to the receiver (e.g. television, radio, newspapers). The consumer interprets the message through a process of **decoding**. If the consumer interprets the message as required, it should have the impact the seller wished for.

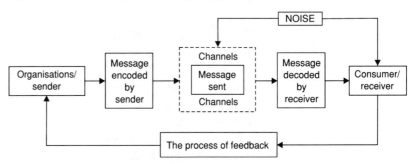

FIGURE 8.2
*The communications'
process*

Though the message flows through to the receiver there is no guarantee that the receiver will either receive the full message or even understand it. This is because the process may be subject to some form of interference which affects the flow of information. This is known as **noise** and may lead to the downfall of the message. It will take the form of any barrier which acts as an impediment to the smooth flow of information and may include linguistic and cultural differences between the sender and the receiver. Noise in the competing environment may affect communication so that the meaning of the message is lost. For example, nearly all promotional activities compete with activities from other organisations. One leaflet put through your door may be lost amongst a sea of direct mail from other organisations.

Another example of 'noise' is the remote control of a video recorder: a survey in the UK showed that, whereas 43 per cent of people watch adverts at the time of watching a programme, if they record a programme 90 per cent 'zap' through the adverts using their remote control.

To improve the chances of a message getting through, it may be necessary to repeat the message several times rather than rely upon one transmission. It might also be necessary to use a variety of channels of communication media to avoid any noise in one particular channel.

**Feedback** from the receiver to the sender enables an organisation to monitor its performance and satisfy itself that the messages are getting through and are having the desired effect.

A number of factors will determine the **effectiveness** of the process of communication. Personal factors such as linguistic, cultural and educational differences are bound to cause problems with encoding and decoding messages. Advertisers and their copywriters have to develop messages and express ideas so that their target market can understand them. Group factors or influences may also affect a message. Feelings about a particular product such as a motor car and its quality may be reinforced by group opinions. Message factors will also determine effective communication. The strength, clarity, duration and frequency of the message will be important as well as the type of media channel chosen.

## CASE STUDY *Targeting women*

The modern woman can be a household's main income earner, managing the family budget, buying pension plans or making family decisions. She might be a housewife, a working mum, a single parent, a successful businesswoman or a senior executive. Given all of these, and many more, roles, advertisers have to consider how to communicate their message to reach the intended recipient as well as how to ensure that their message makes the right impact.

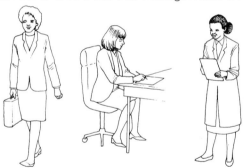

No advertiser will want to reach every woman. The changing dynamics of the female population have meant that advertisers have to choose their media opportunities carefully. Traditional indicators such as demographic trends, social class and age have become less important. Frequently, in order to find a platform for their message, advertisers try to target women through magazines.

Teenagers can be targeted through *Just Seventeen* or *19*, working mums through *She*, pregnant mums through *Practical Parenting*, and women concerned with their weight through *Slimming*. The range varies from popular weeklies through to upmarket magazines such as *Vogue*. In between these two parameters it is possible to target women with increasing precision. By doing this advertisers try to meet womens' specific needs and at the same time use a specifically targeted message to generate sales.

| | | |
|---|---|---|
| **Weeklies** | Family Circle | Hairflair |
| Bella | Woman & Home | Country Homes & Interiors |
| Take a Break | Cosmopolitan | Home & Country |
| Woman's Own | Vogue | Harpers & Queen |
| Woman | Ideal Home | True Story |
| Woman's Weekly | BBC Good Food | Health & Fitness |
| Best | Homes & Gardens | True Romances |
| Hello | Essentials | Parents |
| Chat | Clothes Show Magazine | Vanity Fair |
| My Weekly | She | Tatler |
| People's Friend | House & Garden | Catch |
| Woman's Realm | Elle | Love Story |
| Me | Marie Claire | Here's Health |
| Just Seventeen | Needlecraft | The World of Interiors |
| The Lady | Mother & Baby | Period Living/Traditional Homes |
| My Guy | Country Living | Loving Monthly |
| Girl About Town | House Beautiful | My Guy Monthly |
| Ms London Weekly | '19' | |
| Midweek (London) | Living | **Bi-monthlies** |
| | Looks | Weight Watchers |
| **Fortnightlies** | Practical Parenting | Hair |
| More! | New Woman | Slimming |
| Mizz | Woman's Journal | Brides & Setting Up Home |
| | Company Magazine | Slimmer |
| **Monthlies** | Options | Wedding & Home |
| Prima | Annabel | Elle Decoration |
| Good Housekeeping | BBC Good Health | |

The national press has not been oblivious to what has happened in the magazine industry. In order to compete, they themselves have been targeting women with specialist sections and supplements. The whole industry now believes that it is possible to reach the modern women, by catering for women with different views, lifestyles, frames of mind and attitudes.

**Questions**

1 How do magazines help advertisers to target certain categories of women?

2 Identify, and then describe, two noise factors which might affect the success of the communication process through magazines.

3 How might an advertiser determine whether or not the intended message is achieving its objectives?

# THE PROMOTIONAL MIX

The promotional mix comprises all the marketing and promotional communication methods used to achieve the promotional objectives of the marketing mix. These methods can be broken down into two distinct areas, controllable and non-controllable.

## Non-controllable communication

**Non-controllable communication** consists of marketing messages which take place on the basis of word-of-mouth, personal recommendation and a consumer's overall perception of a particular product or service. For example, consumer opinions are influenced by a number of factors, such as whether the family has regularly used the product. A brand heritage, character, colour and image will also have helped to create brand loyalty and influenced regular purchasing patterns. Perhaps the most famous brand heritage is that of Rolls Royce: the term 'a Rolls Royce' company is frequently applied to organisations which build up a strong reputation for their goods and services. On the other hand, public displeasure with a particular organisation may adversely influence its fortunes.

## Controllable communication

**Controllable communication** consists of marketing messages which are carefully directed to achieve the objectives of an organisation's promotional campaign. There are four main areas (see Figure 8.3).

- *Advertisements* are messages sent via the media which are intended to inform or influence the people who receive them.

- *Sales promotions* are techniques designed to increase sales, such as money-off coupons, free samples and competitions.

- *Personal selling* involves the making of sales and emphasises the importance of salesmanship.

- *Publicity* is a non-personal communication using the media but, unlike advertising, it is not quantified with the success of a particular product. Its key component is public relations.

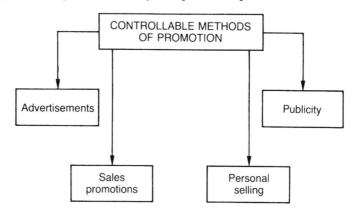

FIGURE 8.3
*The four areas of promotion*

In this chapter we look at advertising. The other three areas of the promotional mix are discussed in Chapter 9.

The controllable methods of promotion are often categorised as **above-the-line** or **below-the-line**. While changes in the law have now extinguished the origins of this system, the terms are still often used. 'Above-the-line' refers to the media such as TV, radio and press, for which commission is paid to an advertising agency. 'Below-the-line' comprises all media and promotional techniques for which fees are paid in preference to commissions – these might include exhibitions, sales literature and direct mail.

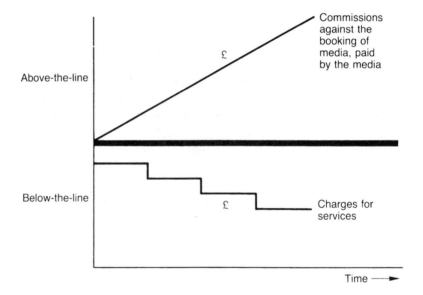

FIGURE 8.4
*Paying for agency
services*

### The promotional mix in international markets

Effective communications are particularly important in international markets. As the producer is geographically and often also culturally separated from the market, it is important that research reveals ways of effectively communicating with customers overseas.

One important issue when promoting overseas is the degree of **standardisation** that is possible. Global standardisation means using the same promotional methods with a roughly similar mix in all international markets. The purpose of this is that it simplifies the role of international marketing and implies the use of a common promotional policy using the same message through similar media across a range of countries. Buying motives are often the same in many markets and standardisation will reduce production costs and create potential for larger profits.

The ability to standardise completely is rare. Language differences are one problem, and another is that there may be national restrictions on promotional methods. Different countries have constraints on promotional methods which restrict what can be stated and the types of media that can be used – for example, many countries have their own rules regarding tobacco advertising.

An important aspect of international promotion in recent years has been **media overspill**. This involves markets other than the target market receiving the message, usually because media have crossed national borders. Possibilities for overspill have increased, particularly with the advent of satellite TV, and some British newspapers have good sales overseas. If greater standardisation is required, then media which reach many overseas markets may be used (e.g. *Reader's Digest*).

The importance of different types of media varies in different markets. For example, in some countries the press is still more important than television. Other more complicated issues also have to be broached: Are statistics available to show coverage of overseas media? What are literacy levels in other countries and how will this affect the ways in which the message should be communicated? How effective is the media in other countries? What is the reproduction quality of the media?

---

## CASE STUDY  *Promotion across Europe*

The European advertiser is faced with a complex and dynamic media market, comprising many very different countries, cultures and environments. With changes to the region adding the availability of Eastern Europe and the united Germany, Europe does not comprise a homogeneous media market. For example, television is a very important media investment in Italy and Greece, while Scandinavia and Germany are still dominated by the press. To reach targeted consumers, the European advertiser has to understand the significance of national differences that exist.

European media regulations are in a state of flux. Further domestic and international regulations are expected. Restrictions on TV advertising airtime availabilities exist in certain countries so that advertisers have to consider carefully the use of other media. One problem is the type of data available on consumers – there is often limited information and many countries use different interpretations of consumption patterns.

The overall effect of all these differences is a need for greater care when marketing overseas. Better planning and better research are required before embarking on a Europe-wide campaign.

**Questions**   **1**   What are (a) the benefits and (b) the problems of trying to standardise a promotional campaign across international markets?

        **2**   Before engaging in a promotional campaign across Europe, what questions might you require the answers to?

## USING THE PROMOTIONAL MIX

An organisation needs to appraise the communications process carefully. It must have a clear idea of what a message should be, to whom it should be sent and the expected outcome of sending it. Promotional requirements will vary with geographic size, demographic dispersion and the nature of market segmentation. The more clearly an organisation can define its particular market segment, the more relevant will be its promotional mix.

To achieve its promotional objectives an organisation has to set its promotional strategy. A common mnemonic used to describe how to persuade a customer to make a purchase is 'AIDA':

**A**   A customer's *attention* is captured and he or she is made *aware* of the product.

**I**   The *impact* of the promotion stimulates the customer's *interest*.

**D**   The customer is persuaded that he or she is *deprived* by not having the product, and this helps to stimulate a *desire* for it.

**A**   *Action* involves the purchase of the product.

The most common method of setting a **budget** for promotional activities involves allocating a fixed percentage of sales revenue to promotion. Some producers of consumables have as much as 10 per cent of their sales revenue devoted to promotion. It is always difficult to assess the effectiveness of promotional expenditure because the results may be delayed. A distinction is sometimes made between *immediate-impact* and *delayed-impact* advertising.

Whereas companies in consumer goods markets may commit anything up to 80 per cent of their promotional budget on advertising and sales promotion to generate **demand-pull**, companies in organisational markets are more likely to rely on personal selling and other forms of publicity to **push** products into markets. For example, in such markets catalogues and technical information may need to be supported by demonstrations, trials and testimonies from satisfied customers.

The promotional mix used must match the stages in the product life-cycle (see Chapter 5). For example, during the introduction stage, consumer awareness must be developed. As the product reaches maturity, it might be necessary to emphasise a brand's heritage to

FIGURE 8.5
*Using the promotional mix to push products into markets or pull products through markets*

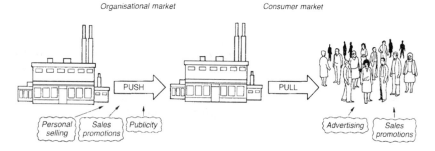

maintain consumer loyalty. Organisations must also react to the promotional expenditure of their competitors. For example, if a brand of confectionery is advertised heavily, the sales of other brands might be affected unless the other manufacturers retaliate. In fact, matching the activities of competitors is often a criterion for promotion, particularly to retain market share during the maturity phase.

## THE BUSINESS OF ADVERTISING

Advertising is a method of communicating with groups in the marketplace in order to achieve certain objectives and results. Advertisements are messages sent through the media which are intended to inform or influence the people who receive them. So, how do organisations advertise? In their literature Vauxhall state the following:

*It is not sufficient for a manufacturer to produce the best products in its field if few people know about them. First and foremost, advertising is essential in letting purchasers know that a specific product exists and in*

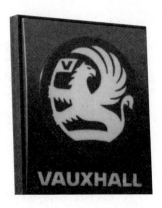

*keeping its brand name uppermost in the consumer's mind. Advertising fulfils a number of important functions by:*

- *Creating or building an image for the product – This 'targets' the particular model so that the consumer is made aware of who the product is aimed at.*
- *Encouraging a desire to own the product – Effective advertising should be persuasive. Its prime function is to sell.*
- *Providing information about the product – Initially, it will let as many people as possible know that the product exists, as well as providing relevant details.*

Advertising messages may be sent through a variety of media forms, such as TV, radio and the press. Promotional materials supplied with a product, promotional events or company brochures are not generally regarded as advertising (see Chapter 9).

At all stages in the advertising process it is important to assess how effectively advertisements have contributed to the communication process. In order to measure objectives, **DAGMAR** has become a fundamental part of good advertising practice. This stands for:

> Defining Advertising Goals for Measured Advertising Results

In other words, before any advertising campaign is started an organisation must define its communication objectives so that achievements can be measured both during and after the campaign.

## CASE STUDY  *Spontaneous recall*

Each week, *Marketing*, a marketing paper, publishes the results of audience research conducted by Audience Selection using 'Phonebus', a weekly telephone survey among more than 1000 adults aged 15 and over. The subjects are asked the question: *'Thinking back over the past week, which commercials can you remember seeing or hearing?'*. This is called 'spontaneous recall.'

The chart reproduced here shows the 'Top 10' for 10–12 December 1993 (published in *Marketing* on 6 January 1994). It also shows how long each product had been in the chart since 1 July 1993.

| Brand | Weeks in chart | Agency/media buyer |
|-------|----------------|--------------------|
| 1 Ford | 24 | Ogilvy & Mather |
| 2 Daz (unspecified) | 21 | Leo Burnett/P&G |
| 3 Nescafé Gold Blend | 5 | McCann-Erickson |
| 4 John Smith's Bitter | 5 | BMP DDB Needham |
| 5 Nescafé | 11 | McCann-Erickson |
| 6 Tesco | 4 | Lowe Howard-Spink |
| 7 Persil | 22 | JWT/Initiative |
| 8 Woolworth | 4 | BSB Dorland/Zenith |
| 9 Andrex | 18 | JWT |
| 10 BT | 8 | Saatchi & Saatchi/Zenith |

**Questions**

1 Why do some advertisements seem to be better at communicating a message than others?

2 Is 'spontaneous recall' a good way of assessing their effectiveness?

3 List ten advertisements you have seen recently which you can 'recall spontaneously'.

## Advertising agencies

To plan a campaign, an advertiser might consult an advertising agency. Such an agency is a link between the advertiser and the consumer. The role of an advertising agency is to create, develop, plan and implement an advertising campaign for its client. The extent to which an agency does so will vary according to its type. Some agencies offer all kinds of services, others only buy media space or time, and others specialise in creative work. Such agencies offer skilled expertise which can be shared with clients.

For example, Lyons Tetley's agency is DMB&B. Their relationship is a very close one and there are some areas of overlap between the functions and expertise of each. The main function of DMB&B is to develop and produce the company's advertising. However, because other functions such as public relations and sales promotions are based upon the same theme, the agency tends to have a role which is wider than just advertising.

One advantage of using an agency is that it would not be economic for the majority of advertisers to employ a full-time team. Agencies also offer the media an economic way of buying and selling airtime and space. The media have to deal with a small number of agencies rather than with thousands of individual advertisers.

The team of experts in an advertising agency services clients, who are known as **accounts**. An account executive supervises the work for a particular client and, together with the account director, works to meet the client's objectives. To achieve this they lead an account group comprising representatives from each of the main departments contributing to the campaign (Figure 8.6).

The account executive has to understand the needs of the client in the context of its operations and its industry, and interpret these to the agency. He or she will also have to present the agency's proposals to the client. The job requires diplomacy in order to keep all the interested parties happy.

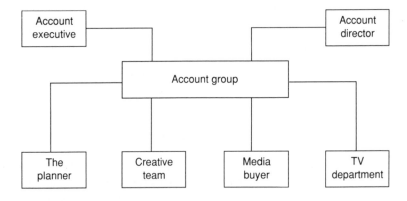

FIGURE 8.6
*Composition of an*
*account group*

The planner assists the account executive, maintains the performance of activities and uses specialist market research to assess the reactions of the public. From such analysis the planner can decide upon a strategy for a campaign and also test adverts to see how the public responds.

The creative team may consist of an art director who will create and develop rough drawings or illustrations called **visuals** and a copywriter who produces the words known as **copy** for an advertisement. They will also commission further artwork for the adverts.

The media buyer buys 'space' in newspapers and/or magazines or 'time' on TV or radio. The media buyer works with a media planner to decide the type of media to carry particular advertisements.

The TV department will, where necessary, commission the production of a commercial, organise the shoot, and edit and supply the finished advert.

When taking an account, an advertising agency will discuss what sort of message the advertiser wants to give to the market. This will initially involve finding out as many facts as possible about the product – for example, to whom it appeals, how it is to be sold, what its market share is and how its price compares with alternatives. The agency will wish to know not only about the product but also about the alternatives. To discover more, market research is used on a sample of consumers and the feedback is analysed.

## CASE STUDY — *The top 20 advertisers in 1992*

Study the chart, which shows the top 20 advertisers in 1992.

| Advertiser | Total (£000) | Advertising expenditure TV (%) | Radio (%) | Press (%) |
|---|---|---|---|---|
| 1 Procter & Gamble | 94 357 | 97.7 | 0.4 | 1.9 |
| 2 Lever Brothers | 74 706 | 88.3 | .. | 11.7 |
| 3 Kellogg Company of GB | 60 777 | 97.3 | 0.1 | 2.6 |
| 4 Ford | 46 424 | 58.3 | 1.8 | 39.9 |
| 5 British Telecommunications | 45 574 | 75.8 | 0.9 | 23.3 |
| 6 Vauxhall (General Motors) | 35 939 | 37.9 | 1.0 | 61.1 |
| 7 Procter & Gamble (Health & Beauty Care) | 35 727 | 94.3 | 0.5 | 5.2 |
| 8 Mars Confectionery | 33 125 | 94.3 | .. | 5.7 |
| 9 Elida Gibbs (Unilever) | 30 905 | 82.4 | .. | 17.6 |
| 10 Dixons | 30 624 | 12.5 | 0.1 | 87.5 |
| 11 Nestlé Rowntree | 29 989 | 95.4 | 0.7 | 3.8 |
| 12 Rover Group (BAE) | 29 833 | 31.1 | 2.0 | 66.9 |
| 13 Peugeot Talbot | 27 826 | 22.9 | 0.8 | 76.3 |
| 14 Bass Brewers (Bass) | 26 983 | 82.5 | 2.4 | 15.1 |
| 15 Renault (UK) | 26 657 | 48.0 | 4.7 | 47.3 |
| 16 Birds Eye Wall's (Unilever) | 26 304 | 92.1 | .. | 7.9 |
| 17 Tesco | 25 908 | 46.6 | 0.6 | 52.8 |
| 18 Cadbury (Cadbury-Schweppes) | 25 196 | 96.4 | 1.8 | 1.8 |
| 19 Kraft General Foods | 24 086 | 97.0 | .. | 3.0 |
| 20 VAG (UK) | 23 850 | 34.0 | 0.8 | 65.2 |

**Questions**
1. How much did the top 20 advertisers spend on advertising in that year?
2. Which medium received the most support from advertisers? Estimate the total spend on this medium, in round figures.
3. Suggest two reasons why radio shows such a low spend.
4. Think of one advertisement from one of these organisations. Comment on how effective this advert is at communicating the intended message.

At this stage, the agency starts to put forward some ideas for the advertising campaign. These are discussed with the client. The agency then provides ideas in the form of **storyboards** which show roughly what the commercials/advertisements will look like. The roughs will be tested on a target audience and the campaign will then be carefully planned. The client will need to approve the ideas. Production then begins on the final advertisement. A production company is signed up to make the TV commercial and the media department books suitable slots in television time as well as space in newspapers and magazines. A **test launch** may be used to assess consumer reaction to the campaign. Researchers follow up the campaign by finding out how the public responds, and this information is fed back to the client.

Agencies have in the past been paid by commission. The agency would book time or space for an advertiser who would then be charged by the media, who would pay a commission to the agency. However, over recent years agencies have become more involved in below-the-line promotional activities and have therefore billed their clients for activities. Many agencies today charge a straight fee for their services and then reimburse any commissions from the media to their client.

The success of the relationship between the advertiser and its agency depends largely upon trust and confidence. It is important at the outset that the advertiser establishes what type of services the agency will provide, the remuneration it will receive and the legal implications of their relationship. For example, how easy is it for an advertiser to ditch an agency and move elsewhere? Four woolly areas often include:

- *Copyright* – This normally belongs to the agency or to the freelance professionals used to produce the materials.
- *Exclusivity* – The advertiser would probably not wish the agency to act also on behalf of competitors for the duration of their relationship.
- *Confidentiality* – Information of a sensitive business nature supplied by the advertiser should be kept confidential.

- *Indemnity* – The advertiser may be legally liable if an advertisement created by an agency infringes a third party's trademark.

### Selecting an agency for an international market

When advertising products overseas a number of options are available. The advertiser may:

- use a domestic agency which will either have agencies and offices abroad or will be prepared to work with overseas media; or
- select a foreign agency in each overseas market.

A number of factors will determine the decision taken, such as the size of the market, the extent of the coverage and the type of knowledge required. In Europe the media market is dominated primarily by three routes: full-service agencies, media specialists, and media buying clubs. The full-service agencies provide a total advertising package for clients. Media specialists offer advertisers an alternative route to the media and are responsible for about 50 per cent of media expenditure in western Europe. Media clubs pool buying power from agencies and specialists to gain significant discounts from media owners.

## CREATIVITY

The interaction of ideas together with **creativity** are a major factor in the success of an advertising campaign. The message might be a combination of words, symbols, characters, colours, sounds and gimmicks. It must be conveyed to the right people in the right place at the right time, as 'good' advertising will not work if it is misdirected.

It is always an important objective of an advertising campaign to develop a good rapport with the targeted consumers. Sometimes this is found out by discovering where interests lie and how they respond to different sorts of advertising strategies.

At the heart of good advertising is good **copywriting**. Copy creates the theme for an advertising campaign and the visualiser/art director will develop ideas from the basic copy. Buzz words such as 'new', 'free' and 'call' are all designed to encourage the consumer to do something. They are *action words*. **Straplines** associated with a brand name can help to create an image or make a statement –

examples are 'Once driven, forever smitten' and 'Everything we do is driven by you'.

Some organisations use a created character to identify with a brand, so that the actions of the character will help to project the qualities of the product or service. These characters have often become valuable promotional assets. Mr Kipling creates a home-baked image for cakes and Mr Sheen helps to reflect the qualities of furniture polish.

## CASE STUDY  *Creativity with tea*

Tetley introduced the teabag in 1953 and has since positioned itself in the market as the 'teabag expert'. Since 1973 it has done this via the animated Tetley Tea Folk. The Tetley Tea Folk have been an identifiable trademark for the brand which has given Tetley a 'common sense, down to earth, warm, friendly and honest image'. They give tea a craftmanlike connotation which helps to provide the brand with a sense of quality, reassurance and homeliness which, at the same time, is also humorous.

Some of the notable straplines have been:

'2000 perforations which lets the flavour flood out'
'Tetley make teabags make tea'
'Tetley bags all the flavour'
'Tetley: every sip blended to a "T"'

This type of campaign provided consumers with a lot of reassurance at a time when most were changing their tea-making habits from loose tea to teabags. The Tetley Tea Folk have been perceived as lively, sociable, family-orientated and reassuring. Their characters have been likened to the product itself – sociable, reassuring, good in a crisis.

Another important innovation for Tetley was the round teabag. This looked better in a cup and was another example of how Tetley could differentiate its efforts. Tetley have also made inroads into TV sponsorship with 'The Darling Buds of May'.

The results of Tetley's efforts are largely self-evident, and 71 per cent of consumers is an almost all-time high recall level for the brand. Innovations, and the continuing success of the Tetley Tea Folk, have provided the brand with a greater depth of penetration than that of competitors.

**Questions**

1  Explain how product innovation combined with creativity have helped to create a successful brand for Tetley.

2  Provide two other examples of similar achievements.

A brand's heritage is often an area that advertisers like to build upon. It helps an organisation to foster **brand loyalty** – grandparents and parents pass on their consumption patterns to successive generations. For example, many confectionery products such as Smarties have been with us for more than fifty years.

Advertisements are enhanced by **artwork** – often the prime means of capturing the imagination of the consumer. Most mass media today have colour facilities; newspapers are the most recent addition to the fold. Good artwork and effective use of colour can help to develop a unique brand or organisational identity which is instantly recognisable as a message as to the quality, reliability and acceptability of a product. Improvements in technology have provided artists with further opportunities to develop their work.

Humour is another area which is open to creative brilliance. For example, in the tea sector, fierce competition for awareness through humour takes place between Brooke Bond Oxo's chimps and the Tetley Tea Folk.

One of the secrets of successful advertising is **repetition**. Brand or company names can appear throughout an advertisement and be regularly repeated. It is also possible to create a sense of motion with a cleverly concocted strapline or invent a combination of words in a catchy style that consumers will probably always remember – such as 'We all adore a Kio-ora'.

Advertising messages help organisations to develop and communicate the identity of their brands as well as to provide a foundation for other areas of the promotional mix.

# THE MEDIA

The characteristics of various media will commend them to creative areas such as sound, vision and script. The success of an advertising campaign depends on using creative skills effectively and making the correct choice of media.

**Media selection** will also depend on the target audience (i.e. the number of potential customers the advertiser wishes to reach), as well as on the number of times the advertiser wishes the message to be transmitted. These are known as **coverage** and **frequency**.

In order to plan a campaign an advertiser must gather detailed information about members of the targeted audience. Television stations will always provide information about demographic distribution, communications, size and nature of companies, spending patterns, leisure activities and incomes of their viewers. The coverage and frequency of media choice may also be limited by financial constraints, so the advertiser must distinguish between those media which are affordable and those which are not. A media choice is then made on the basis of **cost-effectiveness**.

For an advertisement to be cost-effective, it must not only have good coverage but its frequency must produce the required impact upon the targeted audience. The **threshold concept** illustrates that unless advertising for a particular brand reaches a certain level, it will be wasted. An advertisement's effectiveness will therefore relate to advertising expenditure – the number of times people are exposed to a message will help to determine whether they remember it.

Media coverage will help to create preferences for a product or service which could influence a purchase decision. It might also help existing customers to purchase more and reinforce consumers' feelings that they have made the right purchase decision. It will allow organisations to develop a strategy for a brand and take a range of actions, perhaps in response to the actions of competitors, so that market share and other objectives can be achieved.

## Types of media

### Printed materials

**Printed materials** make up by far the largest group of media in the UK. The group includes all newspapers and magazines, both national and local, as well as trade press, periodicals and professional journals. There are about 9000 regular publications in the UK which can be used by the advertiser. They allow the advertiser to send a message to several million people through the press or to target magazines of special interest, from railways to snooker. They also allow the advertiser to communicate with people in a certain trade or profession as well as those in a particular region.

---

**CASE STUDY** *Comparing readership profiles*

Look at the comparison between the readership circulation and profiles of *Country Life* and *Exchange & Mart*.

| | Circulation (000) | Adult readership (000) | (%) | Men (%) | Women (%) | 15/34 (%) | 35/54 (%) | 55+ (%) | ABCI (%) | C2DE (%) | Mono (£) | 4 colour (£) |
|---|---|---|---|---|---|---|---|---|---|---|---|---|
| | | | | | | | *Adult readership profiles* | | | | *Page rates* | |
| Population profile | | | | 48 | 52 | 37 | 32 | 32 | 45 | 56 | | |
| *Country Life* | 42 | 471 | 1 | 49 | 51 | 24 | 44 | 32 | 68 | 32 | 1870 | 3060 |
| *Exchange & Mart* | 136 | 1772 | 4 | 74 | 26 | 48 | 39 | 13 | 41 | 59 | 3360 | 3820 |

**Questions**

1 Provide a brief description of each of these magazines.

2 Describe in what ways readership differs between the two magazines.

3 What type of advertisements would you expect to see in each?

The printed media allows accurate targeting. Types of customers can be identified by analysing **readership profiles**. Long or complex messages can be sent and, as the message is durable, it may be read repeatedly. If an advertisement appears in a prestige publication it may take on the prestige of that particular publication. Colour quality is today offered in an increasing number of newspapers and magazines; tear-off reply coupons which follow up an advertisement are also popular.

Advertisements in the printed media are sometimes criticised for having a poor impact. There are many competing messages which the reader is not forced to read and some publications have a short life-span. Printed advertisements have static rather than dynamic qualities.

### Broadcast media

**Broadcast media** includes commercial television and commercial radio. Television is the most powerful media channel available. It reaches 98 per cent of households and viewing figures can exceed 20 million. TV advertisements are usually of a high creative quality, helped by both sound and colour. Messages are dynamic as they have voice, images, movement and colour and the ability to be repeated over and over again.

The main disadvantage of such an expensive media is that it is sometimes difficult to target a broadcast to a particular group of consumers (see Figure 8.7).

| | Total households (000) | Social grade | | | | Size of household | | |
|---|---|---|---|---|---|---|---|---|
| | | AB (%) | C1 (%) | C2 (%) | DE (%) | 1 (%) | 2 (%) | 3+ (%) |
| London | 4523 | 23 | 31 | 18 | 28 | 27 | 33 | 39 |
| Midlands | 3693 | 14 | 26 | 26 | 34 | 25 | 30 | 44 |
| North West | 2588 | 18 | 24 | 20 | 38 | 27 | 31 | 43 |
| Yorkshire | 2295 | 13 | 24 | 24 | 38 | 27 | 32 | 41 |
| C. Scotland | 1392 | 15 | 26 | 20 | 39 | 26 | 32 | 41 |
| Wales & West | 1830 | 16 | 27 | 24 | 33 | 26 | 31 | 43 |
| South & S. East | 2221 | 21 | 29 | 20 | 30 | 27 | 33 | 40 |
| North East | 1178 | 12 | 22 | 23 | 42 | 27 | 31 | 42 |
| East | 1667 | 15 | 27 | 24 | 34 | 25 | 34 | 42 |
| South West | 657 | 20 | 28 | 24 | 28 | 27 | 35 | 38 |
| N. Ireland | 489 | 13 | 26 | 19 | 43 | 24 | 25 | 52 |
| Border | 274 | 17 | 26 | 23 | 35 | 27 | 31 | 43 |
| N. Scotland | 475 | 17 | 28 | 24 | 31 | 26 | 36 | 39 |

FIGURE 8.7
*Population profiles of commercial TV areas*

Recent developments in television have seen franchise changes and the emergence of Carlton, GMTV and others. There have also been some mergers between television franchisees such as Yorkshire and Tyne-Tees, and this has led to an outcry by some advertisers who believe that the reduction of competition will inevitably lead to higher advertising rates. Direct broadcasting by satellite has been available since 1989 when Sky TV started on the Astra satellite which is reaching an increasing number of households. Cable TV penetration in the UK is still low but is also increasing.

There are more than 120 Independent Local Radio (ILR) stations in the UK, including 12 in London (see Figure 8.8), as well as several Independent National Radio (INR) stations including Classic FM and Virgin. Local radio stations can be geared to different audiences at different times of the day. Radio is a good way of communicating a sense of urgency and action to consumers. Advertisement production costs are low in comparison with those of TV. One of the problems of radio, however, is that for many it is just a background medium, and many rarely listen closely to it.

## Outdoor media

**Outdoor media** include fixed posters and hoardings, advertising on buses, taxis, underground trains and other forms of transport, as

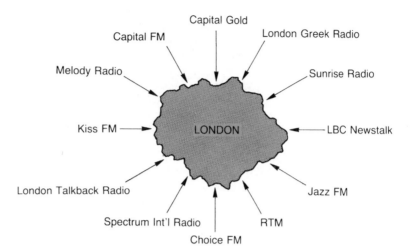

FIGURE 8.8
*Independent Local
Radio (ILR) stations
in London*

well as neon signs and electronic screens. This is particularly useful
for providing frequency and supporting the images created through
the broadcast media.

If an outdoor medium is well sited, its impact may be considerable.
Posters can be in colour and there is a wide choice of locations and
sites with little competition from other advertising matter. In fact
many become a sole attraction where people have little to do except
look at the advert or fellow passengers.

Outdoor media suffer from the intrusion of noise and clutter from
the immediate environment. Advertisements may become part of the
scenery and go unnoticed. Outdoor posters are always subject to
damage from vandalism and graffiti, and many people today feel
that hoardings intrude into the environment.

### Direct mail

**Direct mail** is personally addressed advertising sent through the
post. Every month each British household receives on average six
and a half direct mail items. By using direct mail an organisation
may establish a direct relationship with its customers. The advertiser
supplies promotional literature to encourage a sale and then tries to
cater for the customers' perceived needs.

It often also includes direct selling, which does not involve a long
distribution chain. It is recognised as the most rapidly increasing
form of promotion because it allows an advertiser to reach a
narrowly identified target audience.

FIGURE 8.9
*An inducement to respond to a direct-mail offer*

> Dear Mr Lucky
> First of all allow me, on behalf of my colleagues and myself, to offer you our warmest congratulations, because
>
> YOU REALLY ARE A WINNER
> IN OUR 1994 SUPER PRIZE DRAW
>
> Yes, you're off to a winning start, since one of our fabulous entry prizes is already yours, and may have even gone one better if, as I hope, your personal lucky number 20676646 matches our 1st prize, you will also walk away with the prize of prizes, or the car, or £15,000 cash!

The ability of direct mail to target precise segments in a market makes it cost-effective, as it eliminates the supply of mailshots to those unlikely to buy. Geodemographic and life-style systems such as PIN, ACORN and MOSAIC help the direct-mailer to identify types of consumer according to where they live and the life-styles they follow. The majority of mailshots are read and organisations often use sales promotions such as offers and competitions to encourage a response (see Figure 8.9).

If a good impression is made with the consumer, direct mail can offer an organisation the opportunity to send a long message and some detailed copy. Organisations such as the Automobile Association, Reader's Digest, Consumers Association and the National Geographic Magazine are well established in using direct mail techniques. It is the most easy form of promotion to measure as it is possible to calculate the number of mailshots sent out, the cost of the campaign, the response rate and the number of sales made.

Royal Mail offers its 'Mailsort' services for volume mailings. By pre-sorting mail before handing the posting over, users can be provided with discounts on postage costs. Royal Mail points out that direct mail is the most selective form of promotional message reaching people in their own households, and that it has a high impact in comparison with other advertising messages.

## Cinema

**Cinema** has been declining in importance as an advertising medium over recent years, though it tends to be popular with the young. It may, therefore, be an appropriate way of targeting a younger audience.

A cinema has a captive audience, and the physical size and loud volume of advertisements makes them almost impossible to ignore.

The quality of sound and vision helps the audience to recall cinema commercials better than those on television. Cinema audiences fluctuate widely and are dependent upon the popularity of the films being shown. Commercials tend to be shown once during a programme and are not reinforced unless the recipient is a regular cinema attender.

## CONTROLS OVER ADVERTISING

Controls can be divided roughly into **statutory** and **voluntary** areas. The Trade Descriptions Act refers to the ways in which products are described and may cover statements made in advertising literature. Consumers are also protected by a statutory instrument called the Control of Misleading Advertisements Regulations. These regulations refer to misleading advertisements and allow complaints to be made to the Director General of Fair Trading. Complaints about broadcast media, however, have to be made to either the Independent Television Commission (ITC) or the Radio Authority (RA).

The **British Code of Advertising Practice** is administered by the **Advertising Standards Authority** (ASA) and sets out rules applying to different categories of advertisements. The ASA invites the public to complain about adverts and investigates complaints. Other codes include the Independent Television Commission's **Code of Advertising Standards and Practice**, and the Radio Authority's **Code of Advertising Standards and Practice and Programme Sponsorship**.

## ASSESSING ADVERTISING EFFECTIVENESS

Advertising is often an essential part of the promotional mix and can require particularly high levels of expenditure. It is therefore crucial that organisations try to analyse the effectiveness of their investment. However, it is sometimes difficult to measure how effective an advertisement campaign is in developing a product or brand image.

The effectiveness of a campaign will depend on the way it appeals to the attitudes of its target audience. Advertising will help to create stability in the market. Many customers are intensely loyal and expect to see promotional messages from advertisers of goods they regularly purchase. They often rely on them for product information and for details relating to future purchases.

The most common method of evaluating the success of an advertising campaign is to test the views of a **representative sample** both before and after a campaign. Pre-testing will discover the sample's perception of a product before the campaign. Post-testing involves asking the same questions to discover how far knowledge and understanding of the product has been improved. For example, in the Creature Comforts campaign, customer perceptions were initially investigated. The campaign was 'tracked' with 10 000 interviews per month, and then the success of the campaign was evaluated by looking at the degree to which customer perceptions had changed in line with objectives. During the course of that campaign the proportion of consumers who viewed electric central heating as modern and up-to-date increased from 20 to 30 per cent.

Specialist agencies in the UK carry out audience research. Their results are made known to advertising agencies, marketing departments and market researchers. **British Rate and Data** (BRAD) is the national guide to UK printed media – its publications carry out readership research in many areas. Television ratings (TVR) are carried out by the **Broadcasters' Audience Research Board** (BARB) on behalf of broadcasting organisations. These figures are also broken down on a demographic basis to indicate yields for specific groups of the population.

Apart from when advertising by direct mail, it is not always easy to evaluate the effectiveness of an advertising campaign. One reason for this is that advertising is difficult to isolate from the other ingredients in both the promotional and the marketing mix. Nonetheless, advertising does have an important role to play and is essential for developing a market and stimulating sales.

## ASSIGNMENT

Life-style is the Nesrefresh brand of lemon-tea. Imagine that you work in an advertising agency as an assistant account executive. Work in groups to complete the following tasks.

**Task a**   Identify the target audience for the brand.

**Task b**   What types of media would be suitable for reaching the target audience?

**Task c**   You have been asked to draw up a *media plan* on a form like the one shown on page 209. If your campaign is to be successful it will be advisable to use several different types of media. Remember the importance of targeting the consumer as well as coverage and frequency. Your budget is £450 000.

**Task d**   Explain how you would propose to change or further develop the brand, if at all, over the next 5 years.

**Task e**   Emphasise the use of creativity in your guidelines and produce a dummy advertisement. Present your results and conclusions back to the other groups.

| MEDIA PLAN | | | £ COST | JAN | FEB | MAR | APR | MAY | JUN | JUL | AUG | SEP | OCT | NOV | DEC | SUB-TOTAL COSTS | COMMENTS |
|---|---|---|---|---|---|---|---|---|---|---|---|---|---|---|---|---|---|
| TELEVISION (CENTRAL AREA) | 30 SECOND TV COMMERCIAL | OFF PEAK | 600 | | | | | | | | | | | | | | |
| | OCT, NOV, DEC, MAR, APR, MAY | ON PEAK | 4,000 | | | | | | | | | | | | | | |
| | 30 SECOND TV COMMERCIAL | OFF PEAK | 400 | | | | | | | | | | | | | | |
| | JAN, FEB, JUN, JUL, AUG, SEP | ON PEAK | 3,000 | | | | | | | | | | | | | | |
| LOCAL RADIO | 30 SECOND SPOT | | 100 | | | | | | | | | | | | | | |
| NATIONAL PRESS | ONE INSERTION PER NEWSPAPER | | 5,000 | | | | | | | | | | | | | | |
| LOCAL PRESS | ONE INSERTION PER NEWSPAPER | | 500 | | | | | | | | | | | | | | |
| FREE TRADE PRESS | ONE INSERTION PER NEWSPAPER | | 200 | | | | | | | | | | | | | | |
| DIRECT MAILING | 1000 PACKAGES DELIVERED BY THE POST OFFICE (SELECTED ADDRESSES) | | 450 | | | | | | | | | | | | | | |
| | 1000 PACKAGES HAND-DELIVERED (SELECTED AREAS) | | 300 | | | | | | | | | | | | | | |
| BUS SIDES | 10 POSTERS | | 1000 | | | | | | | | | | | | | | |

# Sales Promotion, Personal Selling and the Role of Public Relations

Though advertising is an important part of the promotional mix, effective promotion includes the use of other ingredients which may be used to support, complement and integrate with advertising so that an organisation can achieve its promotional objectives.

FIGURE 9.1
*Using all areas of the promotional mix to achieve objectives*

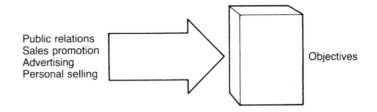

Public relations
Sales promotion
Advertising
Personal selling

Objectives

## SALES PROMOTION

**Sales promotion** describes a category of techniques which are used to encourage customers to make a purchase. These activities are effectively **short-term** and may be used to increase sales, to respond to competitive activities, to help with the task of personal selling or simply as an alternative to advertising.

The Institute of Sales Promotion defines sales promotion as follows:

> Sales promotion is the function of marketing which seeks to achieve given objectives by the adding of intrinsic, tangible value to a product or service.

Sales promotions might include point-of-sale materials, competitions, demonstrations and exhibitions. The essential feature of a sales promotion is that it is a short-term inducement to encourage customers to react quickly, whereas advertising is usually a much more long-term communication process involving the building and developing of a brand.

As you walk down a town high street or through a shopping mall, you will see many different examples of sales promotions. Such promotions may serve many different purposes. For example,

**competitions**, **vouchers** and **trading stamps** may be designed to build customer loyalty and perhaps increase the volume purchased by existing customers. **Product sampling** is a strategy which is often used to introduce new products into the marketplace. **Clearance sales** of overstocked goods will increase sales during seasons when business would otherwise be slack. Many sales promotions are undertaken in response to the activities of competitors to ensure that an organisation remains competitive. Nearly all oil companies and petrol retailers offer competing promotional activities which change from time to time.

Sales promotions can have a more direct influence on sales than other promotional methods such as advertising. They enable the manufacturer to have a direct influence upon the actions of the customer and, in some cases, encourage retailers to stock brands. Sales promotions may also help products in decline by injecting new life, encourage impulse buying, arouse interest in new products, or simply persuade customers to switch brands.

Sales promotions can be divided into two broad areas:

- those which are designed to enhance the sales of a product to the trade

- those which assist the trade in promoting and selling products to the final consumer.

**Selling into the pipeline** is an expression often used to describe promotions which move products from the manufacturer into the distribution system. **Selling out of the pipeline** describes promotions which trigger the end-user to make a purchase.

FIGURE 9.2
*Promotions into and out of the pipeline*

### Promotions into the pipeline

These are techniques used to sell more stocks into the distribution system and are addressed directly at the distributors.

**Dealer loaders** are among the inducements used to attract orders. They might include a 'free case' with so many cases bought – for example, thirteen for the price of twelve is known as a 'baker's dozen'. **Dealer competitions** might be linked to sales, with attractive prizes for the most successful dealer. **Promotional gifts** such as

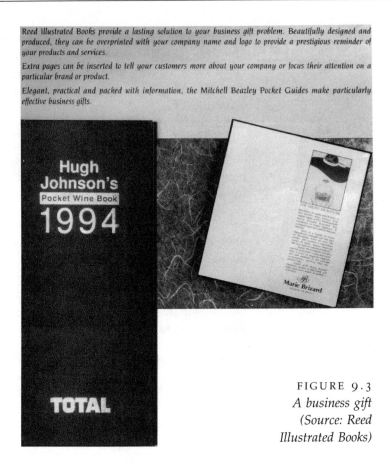

*Reed Illustrated Books provide a lasting solution to your business gift problem. Beautifully designed and produced, they can be overprinted with your company name and logo to provide a prestigious reminder of your products and services.*

*Extra pages can be inserted to tell your customers more about your company or focus their attention on a particular brand or product.*

*Elegant, practical and packed with information, the Mitchell Beazley Pocket Guides make particularly effective business gifts.*

FIGURE 9.3
*A business gift
(Source: Reed
Illustrated Books)*

bottles of spirits, clocks, watches or diaries sometimes influence the choice of goods dealers stock (see Figure 9.3).

**Point-of-sale (POS)** materials such as special displays, posters and racks can be offered against volume orders or offered on loan for a period. Some organisations might offer the use of a video recorder together with a promotional cassette to play for customers.

**Publishing of dealers' names** in advertisements, sales literature or catalogues always encourages the support of particular dealers.

**Extended credit** often encourages dealers to stock goods, particularly if they sell and receive payment for the product before they have to pay suppliers. **Sale or return** can be used to encourage a dealer to stock an untried product and helps to remove the danger of being left with unsold stock.

**Staff training** is often provided for the dealer if the product involves detailed explanations, demonstrations or dealer servicing, such as in the case of cars.

# CASE STUDY    *What is in a gift?*

In the run-up to Christmas in 1993, leading business gift suppliers stated that gift providers were sticking to tried and tested items such as diaries, calenders, pens, calculators, clocks, leather goods, and food and drink hampers. However, because of the recession, many cost-conscious firms had introduced strict guidelines for buying and distributing Christmas gifts and a large number were offering similar gifts as part of an all-year-round business gift programme.

Makita UK, the Japanese-owned manufacturer of industrial power tools, is a major purchaser of business gifts. The company uses gifts to 'target individuals at different levels within disparate customer companies'. The company first decides whether customers should be given gifts and then evaluates the various levels required of gift-giving – so that a director might receive a personalised bottle of champagne while retail counter staff could receive a branded ski-jacket.

The whole point of giving corporate gifts is to provide a gift portfolio that really works. Most companies today carefully target those to whom they send promotional items. Gifts are frequently designed to meet the objectives of the provider and to appeal to those who receive them.

**Questions**   1   Explain why many companies provide their customers with promotional corporate gifts.

2   Describe two alternatives to the provision of corporate gifts.

3   Comment briefly on the ethics of providing gifts. For example, should gifts influence future business decisions, should they be pooled and shared, or should they just be accepted graciously for services rendered?

### Promotions out of the pipeline

These assist the trade in promoting and selling products to the end-users. Manufacturers tend to be responsible for the bulk of sales promotions, though more recently retailers have started to become involved. Sales promotions to the end-user require a careful creative approach, as repeated use, or a tasteless promotion, might damage a brand.

**Sample or trial packs** are either given to customers or sold to them at low prices to encourage them to try the product, in the hope that this will stimulate them to make a full purchase. **Bonus packs** offer customers more of the product for the same price, giving greater value for money – beer and lager cans often offer extra beer for the same price. **Coupon offers** in the form of 'money off' are distributed door-to-door, or appear as part of an advertisement or on a pack.

**Price reductions** are always popular with consumers. They can, however, prove expensive for manufacturers and retailers, as many of those who buy the product might be regular users who would have been prepared to pay the full price. **Premium offers** may offer an extra product for the same inclusive price.

**Competitions** may interest consumers, particularly if there is an attractive prize. Scratch cards, free draws and bingo cards are popular.

**Trading stamps** have largely disappeared from the retailing scene but are still popular at petrol stations. A certain quantity of stamps is given every time a purchase is made, and these can be redeemed later for goods or services. This helps to reinforce brand loyalty.

**Charity promotions** can be popular with young customers, who collect box tops or coupons and send them to the manufacturer, who then makes a donation to a charity.

**Demonstrations** at the point of sale which involve giving away samples or demonstrating a product often generate considerable interest. These tend to be expensive, however, and are often not considered to be cost-effective.

**Point-of-sale displays** are designed to push products to consumers from the location where they are sold. An effective point-of-sale display attracts customers' attention and encourages them to approach and inspect the product before making the decision to buy.

**Merchandising** is the physical process of stocking goods so that they are in the right place at the right time, making it easy for customers to walk around a store, select the goods they require and take them away. It provides a competitive advantage to the retailer by supplying products at the right eye-level and at a location relative to height. Look at the sweet and crisp displays in your local supermarket! It also involves providing access for the physically handicapped, the placing of own brands next to manufacturer brands so that prices can be compared, and the siting of impulse items near to the cash registers.

### Overseas sales promotions

In **overseas markets**, sales promotions are fraught with legal inconsistencies. For example, free draws are not permitted in Germany, Denmark, Belgium, the Netherlands, Luxembourg, Austria, Norway, Sweden and Switzerland, but are permitted in Spain, the UK, Ireland, France, Portugal, Italy, Greece and Finland.

Sales promotions also have differing degrees of importance in overseas markets.

The Department for Enterprise supports overseas store promotions of UK goods. Though this type of promotion is usually geared more towards establishing a place in an overseas market as well as selling, it may include a number of attractions of a British flavour and be used to promote goods which already sell in overseas markets.

### The effects of sales promotions

The effects of individual sales promotions will vary widely. Though most promotions such as free samples will clearly lead to an immediate increase in sales, on the whole sales promotions are a short-term measure and have little effect on brand loyalty over a longer period. For the manufacturers of staple goods such as washing-up liquid and bleach, sales promotions will not affect total market size which will be relatively fixed – though they will encourage buyers to move away from competing brands. Probably the greatest overall benefit of sales promotions is their ability to inject life into a brand in a way which is completely different from, but often just as effective as, a big advertising spend.

---

## CASE STUDY  *Dettox and Vileda in joint partnership*

The following article, by journalist Ken Gofton, describes a joint promotional effort by Vileda and Reckitt & Colman. It appeared in *Marketing* on 14 October 1993 and is used with permission.

Call them what you will – piggy-back, partnership, or third party promotions. The fact is, they're a favourite promotional weapon which tends to be brandished all the more frequently when budgets are under pressure, not least because they allow costs to be shared.

Synergy is the key to successful partnerships, says Peter Le Conte, a director of sales promotion consultancy SMP. And the closer the fit between participating brands, the better.

SMP was the consultancy in what may well have been one of the happiest promotional marriages of the year – a tie-in between Vileda Supermop and Dettox multi-surface cleaner. After all, if you're going to clean the floor with a Supermop, you will need a cleaning agent, too.

In fact, when Vileda approached Dettox manufacturer Reckitt and Colman to suggest a joint promotion for the spring of this

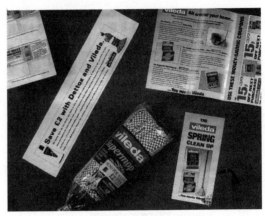

year, it turned out that Reckitt was also casting around for a really powerful means to encourage trials of Dettox.

In the deal hatched by SMP, one Supermop purchase entitled the purchaser to receive by mail a voucher for £1 off a Supermop refill (which retails at about £3), plus a voucher for a free bottle of Dettox multi-surface cleaner, retailing at £1.09. In addition, consumers received two further "bounce-back" vouchers to save money on other leading Vileda brands, all contained in a Handy Household Hints leaflet.

But what took this promotion up a notch was the unusual decision to ask consumers to nominate their preferred store for voucher redemption, and to state if they had previously purchased either brand.

"This gave us a tremendous insight into purchasing habits," says Carol Devins, Vileda marketing manager. "We've already identified that over half the respondents to the promotion had never previously bought either Supermop or Dettox. This partnership has given both of us huge numbers of new purchasers as well as rewarding our loyal users.

"We've also been able to demonstrate to our grocery customers that promotions like this work for them as well. We know exactly how many customers wanted to redeem their vouchers in Sainsbury, Tesco, Safeway and Asda."

The promotion has proved such a success that the two companies are exploring other ways of co-operating on other brands. Reckitt's Windolene trigger packs are currently acting as the host brand this time round, offering consumers money-off vouchers for Vileda Sunsplash and Window cloth, as well as vouchers for Windolene purchases.

Reckitt's senior product manager Helen Taylor says she's impressed with the consumer and trade response to this type of activity – "and the combination of Reckitt and Vileda brands means that we can give our consumers greater incentives without having to bear the full costs ourselves."

Adds Vileda commercial director Andrew Marsden: "Having created such a powerful and natural link between a number of our brands, one of the main tasks for next year is to ensure that we exploit it fully by supporting the promotions with advertising, PR, and tailor-made overlays. We're working towards a win:win situation for both companies and, of course, our consumers."

**Questions**   1   Describe the nature of the Dettox/Vileda promotion.

2   What benefits were gained by the manufacturers of Dettox and Vileda from their partnership?

3   How else do they intend to exploit their partnership?

4   Identify three other possible instances where manufacturers could link products together for the purpose of sales promotions.

---

# PERSONAL SELLING

Every day of your life you are involved in some form of **personal selling activity**. It might be persuading a friend to accompany you to a sports event or a relative to buy something for you. What you are doing is using a relationship to sell your ideas to someone else.

Personal selling involves persuasive communication between a seller and a buyer which is designed to convince the consumer to purchase the products or services on offer. The objective of personal selling is therefore to make the sale and is the culmination of all the marketing activities that have taken place beforehand. It involves matching a consumer's needs with the goods and services on offer. The better the match, the more lasting the relationship between the seller and the buyer.

The role of personal selling will vary from business to business. It can be one of the most expensive ingredients of the promotional mix. Though the high cost of salaries, commissions, travel and hotel expenses are a major disadvantage, personal selling is a two-way process of personal communication which allows an organisation to obtain information about its customers. This personal communication element can be very important as the final sale might come as the result of protracted negotiations.

Personal selling is important in both consumer and organisational markets. In consumer goods markets, advertising is often the driving force which has *pulled* a product through the distribution network so that most consumers know what they want to purchase. In organisational markets, the purpose of a sales force is to *push* the product through the market.

The mnemonic used to describe personal selling and the sequence of events it creates is known as the **five Ps**.

*Preparation*

*Prospecting*

*Pre-approach*

*Presentation*

*Post-sale support*

**FIGURE 9.4**
*The five Ps of selling*

- **Preparation** – Sales staff should be adequately trained and familiar with the product, customers, competition and the market.
- **Prospecting** – This involves identifying customers or *prospects* before selling takes place.
- **Pre-approach** – It is important to learn about the projected customer before the approach.
- **Presentation** – This involves active selling skills and will involve the use of AIDA (see Chapter 8).
- **Post-sale support** – Following up sales helps to create repeat business.

### Preparation

Selling in a highly competitive world means that preparation has never been so important. Though it has been said that sales people are born and not made, skills, knowledge and training can improve everybody's performance. Training is designed to build upon a person's selling skills and to use their personal abilities and understanding to follow the psychological stages of the sales process. Product knowledge is vital as it allows feedback from the prospect's questions about the product's technical specifications, benefits and functions.

Comprehensive records on customers should be kept and updated after each visit. Keeping sales records enables the salesperson to respond exactly to each customer's individual needs. Knowledge of competitors and their products enables the seller to respond to queries about the relative merits and demerits of products. Good preparation improves the chances of closing a sale.

## Prospecting

Identifying customers is a traditional role fulfilled by a salesperson. **Prospects** must be located before any selling can begin. Though sales staff will already have a list of customers or accounts, a salesperson will often have to carry out '**cold calling**'. This involves visiting or telephoning an organisation that the business has not previously had any dealings with. Cold calling by sales representatives has unpredictable results and can be demoralising if there is a poor reception.

An alternative to cold calling might be the use of telephone **canvassers**, whose job it is to find potential customers and then pass on the details to the sales representatives. Sometimes it is possible to use independent **agents** to find customers. Working on a commission-only basis, agents may reduce the need for an organisation to employ as many sales representatives, particularly if there are a large number of low-value accounts. Insurance, for example, is sold by agents.

Many organisations today use **direct-mail** techniques to stimulate enquiries for sales staff to follow up. A good mailshot will make it clear what is on offer and help to initiate the selling procedure.

A growing form of selling approach is through the use of the telephone. **Telemarketing** is often regarded as a fairly cost-effective alternative to cold calling in person.

### Pre-approach

It is necessary to learn about a potential customer. This might involve finding out about the past history of transactions, if any, by researching records; and finding out who they are dealing with and whether they have achieved access to a decision-maker, as well as ascertaining their general needs and aspirations.

### Presentation

The presentation must be made on the basis of a strategy (see AIDA, Chapter 8). **Probing** is quite important at the early stage, in order to find out the prospect's needs and where the priorities lie. The salesperson can try to match the product or service with the prospect's needs. This might involve elaborating on the product's advantages, concentrating on aspects such as savings in costs, design ingredients, performance specifications, after-sales service, etc.

During the presentation, the salesperson must constantly evaluate whether the product is appropriate to the needs of the prospect. It is unethical to sell something that they might not need – although this often happens. The larger and more complex the order, the more complex the negotiations over the conditions of supply. Sometimes sales aids such as product demonstrations, samples and literature will help the process.

The prospect may have a variety of objections to the purchase. These objections might be genuine, as a result of a misunderstanding. There might also be a reluctance to make a commitment at this stage. Logical, well-presented arguments and incentives may overcome such objections.

Timing is crucial to **closing** the sale. A salesperson must look for **buying signals** which indicate that the prospect is close to a decision and almost ready to put a signature on an order form and discuss the contractual arrangements.

### Post-sale support

This stage involves following up the sale. Promises that might have been made during the negotiations will have to be met. If the salesperson guarantees delivery by a certain date, that date must be held. Contacting customers to see if they are happy with the product will help repeat buying and improve the supplier's reputation for concern for its customers.

## The sales force

Sales staff operate as an information link between the suppliers and their customers. As a result, personal selling involves a boundary role – being at the boundary of a supplying organisation and also in direct and close contact with customers. The role is often not only one of selling but also one of interpreting the activities and policies of each organisation to the other.

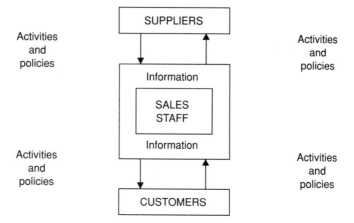

FIGURE 9.5
*The information link
between customers
and suppliers*

The size and nature of the sales force is determined by factors such as revenue and workload. Often large and widespread markets can only be supplied by a massive salesforce whereas small concentrated markets tend to make personal selling cost-effective. No matter what other sales techniques are used in some markets, if customers become used to personal selling they will tend to expect close contact with a representative from their suppliers. In these circumstances, particularly if a competitor uses personal selling, it can become very difficult to do anything but become locked into the use of personal selling techniques.

Having decided upon the number of sales staff to employ, an organisation allocates its territories and, in doing so, tries to provide an equal workload for representatives. Salaries might be in the form of basic pay only, basic pay plus commission or commission only.

The role of personal selling has changed considerably in recent years. Despite improvements in database management, changing patterns of distribution and the concentration of purchasing power reducing the size of the workforce, personal selling will continue to play an essential role in providing buyers with goods, services and information to help them to manage their activities for a long time to come.

## CASE STUDY *Telemarketing*

The idea of **telesales** was born in the USA in the 1960s as a fast-action sales tool. When it came to the UK it failed to develop properly and established a poor reputation. This was the first generation of what is now known as **telemarketing**.

As more sophisticated telephone skills developed for research, account servicing and a little less harsh form of prospecting and appointment setting, telemarketing was viewed as being more acceptable. Despite this, it was still reserved for short-term emergency campaigns and was rarely integrated with other direct marketing and selling activities.

The second generation of telemarketing involved spending large amounts of time and money on an exercise which was proving to be a poor investment – much of the information needed to make the system more efficient already lay around in offices on pieces of paper, in card indexes or in the field in the boots of sales representatives' cars. Potentially useful sales information was being wasted, opportunities were lost and more accurate targeting was made impossible.

From this muddle telemarketing's third generation emerged, with the aim of contributing to a database which could then be managed and integrated as part of the organisation's overall promotional mix. Such information was to provide an opportunity to analyse the market and the position of competitors. It was to create a new and more powerful use of the phone to build, maintain and service accounts, whilst at the same time linking with other marketing activities.

A recent report from Datamonitor predicted that telemarketing will be the big growth area in direct marketing. The value of direct marketing will rise from £75 million to £108 million by 1998, an increase of almost 45 per cent. This surge will involve the setting up of a number of 'carelines' which will be able to monitor customer reaction to sales.

So, how might telemarketing sales techniques change over the next few years? The opening up of 'ISDN' lines and the creation of 'multimedia' packages may in the future mean that more selling will be done 'down the lines', with visual packages being presented PC-to-PC. The opportunities are almost limitless. And, of the savings? – Fewer cars on the road and more time spent selling.

**Questions**   1   What are (a) the advantages and (b) the disadvantages of selling in this way?

2   Explain why telemarketing is set to grow.

## Personal selling abroad

After having taken **etiquette** and **customs** into account, personal selling techniques will be roughly similar to those used in the home market. It is very important to identify opportunities to enter new overseas markets, and trade fairs and missions are occasions when selling can take place.

A **trade fair** or **exhibition** is a useful opportunity for an organisation to create a 'shop window' for its goods and services. These events play an important role in many different markets and in many different countries. In Germany, attending such events is deemed a necessity.

Though trade fairs cover many markets at different levels, they are particularly important in organisational markets, when trying to sell to large distributors. They enable potential customers to see the products on offer and, where necessary, to view them being demonstrated. Trade fairs provide for direct contact between existing and potential customers so that personal selling and the maintenance of good relations can take place. They provide a good opportunity

FIGURE 9.6
*Trade fairs are a
good way of meeting
customers*

to group customers together so that their views can be recorded.
There is also a useful opportunity to look at the products of
competitors and improve one's understanding of what is happening
in the market as a whole.

**Missions** are simply exploratory visits to other countries. Providers
of goods or services can explore the possibilities of selling into
international markets by meeting agents, distributors and
prospective customers. They provide first-hand experience of a
market and enable an organisation to set up and develop contacts.

## PUBLIC RELATIONS

**Public relations** or **publicity** encompasses all of the actions of and
communications from an organisation. The forces in an
organisation's external environment are capable of affecting it in a
variety of ways. The forces may be social, economic, political, local
or environmental and could be represented by a variety of groups
such as customers, shareholders, employees and special interest
groups, and by public opinion. Reacting to such elements in a way
that will build a positive image is very important.

The purpose of public relations (PR) is therefore to provide an
external environment for an organisation in which it is popular and
can prosper. Building goodwill in such a way will require sound
organisational performance and behaviour and the communication
of such actions and attitudes to its many publics. Lord Mancroft

once defined PR quite wryly as *'The art of arranging the truth so that people like you.'*

The direct selling of goods and services is not an objective of public relations. Whereas advertising is about relatively short-term objectives, public relations is long-term; it works by sending free messages to various groups through the activities the organisation undertakes in order to improve its reputation and maintain its positive image.

According to Frank Jefkins, PR involves a transfer process which helps to convert the negative feelings of an organisation's many publics into positive ones (Figure 9.7).

FIGURE 9.7
*The PR transfer process*

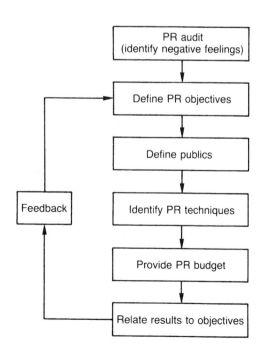

FIGURE 9.8
*Framework for a PR programme*

Public relations can be developed as a strategic device to provide an organisation with a competitive advantage. By identifying the unfavourable attitudes of interest groups and their influence over the external environment, an organisation can develop a **PR strategy** to create a more favourable attitude, to reduce the negative effects, and to build up a more positive profile and image.

One framework for a practical public relations programme is the six-point model shown in Figure 9.8.

**CASE STUDY**   *Where advertising may be bad PR*

Marketing ethical drugs is a complicated business and pharmaceutical companies have had to develop sophisticated ways of communicating their messages though to decision-makers. These decision-makers often include non-medical administrators, health service managers, medical advisors, pharmaceutical advisors, GPs and many other groups.

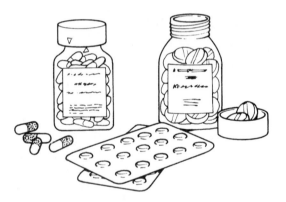

PR strategies targeted at various groups are now an effective way of developing trust and 'building bridges' with customers. PR helps to create awareness of problems, often long-term issues, so that confidence and knowledge is developed before drugs become available. PR is seen as a long-term process which prepares the market. PR events in this industry are also unique. They may include sponsoring conferences or organising satellite links between experts, so that key opinions may be used to educate and debate issues and these filter through to buyers.

Kingston University Business School recently placed PR as the third most important element of the marketing mix for pharmaceutical products. One reason for this is growing cynicism about advertising. The argument is that advertising itself is bad PR for many audiences, whereas PR activities are targeted, more constructive and provide the pharmaceutical companies with greater credibility.

**Questions**  **1**  What are the benefits of using PR rather than advertising?

**2**  Suggest a range of PR activities which could be of use to firms in the pharmaceutical industry.

## Types of public relations activities

**Charitable donations** and **community relations** are good for an organisation's image, often provide lots of good publicity and also help to promote and provide for a good cause.

**Hospitality** at top sporting events is a popular method used by organisations to develop their customer relations. For example, there are opportunities to entertain customers at events such as the FA Cup Final, Wimbledon and the Grand National.

**Press releases** covering events affecting the organisation – such as news stories, export achievements, policy changes, technical developments and anything that enhances the organisation's image – are a useful form of public relations. **Press conferences** are used to cover newsworthy events which are of interest to a variety of media.

**Visits** and **open days** are a popular method of inviting various people to improve their understanding of what an organisation stands for. The Sellafield Visitors Centre, for example, claims to provide a 'window in on the nuclear world' and has become a top tourist attraction in the North West of England (see Figure 9.9).

FIGURE 9.9
*The Sellafield
Visitors Centre
(Source: British
Nuclear Fuels plc)*

227

**Sponsorship** of sporting and cultural events is viewed as a useful opportunity to associate an image with a particular type of function. Examples are the NatWest Trophy, the FA Carling Premiership and the Embassy World Snooker Championship.

**Corporate videotapes** have become increasingly popular over recent years as a method of providing a variety of interested parties with information about company activities.

**Minor product changes** are also good public relations activities. For example, the British Union for the Abolition of Vivisection (BUAV) continually attacks organisations which use animals in the testing of cosmetic, toiletry and household products. Body Shop's reputation has been developed and enhanced by the ways in which it responds to the views of outside bodies in its eco-virtuous approach to bodycare products.

**Magazines**, **publicity literature** and **education services**, in both the private and public sectors, provide strong informed links between organisations and their various publics. For example, most organisations will send out magazines and brochures in response to enquiries in order to indicate what their functions, beliefs and activities are.

Other PR activities have included clubs (the Severn Valley Railway recently set up a club for its younger users), staging of events, appearances on TV, awards, competitions, hot air balloons as well as anything which serves to maintain interest and support for an organisation's activities.

## ASSIGNMENT

Imagine that you have been asked to advise the organisation you either work for or attend on its public relations strategies.

**Task a**   Identify and list all the negative views/feelings that people may have about the organisation.

**Task b**   Given the above, explain what would be the objectives of your PR campaign. In your answer explain all the benefits it could bring to the organisation.

**Task c**   identify all the different groups or 'publics' at whom the PR campaign should be directed.

**Task d**   Suggest and then describe in detail a range of PR activities which would help to meet the identified objectives.

**Task e**   Estimate the possible cost of your campaign.

**Task f**   What results would you expect? Over what period would you expect these results? How would you assess the results?

**Task g**   Explain why your campaign would be worthwhile (or alternatively, why it would *not* be cost-effective).

# CHAPTER
# 10
# International Marketing

When you buy goods, do you look to see where they were made? Have you ever thought about who made the goods you buy and why they have been brought to your country? Think about all of the distribution procedures that may have taken place before such goods arrive in your high street. International marketing makes this process possible.

> International marketing involves the marketing of products in two or more countries.

In some circumstances international marketing will involve trade between one company and customers in just one other country, while at the other extreme a company may sell in many countries and manufacture in many others (see Figure 10.1).

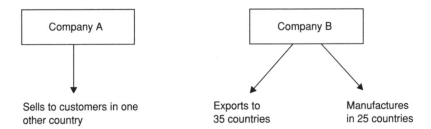

FIGURE 10.1
*Two extremes of
international
marketing*

The key element of international marketing is that it focuses on the differences between selling domestically and selling overseas. In doing so it emphasises the need to understand, develop and then tailor the marketing mix to the requirements of different overseas markets.

## THE NEED TO TRADE INTERNATIONALLY

Imagine what it would be like to live in a country that did not trade with its neighbours. The goods and services which we take for granted today would not be available. Domestic companies would be small because they would not be able to specialise and export their wares overseas. If we measured our standard of living in terms of variety of goods and services, it would be extremely poor.

In an increasingly interdependent world, international trade is an economic necessity. We are not self-sufficient and are therefore dependent upon the imports of raw materials and products from other countries. Exporting overseas helps to maintain our standard of living by making importing possible.

Many companies first enter an overseas markets by chance – they may receive a single foreign order and then decide to follow it up. Trading overseas may then help them to achieve growth, particularly if the domestic market is static or mature. It may also allow them to use up their surplus capacity or to reduce dependence upon the fortunes of a single market and so allow them to spread their risks.

Expanding output into overseas markets enables organisations to benefit from greater **economies of scale**. This means that over a larger output, costs per unit are reduced and provide the supplier with a competitive advantage.

Another reason for trading internationally is in response to **competitive activities**. For example, intense competition in home markets may encourage an organisation to seek markets overseas. Alternatively, where markets are dominated by companies who trade on an international basis, the only way to compete with them may be to trade internationally as well.

Opportunities overseas might arise in **developing countries** where the goods or services produced by organisations in more developed countries are in demand. Sometimes a number of economic benefits such as cheaper labour costs may exist in other countries, which may make it worthwhile producing there. Hong Kong and Taiwan have proved to be attractive places for overseas investment.

Setting up manufacturing units overseas is sometimes called **economic imperialism**. Many of the goods and services we use every day in this country are either from overseas or are produced by overseas subsidiaries which are household names in this country. For example, Ford, Procter & Gamble, Heinz and IBM are primarily American companies. BP, ICI, Glaxo and British Airways probably have a similar effect in countries in other parts of the world.

Many companies trade overseas so that they can sell on discontinued products or seconds without having to sell them cheaply in the home market.

Finally, it may not just be the overseas marketing opportunity which encourages international trade. Often the rules, regulations and economic conditions such as tax benefits and changing currency values within other countries may provide businesses with useful opportunities to prosper from trading links.

## CASE STUDY · *Dell seeks a competitive advantage*

As profit margins in the tough personal computer (PC) market have become slimmer over the last few years, manufacturers such as Dell have been seeking imaginative ways of trimming costs and gaining competitive advantages. Competition in the small-office/home sector of the market has been particularly fierce and many manufacturers are only making about £50 on each computer sold. Sales and support costs in this sector are very high as many buyers need help to use their computers. The solution for Dell Computer Corporation, the American manufacturer, has been to centralise its operations in Europe.

The personal computers that Dell sells throughout Europe are already manufactured in the Irish Republic. Now the company has relocated its support staff and telesales there too.

The Irish operation employs 270 staff. Most have been locally recruited and intensively trained. The company found little difficulty attracting potential recruits from the Irish Republic's pool of unemployed graduates and salary levels are lower than in many other countries. In addition the European Union and the Irish government made substantial grant aid available to Dell. All of this has helped Dell to make huge cost savings which enables the company to compete more effectively in the European marketplace.

**Questions**
1  What benefits does Dell gain from manufacturing overseas?
2  Explain how the marketing of products in Europe may differ from the marketing of products in the USA.

## DIFFERENCES BETWEEN DOMESTIC AND INTERNATIONAL MARKETING

International marketing involves recognising that people all over the world have different needs. Organisations must accept that differences in values, customs, languages and currencies will mean that many products will only suit certain countries and there is rarely such a thing as a **global market**, but rather a number of different foreign markets.

Catering for such differences involves greater risk. Developing products for different overseas markets and also being aware of the changes in currency prices requires careful planning and research. Difficulties are also likely to be encountered when competing with another nation's domestic producers in their own home territory as well as other organisations internationally marketing their products and services. No organisation can hope to be successful unless all its key functions are **integrated** and developed so that the new and unfamiliar elements are provided for effectively.

Before trading overseas, an organisation must develop a thorough understanding of the other country. This involves discovering their policies towards organisations overseas. The organisation will need to be clear about **trade barriers**, such as tariffs or quotas which might restrict the flow of products across borders, and the extent to which home manufacturers are protected against foreign competition. It will also require detailed knowledge of the different legal and financial regulations of the other country; this could involve employing specialist agencies to deal with the various bureaucratic requirements of such markets. Understanding the marketing and distribution **structures** is vital so that organisations can develop a strategy to sell their goods and services.

**Consumer behaviour, culture**, and **customs** vary throughout the world. Patterns of demand will be determined by areas such as life-styles, incomes, use of credit, family and religion. For example, exporting alcohol-based products to Islamic countries would be totally inappropriate. By understanding such influences an organisation can develop its products to make them more relevant to the inhabitants of a particular country.

**Communication systems** differ widely throughout the world. It may be possible to contact representatives easily in the capital of another country but not in other cities and towns. Such a lack of communication may make it difficult to control goods in transit or keep in touch with representatives and channels of distribution. Business activities require written and spoken communication which will influence promotional strategies; for instance, where there is a low level of literacy, television may be an important form of media. Language difficulties might also present a problem, particularly if several languages are spoken in the same country.

A number of economic factors may influence trade overseas, not least the ability of customers to pay for the goods or services they require.

A country's economic wellbeing and guarantees of payment will play an important role in its ability to trade. The use of different currencies makes the process more complicated. If payment from local currency is unacceptable, then trading may depend on the use of foreign currency reserves. Often many developing countries will not be able to earn enough foreign currency to buy in the goods and services they require to satisfy their needs. Counter-trading may be an alternative whereby imports of goods may be exchanged for other goods – for example, imports of cars might be exchanged for coffee. Recent developments in eastern Europe have seen a marked increase in counter-trading.

Transactions overseas depend on the **value of the currency** involved. Currencies are subject to fluctuations in their value against other currencies. For example, the relationship of the yen to the dollar may vary from one day to the next because of the changes in demand and supply of the two currencies. If the pound falls in value, this makes British goods cheaper overseas, and this will determine an organisation's income and therefore the profitability of a transaction overseas.

Trading overseas also involves an assessment of **political risks and events** which might affect an organisation's activities. An unstable regime may create an environment which damages trade and results in a lost investment.

International marketing therefore involves more than simply making goods or services available to people in other countries. It requires an understanding of all the areas mentioned and many more. There may be **protocols** to follow, such as diplomatic channels or negotiations between senior managers and directors. Catering for an overseas market and all its demands will involve considerable organisation to cope with such activities.

### Problems involved in international marketing

Marketing goods and services in other countries is rarely an easy process. Shipping costs, tariffs and legal regulations, credit risks and the high costs of adapting goods to suit the needs of different groups of consumers may cause certain problems. At the same time, there may be strong preferences for home-produced products and this may also make it difficult to enter and develop within these markets.

The benefits, however, from entering these markets, despite the many problems and risks, may be so great as to make the whole process of international marketing worthwhile.

## FREE TRADE

Many people believe that 'free trade' will help organisations to trade widely overseas and that **international specialisation** will maximise **economic welfare** of the world as a whole.

The European Union (EU) stands to gain enormously from the freeing of world trade. A study in 1993 by the Organisation for Economic Cooperation and Development (OECD) and the World Bank showed that the EU would make a gain of 1.4 per cent of its national income in the year 2000, after the Uruguay round of the GATT talks succeed, whereas Japan would gain 0.9 per cent and the USA only 0.2 per cent (see below). These benefits would be gained because without tariffs and subsidies the countries and regions of the world could concentrate on making the things they produce best. For example, China is a leading manufacturer of soft toys, the USA and Japan are leaders in computers, and Germany is the largest manufacturer of hi-tech machine tools (see Figure 10.2).

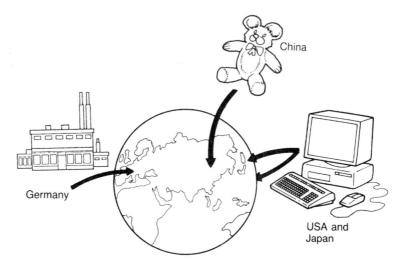

FIGURE 10.2
*Examples of
international
specialisation*

The **General Agreement on Tariffs and Trade** (GATT) was created in 1947. It operates on three levels:

- as a set of trading rules

- as an international agency for helping to resolve trade disputes

235

> • as a means of getting countries together to create free trade and to cut down existing barriers.

At the end of 1993 there were 112 nation members of GATT accounting for 90 per cent of the world's trade. With Russia and China joining the new **Multilateral Trade Organisation** (see below), this has been extended to nearly all of the world's trade.

With the completion of the Uruguay round (a round of talks which started in 1986, the eighth such round of reductions in barriers since 1947) the Multilateral Trade Organisation came into being to replace GATT. The MTO is in effect a powerful umbrella organisation.

FIGURE 10.3
*The MTO – a powerful umbrella organisation*

In the 1990s, world politics and alliances are changing rapidly. Today world trading patterns are dominated by huge internal markets such as:

- the Single European Market
- the North American Free Trade Area (NAFTA)
- the Association of South East Asian Nations (ASEAN).

Each of these markets is made up of millions of consumers.

**CASE STUDY** *The creation of the EEA*

An agreement creating an 18-country Single Market stretching from the Arctic to the Mediterranean came into effect on 1 January 1994. Billed as Europe's answer to NAFTA, the North American free trade agreement that links Canada, the United States and Mexico, the European Economic Area (EEA) has finally arrived.

The agreement linking 372 million consumers was the product of an offer made by Commission President Jacques Delors to include EFTA countries in the European Union's Single Market programme. The deal was, however, held back by Switzerland's 'No' vote in a referendum in December 1992. Negotiations quickly set out to remove Switzerland from the deal and replace it with Liechtenstein which had voted 'Yes' to the EEA.

Liechtenstein is expected to join in July 1994. EFTA's other EEA members – Austria, Finland, Sweden, Norway and Iceland – have offered to make up Liechtenstein's contribution to the new EEA Cohesion Fund. The plan is to compensate the EU's poorest members for incorporating the richer EFTA states.

**Questions**

1 What benefits might many British manufacturers receive from the setting up of the EEA?

2 How will consumers gain from the creation of the EEA?

3 Why do you think that many Swiss voters were not in favour of the EEA?

# ENTERING OVERSEAS MARKETS

Before entering an overseas market, particularly for the first time, an organisation has to consider carefully its mode of entry into that market. There are three main methods of market entry:

- *indirect exporting,* where sales are made to an intermediary who then proceeds to resell to customers overseas
- *direct exporting,* where the company sells direct to customers overseas

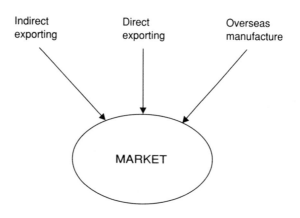

FIGURE 10.4
*Three routes to market entry*

237

- *overseas manufacture*, which might be in the form of a joint venture or the establishment of a wholly owned subsidiary abroad.

## Indirect exporting

Many organisations first venture into the field of international marketing through an **export house**. An export house is not a manufacturer but an organisation whose main activity is the handling or the financing of export trade. Export houses have links throughout the world and play a prominent role in promoting exports and providing valuable knowledge and experience for manufacturers and suppliers. By undertaking this function, export houses enable organisations to enter overseas markets without having to invest in the costly financial and administrative procedures required to cater for customers abroad.

For example, an export house can act as a **merchant** by buying in the home market and re-selling in the export market, and accepting the risks of loss in the search for profit. It may also act as a **manufacturer's or supplier's agent** and hold the sole rights for the promotion and sale of products overseas on an agency basis. Export houses often act as an **export department** and market overseas in the name of manufacturers or suppliers and sometimes bear the credit risk. They might also act as **buyer's agents** on behalf of an overseas buyer and, in doing so, accept responsibility for payment. Other specialist functions include acting as a **confirming house** and assuming responsibility to the organisation exporting for the payment of trade debts, as well as arranging shipping, insurance, finance and credit whenever required.

The export house helps to provide a well-integrated link in the chain of distribution between the UK supplier and the foreign buyer and may act as a stockist or distributor. Doing so enables organisations to broaden their horizons without having to invest in specialist and costly administration.

## Direct exporting

**Direct exporting** involves manufacturers or suppliers shipping their products overseas and selling their wares directly to their customers using their own personnel. This means establishing offices abroad, employing staff to monitor operations and the constant study of overseas trading restrictions. This will require considerable investment in time, money and staff as, even on a limited scale, direct exporting calls for specialised administration or shipping procedures, freight and insurance rates, modes of transport, restrictions, licensing regulations, exchange control procedures, packing regulations and so on.

### Overseas manufacture

Many companies, particularly those who produce bulky products such as beers or carbonated drinks, choose to manufacture overseas rather than export their goods. There are many reasons for this.

Firstly, by locating abroad they are actually established in the overseas market, and this can help them to understand more closely the needs and requirements of foreign customers. Secondly, in many countries production costs are lower. Thirdly, manufacture overseas may overcome the effects of barriers to market entry, such as tariffs.

There are a number of different forms of overseas manufacture. **Joint ventures** exist where two or more firms join forces to make products overseas. Many governments encourage joint ventures with indigenous firms because this means that overseas investors are then helping domestic companies. Sometimes joint ventures involve **licensing** or **franchising**. A licence may be a commercial contract which allows an overseas manufacturer to produce goods or services using a patent or brand name. A franchise is a form of licence that specifies in detail what the franchisee can or cannot do. For example, Pepsi Cola is produced under franchise agreements in different countries.

Establishing a **wholly owned production facility** demonstrates a firm commitment to the overseas market. In doing so an organisation may buy an established or growing company or manufacturing facility overseas or, alternatively, may start from scratch. Toyota and Nissan have made such commitments in the UK. The great benefit of doing this is that organisations retain their independence.

---

## STANDARDISATION OR ADAPTATION?

Just as the marketing environment has to be assessed at home, the overseas potential of markets has to be carefully scrutinised. Finding relevant information might be more difficult, so that it takes longer to build up a knowledge of the territory. The potential market size, degree and type of competition, prices, promotional differences, product differences as well as barriers to trade have to be analysed alongside the cost-effectiveness of various types of transportation. The organisation then has to assess the scale of the investment and consider both short- and long-term targets for an adequate return. A well-constructed strategy will enable the organisation to identify the markets which offer the best financial returns and provide it with a careful assessment of the risks.

Before becoming involved in exporting, an organisation must find the answers to two questions:

> ● Is there a market for the product?
> ● How far will it need to be adapted for overseas markets?

The product must possess characteristics that make it acceptable for the market – these may be features like size, shape, design, performance and even colour. For example, red is a popular colour in Chinese-speaking areas. Organisations also have to consider different languages, customs, and health and safety regulations.

If a company offers a product which is *undifferentiated* between any of the markets to which it is offered, then **standardisation** is taking place (see Figure 10.5). The great benefit of standardisation is the ability to compete with low costs over a large output.

FIGURE 10.5
*Using a standardised product and mix*

In most markets, however, there are many barriers to standardisation. It is not difficult to think about the standard marketing mix for a product and how this might vary from one country to another. For example:

● *Product* – Tastes and habits differ between markets.
● *Price* – Consumers have different incomes.
● *Place* – Systems of distribution vary widely.
● · *Promotion* – Consumers' media habits vary, as do language and levels of literacy.

With *differentiated* marketing, on the other hand, an organisation will, by segmenting its overseas markets, offer a marketing mix to meet the needs of each of its markets (see Figure 10.6).

The great benefit of standardisation is that costs are lowered, profitability is increased and the task of supplying different markets

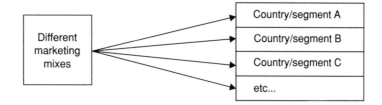

FIGURE 10.6
*Adapting the marketing mix to meet the needs of each market*

becomes substantially easier. However, others would argue that the success of many products in international markets has come about because marketers have successfully adapted their marketing mix to meet local needs.

To a large extent the **standardisation/adaptation dilemma** depends upon an organisation's individual view of its overseas markets and the degree to which it is prepared to commit itself to meeting the needs of overseas customers. Three different types of approach to this are usually quoted (see Figure 10.7):

- *Polycentrism* – With this approach to markets, organisations usually establish subsidiaries, with their own objectives and marketing policies which are decentralised from the parent company. Adaptation takes place in every market using different mixes to satisfy customer requirements.
- *Ethnocentrism* – Overseas operations are considered to be of little importance. Plans for overseas markets are developed at home. There is little research, the marketing mix is standardised and there is no real attention to different customer needs and requirements in each market.
- *Geocentrism* – Standardisation takes place wherever possible and adaptation takes place where necessary.

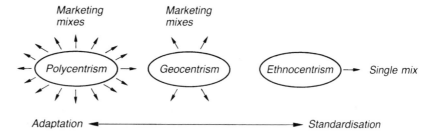

FIGURE 10.7
*Polycentrism versus ethnocentrism*

**CASE STUDY** *Harmonising brands*

Today, it is no longer possible to buy a Marathon chocolate bar. The UK's fourth favourite chocolate bar has been renamed Snickers. This was done to fall in line with Mars' global branding strategy as Snickers was known in every market except the UK.

Many other companies are harmonising brands across Europe. For example, Unilever's Radion washing powder is now identical in most European markets. Such global branding allows economies of scale, enables production to be standardised, and saves on advertising costs because the same images can be used with different words.

Today, greater care needs to be taken when establishing new brands to ensure they have the potential to be successful on an international basis. Denmark's Plopp chocolate would probably not be well received in this country. Apparently Fairy Liquid would raise eyebrows in the USA, and Irish Mist liqueur has a problem in Germany where *Mist* translates to manure! A brand name is therefore something which cannot be ignored.

In a recent survey across Europe, IBM – an American company – was judged to have the most successful pan-European identity ahead of Philips, Mercedes-Benz and Shell. This is probably because IBM is rarely thought of as being American but is seen as local wherever its products are sold. Modern companies are increasingly aware of the need to build core values to meet common needs in all of their main markets.

**Questions**

1   Make a list of brand names which you think have a good pan-European identity. Explain why these goods have this sort of identity.

2   What benefits does an organisation gain from a more standard approach to its markets?

3   To what extent does the consumer 'lose out' when organisations adopt a more standardised approach to their marketing?

## THE DEPARTMENT FOR ENTERPRISE

The UK government provides a range of services designed to help organisations to make the most of business opportunities overseas.

- The *Export Market Information Centre* (EMIC) is a self-help information service for organisations wishing to research a market. It provides statistics such as patterns of trade, production, employment and market reports. A search service may be used to select on-line commercial databases.

- The *Export Marketing Research Scheme* (EMRS) provides professional advice and offers financial support for marketing research studies overseas.
- *Export intelligence* receives information from Diplomatic Service Posts about sources of new opportunities for businesses.
- The department will put an organisation in touch with a *specialist* who will tailor market information to their requirements.
- *Representation* through government departmental representatives will draw upon local contacts and expertise.
- *Other services* include trade missions, trade fairs, seminar support and published information and help.

## CASE STUDY *Is exporting for me?*

The following is adapted from *Trading in Europe*, a DTI publication.

With the whole of Europe as your home market, commitment to customers and consistency in meeting their requirements are no longer a luxury but a necessity.

You will need to give your product and your sales effort as much support as you would in the UK. Look, for example, at the number of sales representatives you employ to cover the UK, and then consider how many you would need to cover other parts of Europe properly. France, for example, is geographically two and a half times the size of the UK. Quite often a company expects big results from a small sales force. If you have limited resources, it may be better to choose one key market (or even one key customer) and concentrate your attention there.

Remember that you may also face increased competition in the British market as other European countries compete to sieze their new opportunities.

To sell to other European countries involves four basic challenges:

- *Adequate management resources* – Successful export marketing requires the near-constant involvement of senior management not just in making decisions, but in making contacts with representatives and customers.
- *Adequate staff resources* – Exporting means more paperwork and more correspondence, much of it in foreign languages. Some of this can be contracted out but even these activities will need careful supervision.
- *Adequate production capacity and flexibility* – The object of export marketing is to obtain extra orders. Have you the capacity to fulfil them

and the flexibility to incorporate the modifications that may well be required in order to meet the needs of different markets?

- *Access to adequate finance* – Laying in extra raw materials, extra packaging, insurance and freight charges, and the longer periods often required to realise payment for overseas orders, will put extra strains on your cash flow. Can you obtain the necessary bridging finance? And can you support other extra activities such as research?

**Questions**
1   What are the main costs of extending your market overseas?
2   Identify and then describe three priorities for overseas markets.
3   What type of business will be less well placed to extend its markets overseas?

## PLANNING AND CONTROL IN INTERNATIONAL MARKETS

Planning for international markets is a much more complex process than for domestic markets. However, as international marketing is only one part of an organisation's total marketing efforts, international marketing planning is likely to be viewed as more tactical and operational rather than strategic. Good planning is very important as it allows decision-makers to analyse the effectiveness of policies which they have developed.

As well as many of the usual ingredients of a marketing plan, an international marketing plan should:

- constantly analyse developments in the international marketing environment
- review an organisation's overseas performance by market, parts of market and by region
- analyse how strengths have been utilised and opportunities developed as well as how threats have been minimised and weaknesses corrected
- relate decisions made to overseas marketing objectives
- indicate how marketing programmes have been coordinated and show budgeted costs.

One model for international marketing is shown in Figure 10.8.

The **screening process** helps an organisation to analyse how it can benefit from entry into each market. It will use screening *criteria* against which to measure the returns to be expected from each market. This will help it to:

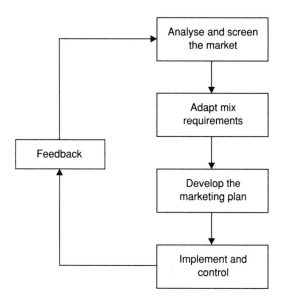

FIGURE 10.8
*A model for international marketing planning*

- identify the best overseas opportunities
- assess the potential of each market
- determine the extent of research required
- show how the mix should be adapted.

**Adapting the mix requirements** involves analysing how the mix should be developed for each market. If a mix requires too much adaptation it may be that entry into that market will not be profitable.

The **marketing plan** will include all of the usual details included in such a plan (see Chapter 4).

The planning process has to include the step when the plan is **implemented**. Finally, **control** is the step of checking that the plan meets the goals and objectives identified so that performance can then be evaluated. If the actual performance diverges widely from planned performance, then action to change the marketing activities will be required.

**ASSIGNMENT**

The Oxfordshire-based company Air Boss Ground Engagement has recently developed long-lasting tyres for the construction industry. At its factory in Didcot, Air Boss is manufacturing a puncture-proof alternative to pneumatic tyres, made from hollow chevron-shaped segments bolted on to a steel rim. The tyres simply cannot deflate and segments of tyre can be replaced where necessary.

Andrew Helby, the MD of Air Boss, feels that the idea for the wheel would not have got off the ground were it not for the European Single Market. The tyre might not have been granted a licence without access to the whole of the European Union market. The Single Market means that the company has access to hundreds of millions of end-users.

Since Air Boss was launched in 1991 it has tested tyres in the UK market and developed connections with Germany, France and Italy. During this time the new ideas have won awards at exhibitions – including the largest construction exhibition, BAUMA, in Germany where the tyres attracted so much attention that the Air Boss exhibitors ran out of brochures.

The first step Air Boss took to enter the European market was to undertake market research. Market intelligence was supplied by the London-based Corporate Intelligence Group, who were able to provide information on sales of tyres by country and type of vehicle. This led to an immediate assault on the German market. At the same time discussions took place with potential agents in France and Italy.

In each case Air Boss decided to work with established distribution outlets. Overseas sales and marketing teams were set up to work with their chosen distributors. German, French and Italian speakers were recruited for the teams and promotional materials were translated into relevant languages. A quality engineer was employed to keep a watching brief on common product specifications, testing procedures and European directives which apply to the company's products.

Over the next few years it is envisaged that 90 per cent of Air Boss' sales will be made in Europe. It is thought that 30 per cent of these will go to Germany and 20 per cent each to Italy and France. At the same time, markets will be developed in other European countries. With such an approach the Air Boss business plan forecasts that the company will become a multi-million pound operation.

Imagine that you are a marketing assistant to the Marketing Manager and have been asked to prepare notes on the following topics to help the manager give a talk at a conference in London.

**Task a** Make a list of the advantages which Air Boss gains from trading overseas.

**Task b** Explain why Air Boss undertook extensive market research before entering the European market. Describe briefly the sort of research likely to have been undertaken.

**Task c** Describe the ways in which the marketing of products around Europe is different from the marketing of products within the UK.

# Responsible Marketing

Business organisations have a prime responsibility to serve their **stakeholders**. These are the individuals and groups who have a stake in the running of the organisation, and in the consequences of organisational activities. Frequently they will have shared **expectations** based on the wellbeing of the organisation. For example, the stakeholders in a large public company include shareholders, managers, banks, unions etc. (see Figure 11.1).

FIGURE 11.1
*Stakeholders*

Shareholders  Managers

Banks

Examples of stakeholders in a
public limited company

Employees

Trade unions

(What other stakeholders
can you think of?)

Whilst most stakeholders will share common expectations, there will be other areas over which disputes arise. Furthermore, expectations can change with time.

Within an organisation, **coalitions** develop between groups of stakeholders (e.g. between managers and shareholders). Most people who work for an organisation will be a member of more than one coalition. For example, there might be a coalition between departments in an organisation, between individuals at the same level in the management structure etc. In an organisation which operates in international markets, these coalitions of stakeholders will be extremely complex (e.g. between unions in different countries, between groups of shareholders, between managers in different national groupings).

The business organisation operates within an external environment which shapes many of its activities. The organisation therefore needs to have a clear understanding of its **social, political, economic and physical environment**.

A modern organisation is fundamentally concerned with the three Cs of business – costs, customers and competitors (Figure 11.2).

FIGURE 11.2
*The three Cs of
business*

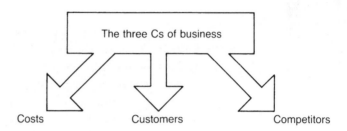

The three Cs of business

Costs          Customers          Competitors

FIGURE 11.2
*The three Cs of
business*

However, it is unacceptable for a modern organisation to ignore the impact of its activities on the wider community. The society in which a business operates should be seen as a very important additional stakeholder. At the same time, business should be seen as a key stakeholder in the prosperity of the wider community.

**Responsible marketing** is therefore based on having an **ethical approach** to business. Responsible marketing means developing a marketing strategy based on responsibility to all of an organisation's stakeholders, including the wider community.

Today many people recognise that development can only be beneficial if it takes into consideration community losses as well as profits. Organisations therefore need to consider carefully how they can strike a balance.

---

## CASE STUDY  *The Co-operative Bank*

In May 1992 the Co-operative Bank announced its new strategy of only taking deposits from and offering financial services to organisations that were not involved in controversial activities, including factory farming, blood sports, production of animal fur, the manufacture of tobacco and the oppression of the human spirit.

Before finalising its new policy it carried out market research on 30 000 of its customers to find out their views. It only put into the policy issues on which it had at least 60 per cent agreement.

The bank believes that it is necessary to have a stance, to show to the public that it is an ethical banker. The Co-op Bank does not hide the fact that its ethical stance is likely to encourage new customers.

**Questions**  1  Is the Co-op Bank's ethical policy market- or product-led?

**2** To what extent is the Co-op Bank's policy based on responsible marketing?

**3** Who are the main stakeholders in the Bank?

**4** Are all stakeholders likely to regard the ethical policy as a good strategy?

**5** Are all businesses likely to develop such ethical policies?

## ENVIRONMENTALISM

Today a company's **environmental performance** is increasingly central to its competitiveness and survival. The following illustrations give a very stark warning to businesses that fail to take environmental action:

- One of the world's largest paper-producing companies committed a minor, technical environmental violation in the American state of Maine. In May 1992 the US government imposed *a three-year ban on government paper purchases from the company*.
- The German government's privatisation programme in the Bitterfield region of the former East Germany ground to a halt when western investors concerned about environmental clean-up costs *were unwilling to buy shares in a single business*.
- An American bank foreclosed on a $1 million building mortgage, thereby becoming the legal owner of the property. However, it also inherited an *environmental clean-up bill of $2 million*.

**CASE STUDY** *Why develop an environmental strategy?*

Sir John Collins, the Chairman of Shell UK, recently made the following comments on this subject:

'We recently carried out a survey of 100 British companies active in the environmental area – doing such things as environmental audits, waste recycling, energy management, emission control and site improvement. We asked why they took these initiatives.

Some two-thirds believed there was a direct financial benefit – in saved costs or increased profitability. Another important set of reasons involved "reputation" and the resulting better relations with regulators, local communities and staff. A quarter mentioned "competitive advantage" and a substantial number "survival" – by meeting customer requirements or making essential financial savings. Better management of energy and other resources, waste control and recycling are obvious routes to profitable environmental improvement.

The question of environmental "image" is important. Hard-pressed business people may feel that it is less so than the financial bottom line. But we all depend on a "licence to operate" from the community. If our reputation is poor – business in general, a particular industry, or a company – profits will certainly suffer in the long run. Regulators will treat us with suspicion, we will lose customer and employee loyalty and legislators will no longer accept our views. And, by "image" I don't mean just a cosmetic one. Good communication is always important but reputation, in the environmental field as in all others, depends on being seen to be taking concrete measures to improve performance.

Competitive advantage is something business people must always pursue – our competitors surely do. I am convinced that environmental improvement offers many opportunities. We all know businesses that have harnessed the power of green consumerism. Again, it is an area where developing opportunities may require ingenuity.

Finally, the question of "survival". The survey mentioned the growing tendency for companies to require their suppliers to match certain environmental standards. This obviously creates great problems for those ill-prepared – but offers the opportunity for those in advance to push their higher standards.'

**Questions**  1  How do the reasons for environmental concern outlined by the survey fit with the three Cs of business – cost, competitors and consumers?
2  Is it sound business sense to build environmental concern into marketing strategy?
3  What is competitive advantage? How can this be achieved through responsible marketing?
4  Are some businesses better equipped to incorporate environmental concern into their marketing strategy?
5  What do you think Sir John Collins meant by 'a licence to operate'? What are the implications in terms of pleasing stakeholders in an organisation?

In July 1993, the UK government identified **seven major environmental sins** leading to the unsustainable use of resources.

These are:

- Emission of carbon dioxide from burning coal, oil and gas
- Worsening local air-pollution, caused mainly by increasing emissions from road transport
- The rising demand for water, threatening to dry out streams
- Water pollution caused by farming, sewage, industry and acid rain
- Loss of countryside to roads, homes and other development
- Damage to habitats and loss of wildlife
- Rising demand for sand, gravel and rock quarries and pits which harm wildlife, landscapes and communities.

A national strategy for sustainable development clearly involves taking action in each of these areas.

A survey of the Annual Reports of the UK's 100 largest companies was carried out by Dr Shailendra Vyakarnam to find out what they were doing about the environment. Dr Vyakarnam breaks down their actions into two main categories:

- *socially responsible actions* which have a direct bearing on the nature of business carried out by a company (e.g. investment in the reduction of toxic emissions by a heavy industrial company)
- *charitable donations and sponsorship* which bear no direct relation to the company's business, and fulfil a useful public relations function for the company concerned as well as benefiting the recipients.

As an example of the second category, Tate & Lyle match employees' contributions to a rain-forest conservation programme. Dr Vyakarman concludes by saying that:

'the charitable donations being made by the companies are clearly based on the principle that charity begins at home, rather than one where it needs to be targeted at the most needy. It seems that the companies are doing things which are right for them, in terms of a strategic fit, whether it is donations, links with education and training, recycling of materials or the use of unleaded (and cheaper) fuel for a large fleet of cars.'

The **environmental lobby** works hand-in-hand with the **consumer movement** to provide protection against some of the excesses of the industrial and commercial world. Many environmental groups (such as Greenpeace) are organised at an international level and have strategies based on integrated worldwide action. These organisations serve to remind firms that they create *external costs* which go beyond their balance sheets. These costs are sometimes known as **externalities** or **spillover costs**:

> **Externalities = social costs − private costs**

At the end of the day, organisations will probably be more interested in weighing up decision-making using their private costs, but will be forced to assess the fuller implications in order to use resources in a more socially acceptable way.

## Pollution

The most obvious social cost of business activity is **pollution**. Many heavy industrial plants choose locations near canals, rivers and the sea so that they can use water in the manufacturing process and pour out effluent into the rivers and the sea. In some countries, firms are charged heavily for causing **water pollution**.

**Air pollution** was highlighted by several horrifying events of the 1980s. In December 1984, the leak of poisonous gas from the Union Carbide plant in Bhopal, India, killed more than 2000 people and at least ten times that number suffered from severe respiratory and eye complications. Even more dramatic – and potentially catastrophic – were the events at the Chernobyl nuclear reactor in Russia in 1986 where wide tracts of land were made uninhabitable and a cloud of nuclear waste was carried airborne across Europe by the release of nuclear material. Emissions from UK plants are said by some to contribute to acid rain which has devastated forests in Scandinavia and Germany – half of the Black Forest has been designated 'a total damage area'. (However, it is also important to point out that a number of scientists argue that the destruction of forest lands may also be as a result of natural processes.)

## The industrial response to environmental issues

Dereliction, traffic congestion, long-term waste and noise are other external effects of business activities which influence the wider environment and determine how organisations are perceived.

At the same time businesses have to be careful about what they produce. For example, what types of additives should go into food and drink? How should the products be tested? Should animals be used in the tests? What use should be made of wood and plastics? The more an organisation analyses environmental issues, the more it is likely to be faced by competing interests.

## CASE STUDY  *An environmental projects department*

In 1986, Body Shop set up an Environmental Projects Department with the responsibility to:

- oversee and coordinate Body Shop's campaigning
- ensure that the company's products and practices are environmentally sound
- check that everything in the product range fulfils the organisation's commitment to customers and that products do not waste energy in production or disposal
- stop unnecessary waste
- make sure that the company does not use materials from threatened species or threatened environments
- avoid practices involving cruelty to animals
- avoid practices which harm other countries, particularly in the developing world.

> # AGAINST
>
> # **ANIMAL**
>
> # TESTING

Body Shop produced a twelve-page environmental leaflet, the first of a series called *Issues*, which set out the arguments for and against using animals to test cosmetics and putting over the organisation's view that it was cruel or unnecessary. These leaflets were printed in millions and distributed through Body Shop outlets throughout the world. Body Shop made it clear that it only tested its products on people who were volunteers either working for the organisation or for Animal Aid. They contrasted this with some of the practices in other parts of the cosmetics industry – like force-feeding lipstick to rats and mice until they died to measure toxicity, and dropping shampoo into the eyes of a conscious rabbit restrained in stocks for seven days.

**Questions**
1. What are the key ingredients of Body Shop's marketing strategy?
2. How did the creation of Body Shop's environmental projects department support the organisation's marketing strategy?
3. How important is it for Body Shop to oppose testing on animals?
4. Why is Body Shop's marketing stance likely to give it a competitive advantage?

### Balancing internal and external expectations

Internally, a business needs to make a profit for shareholders, managers, employees and other stakeholders who have to be content with the way the organisation is run.

Externally, the business has to contend with selling products in the face of competition and the regulatory influences exerted by governments and the pressures from a variety of other interdependent factors. Failing to take heed of organised pressure groups such as Friends of the Earth, the National Anti-Vivisection Society and Greenpeace may lead to the worst possible outcome – a consumer boycott perhaps on an international scale.

In today's more discriminating world, many consumers are genuinely concerned about whether or not dolphins are killed in tuna fish nets or that products are cruelty-free. In fact many consumers develop a sense of purpose and satisfaction at making a contribution to improve the world they live in.

At the same time governments have made international undertakings to work towards sustainable patterns of growth. The Rio summit of world governments in 1992 committed countries to developing sustainable patterns of economic growth with widespread implications for everything from trade policy to electricity generation, from shopping to motoring. In late January 1994, the UK government published its response in setting out ways of creating sustainable growth – reconciling economic growth with protection of the environment and natural resources for future generations; controlling rising emissions of man-made climate-changing gases; protecting the richness and diversity of wild plant and animal species; and conserving and expanding the nation's forests (see Figure 11.3).

There is a strong argument for all organisations today to seek the strategic imperative of **conservation**, at a local, a national and an international level. Modern products frequently depend on non-renewable resources, and many people are worried about how quickly they are being used up. In the past it was possible to have an emphasis on the present at the expense of the future; today it is becoming more important to balance the present with the future.

**Recycling of resources** provides one opportunity. For example, there is a strong case for recycling glass, on both environmental and financial grounds. Recycled glass melts at a much lower temperature than the raw materials of new glass. Less energy is required to collect, process and deliver the glass from a well-organised recycling

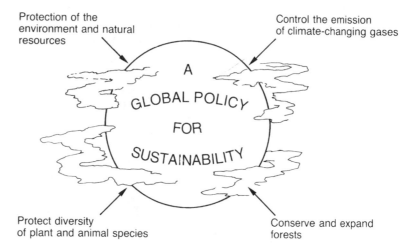

Protection of the environment and natural resources

Control the emission of climate-changing gases

A GLOBAL POLICY FOR SUSTAINABILITY

Protect diversity of plant and animal species

Conserve and expand forests

FIGURE 11.3
*A global policy for sustainability*

scheme than to produce and deliver an equivalent amount of raw materials. To make 1 tonne of new glass requires 12 tonnes of raw materials, or just 1 tonne of broken glass (known as cullet). In all, each tonne of cullet added to the furnace means savings of about 30 gallons of fuel oil.

## CONSUMERISM

Before the 1960s, consumers had few rights and very little say in the bargaining process. They often had to rely upon their own common sense. The Latin expression *caveat emptor* – 'Let the buyer beware' – held true. As large and well-developed organisations often dealt with individual consumers, **consumerism** developed to break down this vast inequality in bargaining power and so provide consumers with more rights and enable them to obtain greater value for money.

The need for consumers to be better protected and therefore insured against the actions of the organisations they bought from arose because of such problems as:

- poor-quality services or damaged goods
- goods or services which failed to match the descriptions applied to them
- manufacturer's or supplier's negligence affecting the safety of the product or service
- breach of contract
- misleading offers, information, advertising, labelling
- unfair terms in contracts

- monopoly control or lack of competition limiting the quantity and/or quality of a product and resulting in artificially high prices.

Greater equality, freedom of speech, improved educational standards, increased governmental regulation, and vastly improved communications are all factors which have encouraged **consumer power**. Consumers today *expect* a product to be safe and to perform its function well. They also feel that it is important to be protected against questionable products or unfair practices. Producers are *expected* to behave in a socially responsible manner. The newspapers and the consumer organisations are there to bring wrongdoers to the public attention, and the law courts are there to punish offenders when necessary.

In response to the consumer movement, many manufacturers or suppliers today pay greater attention to the concept of the **total product**. The total product includes all those aspects which give a product quality aimed at consumer satisfaction. The total product includes accessories, a brand name, a user guarantee, packaging, after-sales service, as well as additional extras such as a customer handbook. Quality and attention to detail help to improve customer satisfaction and to maintain a good public profile. They also help an organisation to show how it bears its responsibility to the community. Such an approach should be seen as adding to the marketing mix. We can see this reflected in the **corporate objectives** of major international companies.

## CASE STUDY *An international organisation and consumer responsibility*

In the early 1990s, Body Shop had over 600 shops trading in 38 countries and in 18 languages producing over 5 million kilos of products. Body Shop had a bigger presence overseas than any other British retailer, and was the fastest-growing company in the UK personal care market.

Anita Roddick who founded Body Shop argues that businesses and consumers working together can help to create social change. Consumers have the power to create change, by asking questions about sources and manufacture, by demanding information, and ultimately by the use of their feet and their wallets to shop elsewhere.

Over 30 million people pass by Body Shop stores around the world each month. Anita Roddick believes that the shop window can be used to educate people about consumer issues. Body Shop sets out to inform consumers clearly about what they are buying, where the ingredients come from and how products are produced. Ms Roddick argues that consumers need to have information so that they can make informed choices. All too often, she asserts, other producers hide the true nature of their products through glossy advertising.

**Questions**

1 Should producers inform and educate consumers, or leave them to find out about products for themselves? Explain your views.

2 What examples can you think of where advertising and sales promotion may mask the true nature of some products?

3 Is it in the interests of organisations like Body Shop to take a stance on consumer issues?

4 How can (a) producers and (b) consumers benefit from businesses and consumers working more closely together?

## Consumer protection

The legal system provides a framework within which transactions can take place and also serves to provide a means of settling disputes. The legal basis of the contract which exists between the buyer and the seller sets out the obligations that individuals and organisations have to each other every time they enter into an agreement.

Over the years, governments have responded to consumerism with successive **Acts of Parliament** designed to protect and increase the powers of buyers in relation to sellers. Such laws cover unfair business activities, poor quality of goods and services and the provision of credit. For example, the Sale of Goods Act 1979 indicates that sellers must provide goods which are of merchantable quality, match the description applied to them and are fit for the purpose for which they are sold. Other important Acts include the Trade Descriptions Acts of 1968 and 1972, the Fair Trading Act 1973, the Consumer Protection Act 1987, the Consumer Credit Act 1974, as well as Acts referring to Food and Drugs and Weights and Measures. The legal aspect of marketing also covers areas such as agency, use of trademarks, infringement of copyrights, insurance, and company law.

Often government actions create a range of organisations or departments designed to represent consumer groups. For example, the **Office of Fair Trading** (OFT) investigates monopolies and mergers, collects information on unfair consumer practices, and plays a key role in developing consumer legislation. The Director General of Fair Trading:

- analyses information affecting the wellbeing of consumers
- refers matters where consumers' rights may be violated to the Consumer Protection Advisory Committee
- encourages the publication of Codes of Practice for dealing with consumers
- takes action against organisations which persist in conduct which is against the interests of consumers
- produces consumer protection literature.

Another body is the **Advertising Standards Authority** (ASA), an independent body which exercises control over all advertising except that on radio and television. The ASA draws up its own codes which it uses to ensure that advertisements are 'legal, decent, honest and truthful'. Advertisements should be prepared with a sense of responsibility to both consumers and society and should conform to the principles of fair competition.

For example, a number of complaints were made to the ASA over a campaign by Rover to extol the virtues of wood-panelling on the Rover 820Se: suspended by the main body of the text appeared a box with the words 'A woman, a dog and a walnut tree – the more you beat them, the better they'll be'. At Rover they insisted that the words were only put there to inject humour! The ASA was also unconvinced of the cholesterol-reducing properties of the showpiece launch of Common Sense Oat Bran Flakes and brought in a team of top nutritional scientists amidst fears that the product and the advert might create needless worry for consumers.

The **British Standards Institution** (BSI) was incorporated by Royal Charter as a voluntary non-profit-making organisation to prepare and publish **standards** for safety, performance, size and testing. They are identified by the now-famous Kitemark displayed on packaging to denote that a product meets BSI requirements.

The **Monopolies and Mergers Commission** investigates possible monopolies and proposed company mergers referred to it by the Director General of Fair Trading. The Commission's role is to assess whether such monopolies and mergers are likely to be against the public interest (see Figure 11.4). For example, in early 1994 the Central and Granada TV companies were told that they could not engage in mergers that would give them more than 25 per cent of ITV's net advertising revenue. This was to prevent any one concern from developing a dominant position in television advertising.

**Trading Standards and Consumer Protection Departments** are departments of local authorities which work with the Office of Fair Trading and help to enforce laws, offer advice for shoppers and traders and watch for unfair trade practices. There is also an

*FIGURE 11.4*
*Assessing whether monopolies or mergers are in the public interest*

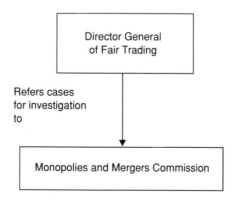

extensive network of **Citizens' Advice Bureaux** (CABs) in the UK which provide advice on consumer complaints and queries.

Another government established body is the **National Consumer Council** (NCC), set up in 1975 to provide independent advice to government and business organisations. It also seeks to further consumer interests by representation on public and other bodies, as well as oversee the development of voluntary codes of practice.

Nationalised industries have **Consumer and Consultative Councils** to influence their policies and ensure that they do not abuse their powers. Privatised industries (i.e. those that have formerly been in the public sector) also have consumer councils which are set up to protect consumers' interests. For example, the Office of Water Services (Ofwat) has a director-general who is responsible for the economic regulation of water and sewage services; its Birmingham-based office has over 130 staff, many of them employed on ten Regional Customer Services Committees. The Office of the Railway Regulator (ORR), as well as issuing licences to new railway operators, is charged with investigating rail-users' complaints which are taken up from Consumer Consultative Councils.

Consumerism has also led to the formation of a number of influential pressure groups and movements. The **Consumers Association** has over 800 000 members and is the largest consumer organisation in the country. *Which?*, its magazine, carries the results of extensive product tests and scrutinises services. The **National Federation of Consumer Groups** comprises a large number of local consumer groups which concentrate upon local issues, such as retail facilities and prices. Other pressure groups which might aim to influence businesses and the government include ecological lobby groups, sports organisations, women's groups, the RSPCA, the Campaign for Real Ale, etc.

There is no doubt that when consumers' rights and obligations are abused, or when dangerous goods are brought into the marketplace, feelings tend to run high. Television and radio have increasingly become a focus for consumer campaigns, through programmes like 'Watchdog'.

In response to consumer pressures and increasing concern about the quality of goods and services, organisations in a number of industries have formed **trade associations** which have established codes of practice to go beyond the basic legal requirements and to provide the highest possible level of consumer satisfaction. For example, the Association of British Travel Agents (ABTA) set up a fund to protect holidaymakers if a company fails to deliver. Other codes of practice apply to products such as cars and car repairs, shoes and shoe repairs, electrical goods and servicing and mail-order trading. Many of these codes have been produced after consulting with the Office of Fair Trading.

The **Chartered Institute of Marketing** has its own code of practice which members are required to adhere to as a condition of their membership. The code refers to professional standards of behaviour in securing and developing business and demands honesty and integrity of conduct. The **British Code of Advertising Practice** is supported by advertisers, agencies and the media whose representatives make up the Code of Advertising Practice Committee. The Code sets out the rules which those in the advertising industry agree to follow, and also indicates to those outside advertising the regulations designed to ensure that advertisements can be trusted.

## The European dimension of consumer protection

Consumer protection takes place today within a local, national and European framework (see Figure 11.5).

Over the years the **European Commission** has set out to create a climate of competition between organisations in the European Union. Agreements between organisations are forbidden if they set

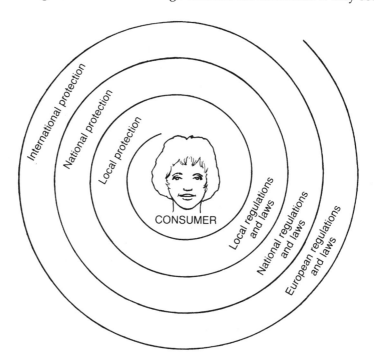

FIGURE 11.5
*Regulations and laws
to protect consumers*

out to prevent, restrict or distort competition within the common market. In particular, agreements fixing prices, sharing markets, discriminating against third parties, or imposing territorial restrictions which split up the common market, are all outlawed. Of course, today this competition policy must also cover the whole of the European Economic Area (EEA).

The European Commission, supported by the **European Court of Justice**, is responsible for safeguarding competition rules in the EU. In addition, a new body – the **EFTA Surveillance Authority** (ESA) – has been set up to maintain these rules in the EFTA area supported by the EFTA court. The two bodies will work closely together. It seems inevitable that these bodies will merge at some stage in the future.

- *Restrictive agreements and monopoly abuse* – The Commission will handle cases where trade between EU Member States is affected and cases where more than 67 per cent (two-thirds) of the EEA turnover of the undertakings concerned is within the EU. However, responsibility will pass to the ESA if the effect on trade within the EU is not great.
- *Mergers and takeovers* – The Commission will handle all cases where the combined worldwide turnover of the organisations concerned is greater than 5 billion ecus, and where the EU turnover of at least two of them is in excess of 250 million ecus.
- *Pricing and exclusive distribution* – As a general rule, firms are free under EU competition law to charge different prices for the supply of their goods in different parts of the Union or to different categories of consumer. The exception to this rule is where prices are fixed *by agreement with other firms*.

### Some aspects of EU consumer law

In addition to measures covering competition between organisations, the EU has introduced many directives aimed at protecting consumers. The following are some examples.

- The **Misleading Advertising** directive, introduced in 1984, aims to protect businesses and the general public against the effects of misleading advertisements.
- The **Product Liability** directive, introduced in 1985, makes manufacturers and importers strictly liable for injuries caused by defective products.
- The **Doorstep Selling** directive, introduced in 1985, brought in a seven-day cooling-off period for certain sales contracts concluded at the consumer's home or place or work.

- The **Consumer Credit** directive, introduced in 1987, protects consumers entering into credit agreements.

- The **Toy Safety** directive, introduced in 1988, harmonises toy safety standards.

- The **Price Indication** directive, introduced in 1988, requires the selling prices (and in some cases unit prices) of food and non-food products to be displayed.

- The **Package Travel** directive, introduced in 1990, established minimum standards of consumer protection for packaged travel and package holidays and tours.

---

## MARKETING ETHICS

**Ethics** are **moral principles** or **rules of conduct** which are generally accepted by most members of a society. They involve what individuals and groups believe to be right and what is considered to be wrong. An ethic is therefore a guide as to what should be done or what should not be done.

From an early age, parents, schools, religious teaching and society in general provide us with moral guidelines to help us to learn and form our ethical beliefs. Many ethics are reinforced in our legal system and thus provide a constraint to business activities, while others are not. In areas not covered by law, there may well be social pressure to conform to a particular standard. Pressure groups often set out to force individuals or organisations to operate in an 'acceptable' way.

Through the media we hear about questionable business activities – issues such as insider trading, animal rights protesters involved in disputes with organisations producing cosmetic and pharmaceutical products, protests about tobacco sponsorships, and trading links with unfriendly or hostile nations. As a result, consumers have become more aware of the ethical and moral values underlying business decisions. Today's consumer is more concerned than ever before about what an organisation stands for, who it trades with, what it does, whether it supports any political party, whether it is an equal opportunities employer and how it behaves in the community as a whole. When *Which*? carried out a survey, 63 per cent of those who responded were concerned about the activities of companies they might invest in.

## CASE STUDY  *Responsibility for what?*

The philosopher Robert Frederick poses some important questions about the responsibility of businesses to the community. He puts forward his arguments in the following manner.

- A number of people seem to think that it is obviously true that businesses have a responsibility to protect the environment. These responsibilities go beyond what is required by law and regulation. Businesses frequently have the knowledge and the resources to limit environmental damage from their activities. To refuse to take responsibility for these actions can be seen as irresponsible and a neglect of moral duty.

- A business person may reply that businesses have only a limited power to serve the economic needs of society and must operate within the bounds of law and regulations. However, a business has no moral obligation to try to solve other social problems which may be partly caused by its activities. Businesses have no moral duty to do more than meet the requirements imposed on them by law and regulation.

- A basic ethical principle is that you should 'do no harm', because creating harm violates the rights of another person not to be harmed. However, perhaps this should be limited to a statement that you should do no *'unwarranted'* harm.

For example, in a football game if one person is accidentally hurt in a tackle, then this is acceptable because the injured party must have been aware that going into a fair tackle sometimes causes hurt. If a knowledgeable and competent investor loses money on the stock market, his or her rights have not been violated. The harm in both examples is an acknowledged risk of participating in the activity.

If, on the other hand, the footballer were to have his watch stolen while he was on the floor, or if the investor were to be trampled underfoot in a rush by floor traders to sell on the announcement of bad news, then their rights would have been violated.

- The same principle can be applied to business life. If individuals or groups are harmed by business activity, and the harm is *unrewarded* in that it is not offset by a balancing benefit, or if the harm is *unnecessary* in that it is a preventable rather than an inevitable peril of ordinary life, then there has been a violation of the right not to be harmed.

**Questions**
1 What is your view on the nature of harm outlined by Robert Frederick?
2 What are the implications for developing a set of principles for defining responsible marketing?
3 How could a set of principles related to the notion of harm be built into 'marketing strategy'?
4 Make a list of ten examples of where 'harm' may be caused by business activity.

The idea of organisations working in and for the community is not new. Many of the great entrepreneurs of the past such as William Hesketh Lever took action to support their ethical beliefs. Marks & Spencer today contributes to a programme which it claims touches all areas of the community; it includes contributions to 'health and care', with involvement in projects for the elderly, the mentally ill and handicapped, the abused, to hospitals and Childline. It also includes contributions to 'arts and heritage' as well as 'community services, education and training'.

Health and safety is an area that has come to the forefront of company policies over recent years. Accidents at a chemical plant or in the North Sea can permanently tarnish an organisation's image. There is always the example of the American corporation which discovered that it was more cost efficient to pay compensation to ill, injured and dying employees than to invest in research to improve safety.

At the same time, organisations have become increasingly aware of the adverse effects their products can have on the health and safety of consumers. A recent report attacked standards in the food industry and called for the government to fund better research and better training for environmental health officers, and to legislate against farmers who produce infected stock. Food scares such as the salmonella egg scandal, listeria and 'mad cow disease' (BSE) shocked consumers and led to sudden short-term changes in demand. Cancer links with the use of chlorine bleach rocked the paper industry.

Buying cheap imports from 'sweat-labour' overseas, Sunday-trading, dumping of goods on foreign markets, the need to invest in areas of high unemployment, contributions to political parties, encouragement of trade unions, treatment of employees, investment policies, pension and insurance schemes, social clubs etc. – the list of issues facing industry is almost endless. No organisation is ever going to be able to give the sort of response to these pressures that will please all parties all of the time. However, by becoming good corporate citizens and being socially responsible for their actions,

265

organisations can generate considerable goodwill and develop a useful marketing advantage whilst, at the same time, pursuing their other business objectives. However, many environmentalists would argue that being 'green' is not an optional extra but a vital – and tardy – step to preserve the future of mankind.

Ethical and environmental perspectives need to be built into corporate strategy. In his book *The Age of Eco-Strategy*, Dr Matthew Kieran has argued that, in order to manage a global shift to environmentally sound practice, organisations will need at a strategic level to provide three key elements of competitive weaponry:

- the capacity to manage organisational learning, innovation and change
- powerful new tools for environmental management
- new, 'greener' sources of investment capital.

The new tools of environmental management will include (Figure 11.6):

- *Environmental impact assessment* (EIA) – carrying out an assessment of the likely impact of major capital projects.

- *Environmental audits* (or eco-audits) – carrying out an audit of current activities to create a snapshot of the environmental impact of these activities.

- *Product life-cycle analysis* – looking at the environmental impact of a product throughout its life-cycle. Such an analysis would examine what happens to a product from the sourcing of raw materials to the ultimate disposal of waste (an analysis that led McDonald's to discontinue its styrofoam 'clamshell' hamburger).

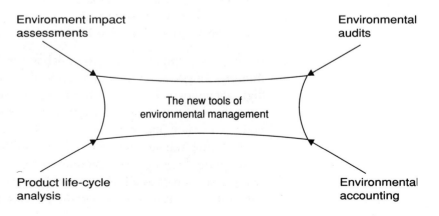

FIGURE 11.6

*Tools of environmental*
*management*

- *Environmental accounting* – accurately recording the value of environmental assets and their depreciations, as well as the true size of environmental liabilities and pollution costs.

There is no doubt that in the future, in the world of the articulate consumer, we will see more **'social' marketing** linking consumer, environmental and ethical issues. For example Ark, the environmental group, which as part of its activities markets environmentally responsible products, concentrates its activities on the individual and how each person can make a positive step to restore the health of the planet. By doing so it hopes to make people aware that everyone has an impact upon the environment, and that if we endanger the planet's health by our activities, our own health will be at risk. Ark carries out its work by establishing a network of local groups, educational publications to provide them with information, celebrity endorsement and environmentally responsible consumer products. Such products provide the consumer with choice, educate individuals about environmental issues, show their potential to the industry and increase consumer awareness of their impact upon the natural world.

In the future, organisations will have to respond with increasing sensitivity by constantly analysing their activities and revising their strategies to match the wishes of their consumers. Many consumers may be willing to pay more to support a principle or even forfeit something they want in the short term in pursuit of a more permanent gain. Perhaps the three Cs of business should become the *four* Cs.

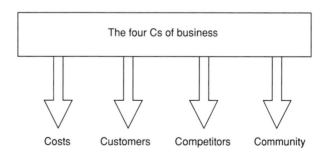

FIGURE II.7
*The* four *Cs of business*

**ASSIGNMENT** Set out a table showing the stakeholders in an exporting company selling English language books in overseas markets, and the sorts of expectations they might have of that company. We have given a few examples to start your list off:

| Stakeholder | Expectations |
|---|---|
| Customers | Clear, easy-to-understand books by reputable authors at affordable prices |
| Government | Taxes, job creation |
| Shareholders | Dividends, an increase in value of shares, a secure investment |
| Community | Employment, use of ecologically sound paper, etc. |
| Suppliers | ? |
| Banks | ? |
| Managers | ? |
| Trade unions | ? |
| Employees | ? |
| Any others | ? |

**ASSIGNMENT**

The market research group Euromonitor recently predicted that the £6 billion tobacco industry faces total extinction within 30 years. Over the last three years cigarette sales have dropped by 10 per cent. The report's editor feels that tobacco smoking is today viewed as anti-social but the tobacco industry does not seem to have faced up to the facts.

Euromonitor critised manufacturers for being far too concerned about Far Eastern markets (which are still growing) to consider the UK crisis where retailers are becoming increasingly disenchanted with the poor returns from cigarette sales. Some companies have responded to changing trends. For example, Nabisco has diversified away from its tobacco interests in Winston and Camel, into other markets, such as breakfast cereal production.

In this assignment you will be expected to carry out the following activities.

Collect and research information produced by the tobacco industry and by groups opposed to smoking.

**Task a** Make a list of six major costs and benefits of the tobacco industry for the UK. Wherever possible try to quantify these costs and benefits (e.g. revenues from cigarette sales, costs of smoking-related illness).

**Task b** Set out a brief statement clarifying your views on the activities, ethics and importance of the UK tobacco industry.

**Task c** Set out a strategy for tobacco firms showing how they can change to survive their rapidly declining market.

**Task d** Set out a strategy for pressure groups seeking to reduce the amount of cigarette smoking in this country (and perhaps the total ban of cigarette smoking).

# Marketing Planning

**Marketing planning** is concerned with identifying clear **objectives** and setting out how these objectives can be achieved. The marketing objectives need to be built into all strategic and tactical thinking within an organisation, and govern the way in which an organisation operates.

The aim of any organisation is to satisfy the stakeholders who have most power and influence. One of the main proposals put forward in this book is that marketing is primarily concerned with satisfying the consumer. The objectives of a market-driven organisation will therefore be chiefly concerned with satisfying the requirements of the consumer in the marketplace.

Marketing planning can therefore be said to be concerned with:

- establishing objectives and goals, allocating resources to meet these and setting out a clear plan of action

- setting out ways of evaluating performance against marketing targets

- assessing the position and performance of the organisation in the various markets in which it operates, and its strengths and weaknesses.

An action plan is established with a clearly established time line for ongoing developments. At the same time a review process is set in motion to track the performance of the marketing strategy. A SWOT analysis is an essential ingredient of the plan. A key component of all planning stages is providing mechanisms that enable the company to evaluate marketing and product performance in the market as a whole and in individual markets in which the organisation carries out its activities (see Figure 12.1).

Having a European and international approach to marketing involves putting a European dimension into all of these activities. For example, an organisation may set out to make its product the number one brand in Europe based on meeting the needs of an identified segment of 'European' consumers. Resources will need to be allocated to researching the requirements of these consumers and to producing a product that provides the required benefits.

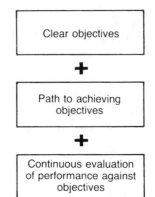

FIGURE 12.1

*From objectives to performance valuation*

## THE FIT BETWEEN CORPORATE AND MARKETING PLANNING

In 1985, the Chartered Institute of Marketing adopted a new slogan:

> # "Marketing means Business"
> ## – it does

Marketing is now accepted in most well-run businesses as a **strategic discipline** or general management function and in this respect must care for the health of a business in the future – especially against competitive influences. This is because it is increasingly realised that although making a profit is important, an organisation should also develop its market share and search for brand leadership as well. So the marketer must monitor the profitability of the business and attempt to anticipate the likely trends. At the same time rival companies should be monitored and examined for vulnerable points.

Successful marketers must therefore be concerned with every aspect of their business, including future projects and other areas of their industry. Successful companies plan five or ten years and more in advance and often know as much about the competition as they know about themselves!

### Thinking marketing

Marketing is not just a series of business-related functions, but more wide-reaching than this. It is a business philosophy designed to develop an attitude of mind which should be shared by everyone in an organisation and is often enhanced by both frequent and open communication. Developing such an attitude of mind reduces the likelihood of crisis and contributes to the development of the overall future of an enterprise at both strategic and tactical levels.

At the heart of marketing lies the degree to which an organisation becomes marketing-orientated. The more committed a company is to its marketing activities, the more able it will be to pursue its corporate objectives and develop and retain customers. Every business in existence relies upon its customers for survival, and those who best meet customer needs will always survive a period of change.

With the accelerating increase in consumer power, the business which does not have the consumer at heart will become a dinosaur and will soon go the way of all dinosaurs!

*The marketing function is therefore an essential ingredient of corporate strategy, and this marketing focus should be communicated through marketing planning into all aspects of business activities* (see Figure 12.2).

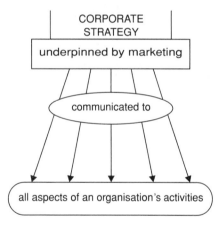

FIGURE 12.2
*The marketing function is an essential ingredient of corporate strategy*

## PUTTING TOGETHER A MARKETING DEVELOPMENT PLAN

Planning means taking decisions today about what is to be done tomorrow. Planning helps to bring your objectives out into the open. There is a famous saying that 'if you don't know where you are going then any road will take you there'. The point is that without clear planning you may achieve something, but it is unlikely to amount to much. If company objectives are clarified then individual departments have clear guidelines and it is possible for them all to work in a coordinated way.

Planning also makes it possible for management to evaluate performance. Without evaluation you have no control. Of course, plans are unlikely to be met in every detail. However, they establish guidelines against which performance can be checked and if necessary modified.

A useful model is set out in Figure 12.3. Start out by establishing objectives, clarify the planning assumptions that are being made, collect and sort out useful data, evaluate alternative courses of action, select an appropriate course of action, then re-evaluate the chosen course, and modify planning in the light of results.

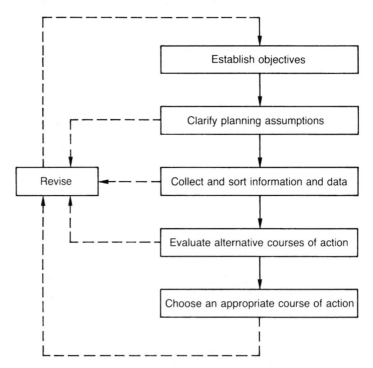

FIGURE 12.3
*A model for action planning*

Another way of approaching planning involves the following (see Figure 12.4).

- *Diagnosis* – Where are we and why? This usually involves some form of audit of company performance, which will then be analysed.
- *Prognosis* – Where are we going? This involves looking at possible future scenarios in the light of present performance and trends.
- *Objectives* – Where do we want to go? What is important?

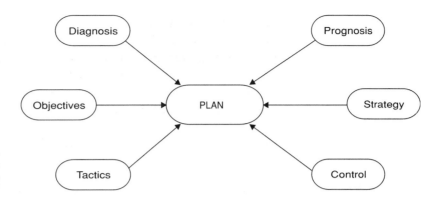

FIGURE 12.4
*An alternative planning model*

- *Strategy* – What is the best way of achieving our objectives?
- *Tactics* – What specific actions will enable us to meet day-to-day targets?
- *Control* – How far have we progressed? A company will need to establish performance indicators against which it can measure its success.

## PLANNING AND THE EXTERNAL ENVIRONMENT

Anyone involved in marketing will tell you that you should always be wary of the environment in which you operate. For example, within the legal environment in which a business operates laws frequently change. A European Union directive on the transport and movement of goods may suddenly slash the profits of a haulage company. Booms and slumps in the economy may harm or improve the chances of a new product just entering the market. Tastes and

FIGURE 12.5
*The changing environments in which marketing planning takes place*

273

fashions frequently change with social attitudes. Environmental awareness changes the ways in which consumers like to see products packaged etc. You may have what appears to be the right product and have made all the right planning moves only to find that technology or consumer requirements have moved on to something new. Marketing planning therefore takes place within a constantly changing political, social, economic, legal, physical and technological environment (see Figure 12.5).

## CASE STUDY  *A changing environment for Philips*

Over the past few decades the Philips laboratories have come up with the Video 2000 video-recorder system, the Laservision video-player, combining pictures with digital sound, and the compact disc. But only the compact disc has turned into a clear success.

The biggest failure was the Video 2000. When the product was introduced in 1979, technicians acknowledged that it was far superior to the competing Betamax and VHS video systems, launched by the Japanese Sony and Matsushita companies respectively. But production failed to get off the ground, and one year after the official launch the product was still not on the shelves around Europe.

Later, the Video 2000 was nicknamed the homing pigeon, since nearly half of the machines returned to Eindhoven for repairs.

The product failed partly because it was beaten to the market, and partly because of the mistaken belief that users would have little interest in hiring commercially produced videos from a video shop. The hardware was thus launched with no software backup! After four years Philips was forced to bring out its own VHS machines, using Japanese technology.

The Japanese companies were thus able to make their products the standard ones and Philips lost over a billion guilders.

Another criticism of Philips at the time was that the national companies within the Philips group were too powerful. For example, the North American Philips Corporation had nothing to do with Video 2000 and sold Japanese systems instead. Many of the national companies ran their own campaigns and demanded specific designs.

Today things have changed at Philips. Managers of Philips divisions coordinate product launches and campaigns all around the world, while managers of business units are responsible for the entire life-span of a product, from development to sale.

**Questions**

1 Was Philips' failure with Video 2000 due to product inadequacy or to marketing failings?

2 What indications are given that Philips' corporate strategy at the time was not underpinned by a marketing philosophy?

3 How many of the problems that Philips encountered would you describe as (i) external influences over which the organisation had little control, and (ii) internal weaknesses?

4 How can an organisation plan for changes in its external environment?

5 How might giving business units responsibility for the entire life-span of a product help to give an organisation more of a marketing focus?

---

# CASE STUDY  *Learning from the Japanese*

The process of *simultaneous engineering* gives us an important insight into how a company can plan for success in the marketplace. Simultaneous engineering is simple but brilliant.

Until recently, in the West many products have been created by what is called *sequential engineering*. Product ideas are dreamed up, the products are designed and then handed to the marketing department. The production engineers calculate how to make them, the suppliers gear up to produce the components, and finally, the manufacturing department starts production.

Quite often at the first attempt it is found that components do not fit together, so that tooling needs rejigging, or there is some other problem, and time is lost sorting it out. It is an exhausting process. As a result, the period from a product's inception to the point when it starts rolling off the production line might be measured in years rather than months.

The idea behind simultaneous engineering is to attend to all the aspects at the same time. Once an idea for a new product has been accepted, the project is handed to a special project team which assumes responsibility until first deliveries. The team contains people from all areas – design, marketing, production, engineering, manufacturing and purchasing. Instead of each department completing its task before passing it to another, the team acts simultaneously.

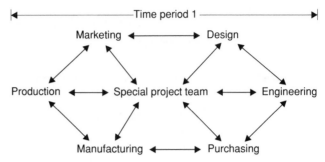

While the design is being finalised, the marketing implications are relayed to produce further refinements. At the same time, production engineers start working on manufacture, teaming up with design engineers to facilitate production. The purchasing department and engineers work with suppliers to incorporate their ideas.

The team approach provides an excellent way of getting around the delays that hamper introducing a product. Decisions can be taken quickly, inter-departmental conflicts are readily resolved, and clear lines of authority are established. Above all, members of the special project team can focus on market-driven planning.

The Japanese way is to spend more time on conceiving the product so that it is virtually free of problems by the time it reaches the consumer. Honda, for example, has cut two years from the five-year development cycle needed to introduce a car.

The results from western companies that have used simultaneous engineering have been remarkable. American Telephone & Telegraph (ATT) halved the time it took to produce a new cordless telephone. Hewlett-Packard cut the time it took to develop a new laser printer from four and a half years to 22 months.

The product that is first on the market often becomes the standard that the others will be forced to emulate.

**Questions**
1 What benefits might a company reap from practising simultaneous engineering?

2 What difficulties do you see in trying to introduce simultaneous engineering into companies that currently use sequential engineering?

3 How does simultaneous engineering help companies to become more marketing-orientated?

# STRATEGIC MARKETING PLANNING

Any organisation that takes strategic marketing to heart will be involved in three interrelated activities. Strategic **analysis** involves building up a view of factors which are likely to influence the short-term and the long-term wellbeing of an organisation. This analysis will help planners to develop a menu of **choices** for strategic development. One or more of these alternatives must be chosen and **implemented**, leading to a further ongoing cycle of analysis, choice and implementation (see Figure 12.6).

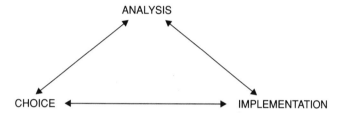

FIGURE 12.6
*The process of strategic marketing*

The process of strategic marketing analysis and choice will clarify the objectives that an organisation is working towards. Today most large and many small organisations express their overarching objectives in a **mission statement**. This sets out what lies at the heart of an organisation's thinking.

For example, Pedigree Petfoods, leading producers of pet food in this country, state that:

> 'We work constantly towards identifying and satisfying consumer needs. It is the activity from which all else springs. We never forget that we cannot influence millions of consumer choices until we have convinced first one, then a second and a third consumer that our product is worthy of purchase. Our success is based on thorough research of the wide range of needs for pet animals and their owners. The knowledge which we gain is translated into a range of quality products which satisfy these needs better than any of our competitors.'

You can see clearly from the mission statement that Pedigree Petfoods is a market-driven organisation.

Today it is fashionable for large organisations to place their mission statements in prominent locations in the workplace so that employees are constantly reminded of the mission.

The **corporate objectives** of an organisation are often expressed in financial terms which are formulated by senior managers. These objectives are likely to express the expectations of stakeholders.

Marketing and financial objectives are brought together in a **total marketing plan**. The financial objective of a company is usually tied up with the strategic objectives, which may, for example, be described in terms of profit-making and growth (although there are many possible objectives depending on the vision and relative strengths of coalitions of stakeholders).

For example, a company may seek to *maximise long-term revenues* for shareholders by clearly identifying a target market and giving priority to satisfying the market with a quality product.

Developing an effective marketing plan therefore involves investigating buyer expectations in order to make decisions about Product, Price, Place and Promotion. If the plan is effective, then not only will consumers be satisfied, but so too will be other strategic objectives of the company such as meeting particular financial targets (see Figure 12.7).

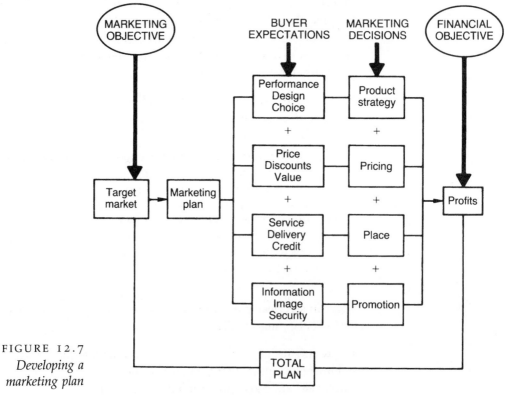

FIGURE 12.7
*Developing a marketing plan*

# TACTICAL MARKETING PLANNING

Formulating a marketing plan for an organisation must be grounded in strategic marketing. However, it is also essential to plan carefully the **tools** and **tactics** of marketing.

On an ongoing basis the various units involved in marketing (and indeed in all other areas of an organisation) will develop **action plans**. These plans need to be *realistic*. They should not be too ambitious nor lacking in demand. The main tasks are to decide on priorities and on how control mechanisms and evaluatory tools can be developed. The sequence shown in Figure 12.8 for preparing an action plan should be helpful.

The marketing plan in a large organisation is made up of a number of plans from each of the sub-groups within the marketing department. It will build on the vision created by the mission statement and other ingredients of the marketing strategy of the organisation.

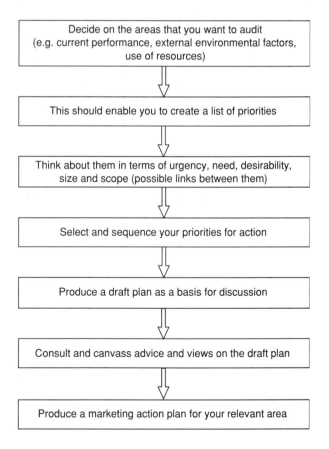

FIGURE 12.8

*Developing tactical action plans*

279

The key ingredients of tactical marketing planning will be:

- assessing current performance using quantitive methods such as ratios, and qualitative analysis
- clarifying objectives
- establishing ways of implementing plans.

The marketing plan will also include plans for the following:

- product mix
- pricing
- distribution
- promotion

- market research
- sales
- advertising.

## *The product mix plan*

An internal audit of the current product mix involves listing the products and examining their performances over a period of years in order to identify *trends*. It will be important to examine market segments and the relationships between them. Useful **ratios** are the net profit made per product and per region, the net profit as a percentage of sales, and the market share per region and country.

This will help the organisation to identify which products should be phased out, which should be modified, and which new products will enter the portfolio and at what time. It should set out objectives for volume of sales, turnover and profits. It should establish how each of the products will be supported within the company, for example by sales staff. Product objectives will also be concerned with the type of packaging used.

The product mix plan should also set out the contribution and/or volume objectives for individual products, market segments and customer groups.

## *The pricing plan*

Pricing is important for any company. A starting point will be to evaluate the quality of pricing decisions that have been taken in the past and the effects of competitors' pricing policies.

The business may want to explore the price elasticity in the various markets which it serves. The pricing plan should set out the principles that cover pricing and discounting of products. Lower prices do not always mean more or better business. It may be better to build a sound long-term business than price to attract short-term or specific orders. If in doubt, it usually makes sense to price high as you can always reduce price or give special offers. If you price low you will find it difficult to put up the price in the short-term. It could also put you out of business. The pricing plan should answer questions such as 'Do we need big volume turnover and can we manage it?' and 'Do we need to aim for lower volume with a bigger margin?'.

## The physical distribution plan

As we saw in Chapter 7 on distribution, effective channels can give a critical competitive edge. Where physical distribution costs are relatively high it is important to use the most effective channels, to control stock efficiently and to minimise breakages and delays. The physical distribution plan needs to be integrated with other key areas of the marketing mix. A useful ratio to compare distribution performance over a number of years is:

$$\text{Distribution effectiveness ratio} = \frac{\text{Distribution costs}}{\text{Sales}}$$

As part of an ongoing distribution analysis an organisation may introduce new objectives, such as the development of a new channel, adding or cutting out distributors, identifying ways of improving distributors' performance, etc.

## The promotional plan

In many large companies, promotions are tied to the life-cycle of a product. Promotional activity will be required at launch and periodically to inject new life into a product.

Promotion will also be closely tied to seasonal fluctuations and other short-term influences on demand. Advertising will be a key ingredient of the promotional plan, but it is only a very small part of promotion. Advertising on its own seldom, if ever, succeeds.

A satisfied customer is the best form of promotion, and planning thus has a lot in common with market research in that the aim is to be consumer-led.

## The market research plan

Market research planning is particularly important for products whose nature and market are constantly changing. The market research plan will cover three main areas:

- gathering of market data

- constantly checking on performance in the marketplace, as well as the performance of competitors
- regularly testing products, markets, operations and ideas.

### The sales plan

Many organisations will also have a discrete sales plan. This will set out targets and intended activities for the sales function in areas such as customer service, and sales penetration. Specific plans are likely to be formulated for given groups of customers and specific accounts. The plan should also set out how the sales force is to be recruited and trained. A useful ratio for assessing sales performance is:

$$\text{Selling performance} = \frac{\text{Selling costs}}{\text{Sales}}$$

A business may want to assess the expenses of selling activities as a percentage of sales:

- per market
- per order
- per product
- per salesperson.

### The advertising plan

Large organisations may also have advertising plans which are separate from other promotional plans. However, the two will clearly need to complement each other. The advertising plan will contain details of which media to concentrate on, how to allocate the advertising budget, the type of audience to be reached, procedures for tracking the success of campaigns, and other features.

Objectives of advertising (and promotion) will include:

- awareness of levels (how many people know about our product?)
- image objectives (how can we improve and monitor perceptions of the image of our brands/company?)
- technique objectives (e.g. to use displays, demonstrations, leaflets).

A ratio that can be used to assess advertising performance is:

$$\text{Advertising performance ratio} = \frac{\text{Advertising cost}}{\text{Sales}}$$

All of the planning activities which have been outlined above should be set out in an action plan that indicates objectives and priorities, resources to be used, programme/timetable/checkpoints, and controls.

# CONTROLLING MARKETING EFFECTIVENESS

In a market-conscious company the cost of marketing will be high. A major problem faced by most companies is that it is very difficult to apportion costs to marketing activities. For example, how can you tell what effect advertising at sports grounds will have on the sales made of an organisation's products? It is very difficult to ascertain how marketing activities translate into profitability. However, an organisation that fails to spend money on marketing activities will find that its sales can dip dramatically.

A rough and ready ratio that can be used to measure marketing performance is:

$$\text{Marketing performance} = \frac{\text{Marketing cost}}{\text{Sales}}$$

However, it is virtually impossible to draw a boundary around 'marketing'. Does this mean that we should include all of an organisation's activities as 'marketing'? (What do you think?)

In the USA a number of people have said that over a half of the costs of many organisations is accounted for by marketing activities. The suggestion is that there should be some control mechanisms to monitor how these costs can be broken down and apportioned. Evaluation should be based on using an organisation's resources in the most effective ways, and should help to answer questions such as:

- What is the optimum sum that should be spent on public relations, given our current budget?
- How can we compare the effectiveness of a quarter of a million pounds spent on Europe-wide promotion of our product with spending the same money on a new production technique?

It is possible to use a number of **quantitive techniques** to provide controls for marketing activities.

- **Marketing profitability analysis** can be used to calculate the relationship between particular (or general) marketing costs and the profits from individual products, markets, consumer groups, distribution methods, etc.
- **Budgets** can set out marketing targets, costs and revenues so that expectations can be compared with actual returns.
- **Sales controls** provide targets and assessment points for the selling operation and individual sales staff.

- **Store audits** can be used to check on quantities of goods moving through distribution channels.
- **Tracking** of advertising and promotion effectiveness is possible.
- **Buyer surveys** can be used to detect reactions and attitudes to particular campaigns and products.
- **Systematic audits** can be conducted of the marketing functions and of all the ingredients of a marketing plan, and marketing activities.

## CASE STUDY  *Planning a new product line*

'Persil washes whiter' is a slogan that can have bypassed few of us since the 1950s. Now we have a new proposition: Persil also washes dishes. Persil washing-up liquid was launched in September 1990 with an £8 million advertising campaign aimed squarely at the undisputed champion of the kitchen sink, Fairy Liquid.

In 1989, Fairy took on Persil on its home turf, by launching an automatic washing powder and liquid. This has led to a counter-offensive by Persil. The initiative is bound to stir up the long-running battle between the two largest companies that make up the detergent market, Lever Brothers and Procter & Gamble. Fairy (owned by P&G) accounts for half the money spent on washing-up liquids each year.

Inevitably this battle will have repercussions. Procter & Gamble is recognised by many to be one of the world's most dynamic marketing organisations. Marketing tactics at P&G are concerned with giving products a high visibility, clear branding, and an aggressively competitive edge.

In 1989, Procter & Gamble discovered that Lever planned to launch a new detergent, Radion, with the promise that it would remove 'stale odours'. Before the Radion advertising had hit television screens, Procter & Gamble was on air with its own commercal for Ariel Automatic which asked a housewife if her clothes smelled. 'Don't be daft,' she replied, 'I use Ariel'.

The now well-established Persil washing-up liquid is targeted at the premium/concentrated segment of the market, a direct challenge to Fairy. Persil's product reflects the 'caring and family values' that Persil claims to represent.

**Questions**  I  What do you understand by the following terms that are used in the case study?
- launch
- slogan
- marketing tactics
- targeted.
- segment of the market

2   Identify the tactical planning areas that would be involved in planning the launch of Persil washing-up liquid. Explain the sorts of plans that you would expect to be made in these areas.

3   What would you expect to be the key ingredients in the strategy of a detergent giant?

4   What tactical decisions would support such a strategy?

5   Why do you think that Lever decided to extend the Persil brand?

## CONCLUSION

In this chapter, we have set out to show that marketing planning is crucial to success and that it underpins the whole process of corporate planning. Marketing activities are carried out to meet organisational objectives shaped by the marketplace. The pursuit of marketing objectives should lead to an effective and efficient use of resources both for individual organisations and for society. They should also maximise returns in terms of the objectives set.

The company should know where it is going while always being prepared to adjust rapidly. The marketplace moves on. For example, in the 1960s not many people would have imagined that in the mid-1990s middle-aged men in 'comfy' cardigans and cavalry twills would have become the battleground for the fashion industry. A marketing survey in 1994 revealed that the over-fifties have a disposable income of over £150 million a year, more than the entire contents of the nation's building societies and double that of the 16–34 age group. Not only are the over-fifties affluent, their number is increasing even as the number of teenagers falls. This particular age group is known in the clothing trade as the 'grey market'. Stylish clothes for the 'fuller figure' are becoming a key new growth area for clothing designers. The Burton Group has resurrected its 60-year-old company, Huttons, selling suits and casual wear. Not to be outdone, the 106-year-old Dunn & Co., which boasts a customer base with ages 19 to 90, has called in an image specialist to update its look without alarming some of its more 'sober' customers.

So, marketing planning needs to carefully look ahead, to foresee future trends and to plan for them!

**ASSIGNMENT**   In 1990 Gillette, maker of razors and blades, already boasted a 62.5 per cent value share of the UK wet-shave market and a 67 per cent value share in North America and Europe. However, to stay still in business frequently leads to going backwards.

Throughout the 1980s Gillette was researching and testing new products for the 1990s. Gillette (like Coca-Cola and Kodak) is a believer in global marketing and advertising. In the middle of 1991 the company launched its new razor (Sensor) simultaneously in 19 countries.

The same commercial was used throughout North America and Europe. A new slogan was developed for the campaign: 'Gillette – The best a man can get'.

In the mid-1990s Gillette is already looking to the year 2000. In particular it is interested in a new process for brushing diamond particles to create a long-lasting coating for razor blades. It recognises that the competition is always trying to steal a march on it. It therefore needs to identify fresh marketing opportunities and to build on its existing strengths.

The most important reason for planning is the possibility of change and uncertainty. If marketing took place in a safe and predictable environment then planning would not be difficult. However, change is ever-present and needs to be accounted for.

**Task** **a** Carry out some appropriate research to compare consumers' perceptions of the relative merits of the benefits offered by Sensor and its main rivals.

**Task** **b** Carry out a SWOT analysis on the Sensor razor.

**Task** **c** What new planning developments may help Gillette to maximise its strengths, minimise its weaknesses, make the most of its opportunities and meet the threats in the marketplace?

**Task** **d** Why must the corporate strategy of an organisation like Gillette be underpinned by a marketing philosophy?

# Index